JAPAN

A TRAVELER'S COMPANION

VANGUARD PRESS, INC.   NEW YORK

COPYRIGHT © 1979 BY LENSEY NAMIOKA
PUBLISHED SIMULTANEOUSLY IN CANADA BY GAGE PUBLISHING CO.,
AGINCOURT, ONTARIO.
ALL RIGHTS RESERVED.
NO PART OF THIS PUBLICATION MAY BE REPRODUCED OR TRANSMITTED IN ANY
FORM OR BY ANY MEANS, ELECTRONIC OR MECHANICAL, INCLUDING PHOTOCOPY,
RECORDING, OR ANY INFORMATION OR RETRIEVAL SYSTEM, OR OTHERWISE,
WITHOUT THE WRITTEN PERMISSION OF THE PUBLISHER, EXCEPT BY A REVIEWER
WHO MAY WISH TO QUOTE BRIEF PASSAGES IN CONNECTION WITH A REVIEW FOR A
NEWSPAPER, MAGAZINE, RADIO, OR TELEVISION.

LIBRARY OF CONGRESS CATALOGUE CARD NUMBER: 78-63639
ISBN: 0-8149-0810-1, CLOTH
ISBN: 0-8149-0816-0, PAPER

DESIGNER: ELIZABETH WOLL
MANUFACTURED IN THE UNITED STATES OF AMERICA.

TABLE OF CONTENTS

INTRODUCTION vii

ESSENTIALS

1. GETTING AROUND 3
The shape of Japan, luggage, taxis, walking, driving, subways, trains, planes, ferries.

2. LANGUAGE 25
Phrase books, social traps, pronunciation, writing (Romaji, Kanji, Kana), Japanized English.

3. FOOD 41
Traditional cuisine, dining towers, model dishes, shokudō, Western-style dishes, tempura, sushi, noodles, lunch boxes, snacks, coffee houses, beer halls, vendors, table manners.

4. HOUSING 64
Traditional house, slippers, furniture, movable wall panels, heating, garden, modern apartments, inns, people's lodging, hotels.

5. BATHS, BATHROOMS, AND TOILETS 85
How to use Japanese-style toilets and baths, water temperature, public bathhouses, hot-spring resorts.

v

CONTENTS

ENTERTAINMENTS

6. AMUSEMENTS   103
Night life, drama (kabuki, bunraku, noh), all-girl revues, geisha parties, TV, pachinko, mahjong, go, department stores, street entertainment, festivals, flower viewing.

7. SPORTS   126
Sumo, judo, aikido, karate, kendo, kemari, tennis, golf, swimming, running, hiking, cycling, climbing, skiing, team sports.

8. ARTS AND CRAFTS   145
National treasures, living national treasures, folk art, museums, museum cities (Nara, Takayama, Kyoto), lessons.

9. CASTLES AND SAMURAI   161
History of the samurai, early shoguns, suggested tour of castles, structure of a castle, famous castles (Nijo, Himeji, Osaka, Ako, Kanazawa, Kumamoto).

10. CHURCHES, SHRINES, AND TEMPLES   179
Shinto, Christianity, Buddhism (Shingon, Jodo, Nichiren, Zen), new religions, visiting a Zen temple.

11. GENERALIZATIONS   198

APPENDICES   211
Maps, list of characters, table of kana, useful addresses, suggested reading.

INTRODUCTION

Why visit Japan?

We go because of the sheer physical beauty of the country — the volcanic peaks, the thousands of tiny islands with their twisted pines, the huge, pillar-straight cryptomeria trees, the swaying, rustling bamboo groves, the hills of tea bushes groomed like velvet.

We go to feast our eyes on the brilliant colors — the vermilion torii gates, the red-lacquered shrine floors, the blue-glazed tiled roofs, the crimson maple leaves, the pastel cherry blossoms, the young girls in their kimonos, the cloth carp streaming in the wind, the bright kites depicting butterflies, centipedes, or ancient heroes.

The colors of Japan are stunning, but even more stunning is the absence of color. We admire the baroque extravagance of Nikko, but also the spare elegance of Katsura. We stay at inns and traditional houses to enjoy the muted beauty of unpainted wood, natural rush matting, clay walls, and thatched roofs of reeds or cypress bark. There are gardens with no colors other than the soft greens and grays of the trees and moss. There are gardens with no plants at all, only white sand and gray rock.

INTRODUCTION

The pace of Japanese life can be frantic. Rush-hour crowds pack into trains where reading over your neighbor's shoulder is not only permissible but unavoidable. Taxis careen wildly in and out of traffic. Throngs of youngsters crowd into shrines to pray for success in passing entrance examinations. Other throngs of youngsters crowd into coffee shops, beer halls, or discos to dance to the beat of Western rock music. During the frenzy of a festival, rival gangs of half-naked youths carrying portable shrines push at one another until there is only a tangle of thrashing limbs.

Life in Japan is frenzied, but it is also serene. Hard-driven executives relax by playing simple tunes on a bamboo flute. We can learn from the Japanese to sit quietly in a park or temple garden and listen to the buzzing of insects, or stroll through a small back street where the only sound is the mournful toot from the horn of a roast-potato vendor, or the clack of an old man's wooden clogs. After returning to our inn, we slough off tension and tiredness the Japanese way with a hot bath, and sit down to dinner in a clean cotton kimono. We find rest in the tranquillity of the uncluttered room and the diffuse light coming through the paper screens.

Japan boasts the most modern technology — punctual bullet trains and computerized seat reservations, efficient postal service and instant telecommunication. The Japanese have a passion for the newest and the latest. The downtown stores display the most up-to-date fashions and trends — Paris models and new skirt lengths, TV games and remote-controlled toy racing cars. Japanese homes contain the latest appliances — electric rice cookers, blanket toasters, feather-touch TV tuners, and video tape recorders.

But together with a passion for the new and the trendy is an equal passion for the old and the traditional. When the color TV set is on, the program is quite likely a *sumo* match, a sport whose history goes back to 23 B.C. *Gagaku*, a court entertainment with masked dancers brilliantly dressed in brocades and accompanied by flutes, drums, and the reedy *sho*, is performed just the way it was a thousand years ago. Worshipers visit the Ise Grand Shrine, which is periodically rebuilt, but rebuilt in a style going back to prehistoric times.

Mammoth department stores sell seven-thousand-dollar kimonos and ten-year-old bonsai, and their service includes gift-wrapping beefsteaks and tracing family trees. For bargain hunters there are maze-like shopping arcades, where prices are sometimes forty percent lower than in the big stores. Shoppers, with appetites whetted by the smell of soy sauce, fried onions, and grilled meat, stop at little stalls to eat noodles, roasted corn, or chicken meat on skewers. At the morning markets spread out on sidewalks, country people come to sell fruits, vegetables, seafood, and handmade toys.

The crime rate is low, and the atmosphere in stores, hotels, and other public facilities is relaxed because stealing is rare. It is safe to walk alone through a park at night, and guests can leave their doors unlocked at inns. But political assassinations are still carried out with a sword, and students and police clash, armed with lances, helmets, and shields like medieval knights.

In Japan unbridled luxury is combined with painstaking thrift. The costs of dinner parties can run into four figures, and hotels have ponds containing prize carp worth hundreds of dollars each. But there are other hotels and resorts where frugal guests bring their own cooking utensils and buy fresh food from local farmers. Wooden lunch boxes are thrown away by the millions every day, but pine needles are carefully swept up to be used as fuel.

With its extreme contrasts and its brilliant colors, Japan appeals to travelers who love the exotic. But because of the language barrier and the Japanese reputation for being

INTRODUCTION

inscrutable, tourists feel timid about venturing out alone and usually surrender themselves to closely guided tours that effectively insulate them from the country and its people.

The purpose of this book is to encourage you to go out alone, to travel the way the Japanese themselves do, to eat their food and stay at their type of lodging. Away from the main streets of the big cities you can see traditional Japanese life, and you will experience not only a sense of adventure, but also a way of life that may appeal strongly to your tastes. Japan is a country of contrasts — occasionally bewildering, sometimes exasperating, but always fascinating.

ESSENTIALS

1
GETTING AROUND

What kind of country is it that we shall see?

CLIMATE

The northern part of Japan resembles the northeastern part of the United States, with long, severe winters and lots of snow. The populous, central part of the country has milder winters, but is very uncomfortable in the summer because of high humidity. For about three weeks in June, there is a rainy season, called the *tsuyu*, which the tourist would do well to avoid. The crisp, bright days of autumn come as a wonderful relief from the oppressive heat and humidity of summer. Spring comes early in central Japan. By the end of February, there is a mildness in the air, and by March, the Japanese shed their heavy winter clothing and start leaving their windows and door panels open. The southern part of Japan is semi-tropical, with lush, exotic vegetation.

SHAPE

In shape Japan is an archipelago consisting of four main islands and many small ones. Starting from the north, the main islands are Hokkaido, Honshu, Shikoku, and Kyushu.

Hokkaido

Compared to the rest of Japan, the northernmost island of Hokkaido is less developed and sparsely settled. Its main tourist attraction is its scenery: rugged mountains (there are a number of active volcanoes), pure lakes, and primeval forests.

Honshu

The main island of Honshu is separated from Hokkaido by the Tsugaru Straits. The largest of the four islands, Honshu is shaped roughly like a boomerang, with Tokyo almost at the apex. Starting from Tokyo, the right arm of the boomerang runs north by northeast, while the left arm runs west.

The right arm is the region known as Tohoku. A spine of mountains divides this arm into two halves. The side west of the mountains faces the Sea of Japan, and in winter cold winds from the Asian mainland dump huge amounts of snow, giving the region the name Snow Country. The side east of the mountains faces the Pacific, and has less snow.

The thick, middle part of the boomerang contains Mt. Fuji and the Japan Alps, the country's highest range of mountains. But the only two sizable plains of Japan are also located in the central part of Honshu, as is the industrial heart of the country.

The left arm of the Honshu boomerang runs straight

west. When the Japanese speak of regional differences, they are usually contrasting east and west. Tokyo is considered the eastern end of the main axis, while Kyoto and Osaka are considered the western end (although there is a lot of Honshu west of Kyoto and Osaka). The region around Tokyo is called *Kantō*, and the region around Kyoto and Osaka called *Kansai* (*Kan* means "barrier," *tō* means "east" and *sai* means "west"). In feudal days, the central government placed various barriers, or checkpoints, along the major highways in order to monitor traffic and keep an eye on subversive activities. One of the main barriers along the famous Tōkaidō highway was at a point about halfway between Tokyo and Kyoto. *Kantō* referred to the region east of the barrier and *Kansai* the region west of it.

On the left half of the Honshu boomerang, the southern coast faces the Inland Sea. Called the Seto Naikai by the Japanese, the Inland Sea is not really a body of water mostly surrounded by land, like the Mediterranean, but actually a channel separating Honshu from the island of Shikoku.

SHIKOKU

The smallest of the four main islands is Shikoku. On its north coast, facing the Inland Sea, are many pleasure resorts. The rest of it is quiet, with fruit orchards and farms, except in the spring when thousands of pilgrims come to the island to visit its many temples (see Chapter 10, CHURCHES, TEMPLES, AND SHRINES).

KYUSHU

At the western end of the Inland Sea is the island of Kyushu, the last of the four major islands. Kyushu is interesting historically because it is geographically closest to the mainland and thus is the first place to be visited by people from the Asian continent.

Besides these four main islands, there are many smaller ones. Of these the most notable are the Okinawa Islands, 685 kilometers (about 425 miles) from the southern tip of Kyushu.

Now we are ready to travel.

Let us begin with a word about luggage, since luggage problems can ruin a trip. In most Japanese trains and buses, your luggage is kept on an overhead rack. Western suitcases tend to be too flat and wide to fit into these racks. Japanese travelers, on the other hand, carry bags whose shape is more cube-like. This may not be good for suits or party dresses, which is why most Japanese wear their better clothes while traveling. We do the opposite: we wear comfortable clothes and bring our party clothes in our suitcases. Duffel bags and rucksacks fit much better into the overhead racks if they are not too long. Many train and air terminals sell large fabric bags with wheels on the bottom. They are perfect for train and plane trips, and you can stuff all your underwear and sports clothes in them. But they won't take heavy use and are not recommended for camping.

For short trips many Japanese carry their belongings in a square piece of cloth called a *furoshiki*. When in use, the opposite corners of the cloth are tied together, forming a neat bundle easy to carry, and when not in use, the cloth is folded flat. Furoshiki come in all sizes and patterns, and they make marvelous souvenir gifts.

TRANSPORTATION WITHIN TOKYO

The information that follows will apply to other large cities as well.

Taxi

Japanese taxis are relatively inexpensive compared to those in other countries. The fare depends on the size of the taxi, although the difference in the fare is so small that you may as well take the large taxi if it happens to come along first. There is an additional charge for going through slow traffic, using toll roads, and for late hours. If you are tired, or if there are three or four persons in your party, a taxi is really worthwhile. But don't try to cram more than four into a small taxi, because this is against regulations. If your luggage is outsized, you may also have trouble, since the trunk of a Japanese taxi is intended for Japanese luggage.

The best way to get a taxi is to wait in line at a taxi stand, which can be found at train stations, airports, major subway stations, department stores, and large hotels. Stopping a cruising taxi is harder, since many drivers are reluctant to take foreign passengers for fear of the difficulty in communication. A crafty friend told me that she would ask a Japanese to stop a taxi for her while she lurked in a doorway out of sight.

By the way, as you prepare to enter a taxi, don't try to open the rear door yourself, but stand clear and wait for it to open automatically. More than one tourist carry scars from the sharp corner of a taxi door opening unexpectedly on their legs. Once inside, you can't open the door yourself, but have to wait for it to open automatically after you first pay your fare.

There are a lot of horror stories about the recklessness of Japanese taxi drivers. The most common is that they are ex-Kamikaze pilots who have been cheated of their death wish during the war. Most of these stories arise from the fact that taxi drivers like to start fast, throwing the passengers back violently against their seats. Also, they like to weave in and out a lot. But statistics show very few casualties among taxi passengers, and when there is a traffic accident, it is usually a pedestrian who is smeared against the wall.

In Tokyo, don't expect every taxi driver to know where he is going. The city is so vast and complicated that drivers often have to stop at police boxes to ask for directions. Your driver is not trying to cheat you: he is genuinely lost. First of all, most streets have no street signs. Moreover, houses are not numbered consecutively. If there is any logic to the numbering at all, it is probably based on the age of the house: that is, house #34 was built before #35, but not necessarily next to it. Tokyo was built on the site of a castle town, and Japanese castles were constructed like mazes, whose purpose was to bewilder the would-be attacker (see Chapter 9, CASTLES AND SAMURAI). This means that your Tokyo taxi driver is bewildered too. If you want him to find an obscure private house in an obscure street, have someone write the full address in Japanese on a slip of paper. It also helps if you can tell him of a nearby landmark, such as a prominent building. But don't be surprised if the driver still has to stop several times at police boxes to ask for help.

WALKING

The best and simplest way of getting around is, of course, to walk. You can dawdle all you want. You can wander into fascinating little streets where you will see the old and traditional Japan. But there are certain things to watch out for while you're walking. First of all, you keep to the left, as in Britain. When asked why they are so stubbornly different, the British and the Japanese say that the rest of the world is on the wrong side of the road. Keeping to the left probably stems from the time of feudal Japan, when people wore their swords on their left side. Since clashing swords with someone was an insult to be wiped out with blood, it was prudent to walk on the left side of the road and keep your sword out of the way. It was also easier to draw your sword and defend yourself from attack.

As a pedestrian, remember that cars drive on the left side of the road, and you must first look to the right before crossing the street. Many small streets have no sidewalks, and when a car comes along, you practically have to flatten yourself against a wall. Cars don't slow down or swerve for a pedestrian. Though the Japanese are noted for their politeness, they sprout fangs when they get behind a wheel. The attitude of the driver toward the pedestrian is that of a samurai toward a peasant: the pedestrian had better get out of the way and be quick about it.

After the car, the greatest menace to the pedestrian is the cyclist. If you hear a bell tinkle behind you, watch out. In the busy streets of large cities, sidewalks are wide, but they have to be shared with cyclists. Strictly speaking, cyclists are supposed to use only the left side of the walk, but they are always weaving in and out.

Another natural enemy of the pedestrian is the watering can. For some reason — perhaps to settle dust — shopkeepers and home owners frequently sprinkle the ground in front of their house with a watering can. Sidewalks in Japan are smooth, not textured, and when you're wearing an old pair of crepe-soled shoes, a wet sidewalk is as slippery as if it has been oiled. Train platforms are also regularly sprinkled. Once I nearly skidded right off the platform into the path of a moving train. You are always told not to wear new shoes when traveling, but neither should you wear your oldest pair of crepe soles. Actually, a pair of *geta*, or Japanese wooden clogs, is the best for muddy ground or slippery sidewalks.

Rain, too, makes the sidewalks slick. It also produces an outbreak of umbrellas. In Japan, not many of the older homes have a clothes dryer, and in the spring and summer the humidity is so high that if you get soaked in April, it may be September before your cotton T-shirt dries. Hence the millions of umbrellas that pop open whenever it rains.

A sidewalk wide enough for three abreast is not wide enough when people are carrying open umbrellas. When two people are approaching each other, one will raise and the other lower his umbrella as an act of courtesy. Until you are used to doing this, you will find it a bumpy experience to go out on a busy street with your umbrella. (It may be a bumpy experience even without your umbrella.) Fortunately, umbrella bumping, unlike sword bumping, is not an insult to be wiped out with blood.

An umbrella does have its uses in narrow streets without sidewalks, especially if it has a sharp metal tip. Hold the umbrella horizontally, with the sharp end pointing toward the middle of the street. Seeing this, drivers will be cautious about coming too close to you. Blood or hair on the bumper is one thing; a deep scratch in the paint work is troublesome to remove.

All this makes walking sound dangerous. But walking is truly one of the greatest pleasures in Japan, more fascinating than going to a museum or a movie. Many Japanese craftsmen work in their front room, which is open to the street. A pedestrian can watch tatami mat-makers with their five-inch pins, carpenters using their traditional tools, and noodle makers rolling out their dough. You're closer to people when you are on foot. And it doesn't always rain.

You are also safe from dog feces, since Japanese dogs are among the most tightly curbed in the world. Dogs are not plentiful in Japan anyway. With hamburger at four dollars a pound, feeding them is a problem. Blind people don't have Seeing-Eye dogs, so crossing a busy intersection is difficult for them. For the benefit of the blind, the large intersections in some cities have recorded music: one tune is played when the light is green for east-west streets, another when the light is green for north-south streets.

Speaking of dogs, we advise against trying to make friends with strange dogs in Japan. In a country where animal protein is expensive and land scarce, dogs neither eat well nor exercise properly — in short, they lead a dog's life. They are chained up most of the day, and take out their frustrations on anyone within snapping distance. Remember the opening scene in *Yojimbo*, showing a dog trotting by with a severed hand in its mouth? The hand might have belonged to a rash tourist who ventured too close.

The rights of pedestrians are beginning to be recognized by politicians and, even more importantly, by businessmen. In certain cities cars are banned from some of the downtown streets on Sundays. You can now walk down the middle of the Ginza on Sunday without fear of being maimed. (But watch out for the mobs!)

Driving

After being a pedestrian for a while, you begin to get quite paranoid about drivers, especially when you see the air pollution resulting from car exhausts. It's a rare treat to see Mt. Fuji above the photochemical smog these days. Many downtown streets post the current air-pollution level, but these figures are more depressing than useful. What can you do when the pollution index reaches a dangerous level? Stop breathing?

If you are the vindictive sort, you may feel a strong urge to rent a car and get into the driver's seat yourself. Don't do it. Japan is the worst of all possible worlds for an American driver. As in Continental Europe, the metric system is used for signs and for selling gasoline, but you keep to the left side of the road as in Britain. Gasoline costs about three times as much as in America. Worst of all, signs are in Japanese characters. On toll expressways, the signs are sometimes also spelled out in English, but in city streets and on small roads the signs are in characters. Finally, the roads are narrow, crowded, and crooked. All the other drivers seem demented. Riding a motorcycle is even more dangerous.

Bicycling

Riding a bike in small or medium-sized cities is not too bad, but it is risky in large cities like Tokyo. Since bicycles share the sidewalk with pedestrians, you have to devote all your attention to dodging mothers with babies strapped to their backs, students walking three abreast, and old men doubled over canes. In streets without sidewalks, the cyclist is at the mercy of cars. Above all, it is fatal to tangle with noodle delivery boys who ride their bikes with one hand, balance a tray of noodle bowls with another, and carry an umbrella with a third. They are probably descended from a long line of acrobats, and it's hopeless trying to compete with them.

Riding a bike in the streets is hazardous, but riding in parks, along trails, and in the country is a pleasure. We shall discuss bicycling for pleasure in Chapter 7, SPORTS.

Streetcars and Buses

Aside from sedan chairs and rickshaws, the oldest form of public transport in the city is the streetcar. But their tracks interfere with motor traffic and they are fast disappearing. Even Kyoto, which used to have the largest streetcar system in Japan, took them out of operation in 1978. Like the cable cars in San Francisco, these lurching, stately old streetcars have a homely charm, and thousands of nostalgic tourists mourn their passing.

For short distances in the city, buses are now the most common form of public transport. If you have time to make a study of the routes or have a friend to explain them to you, buses are a cheap and convenient way to travel. On buses with a front entrance, you pay as you enter, but on those with a rear or middle entrance, you pay as you get off. Buses are not easy for the newcomer. The stops are difficult to read and are always in Japanese. There is a recording that announces the next stop, but it is often out of sync, giving you the name of the stop when it's too late, or giving it prematurely, so you jump off too soon. What you can do is have a friend write the name of your stop on a piece of paper. Wave it around at the passengers near you, and when your stop comes, they will tell you or even help you to the exit. This willingness to help a stranger or a foreigner is something you will meet all over the country. Don't expect it during rush hour, however. Then it's everyone for himself.

Some buses go a longer distance to and from suburbs and adjacent cities. For these, the procedure for paying the fare is different. You enter from the rear and take a ticket from a dispensing machine. On the ticket is a number, which indicates the zone where you got on. (If you enter the bus at the start of its route, the number on your ticket will be #1. When the bus crosses into the next zone, the machine starts dispensing tickets marked #2, and so on.) Above the driver's seat is a lighted panel showing what the fare at the moment is for each kind of ticket. When you get off, you pay the fare indicated for your kind of ticket. All this sounds complicated, but it is quite easy to understand when you're actually on the bus.

Besides these public buses, there are many tour buses of the hit-all-the-high-points-of-Tokyo-in-three-hours variety. They are good for a first, overall impression of Tokyo, but after a while you may get tired of being at the beck and call of the tour guide.

Subway

For longer distances within Tokyo, the subway is the most efficient way of getting around. Subways are called *chikatetsu*, literally "underground rail," and their entrances are marked by a stylized wheel or a stylized "S,"

ESSENTIALS

which looks like a circle with a horizontal dash. (A subway map of Tokyo can be obtained from the Japan National Tourist Organization [JNTO]).

The Tokyo subway is simpler to use than the London or New York systems. You know where you are, where you've been and where you're going, because not only the present station, but the previous and the next are indicated. A friend of mine claims that he gets easily lost aboveground in Tokyo, and when that happens he plunges into the nearest subway entrance to orient himself — like going back into the safety of the womb.

There is just one hitch about using the subway: although the station names are in English, the charts that give a schedule of the fares are in Japanese characters. In order to pay the fare, you can do one of four things. The first is to learn the characters for your location and your destination. But some people resist learning characters (I've known singers who would rather learn a whole opera by heart than learn to read music); they can use the second way — consult their little English subway map and count the number of stops to their destination. Then they look at the fare chart and count to the right number of stops to find out the charge. The third way is to buy the minimum ticket, ride to the destination, and before approaching the exit, go to a window which says "Fare Adjustment." There you learn what additional amount, if any, you have to pay. Of course you have to understand the man when he says, "That will be an additional 70 yen, please." Finally, the lazy wastrel's way is to pay the maximum fare wherever you go. Actually, this is not as extravagant as it sounds, since even the maximum fare is not so much.

The Tokyo subway system still has human guards at the entrances and exits. You hand the guard at the exit your ticket (which you have carefully kept), and if you haven't paid enough, he will order you to the fare adjustment window. In some cities, the subways are completely automated. You insert your ticket into a machine at the turnstile, and it spits out the ticket after registering your passage. Don't forget to take it with you. At the end of your ride, you feed the ticket into the slot at the exit, and if you've paid too much, the ticket pops up again when you go through, so you can use it some more. If you've paid too little, a barrier crashes closed at the turnstile, and a disembodied voice tells the sinner to go to the fare adjustment window.

INTERURBAN TRAINS

The subway system covers central Tokyo. If you want to reach an outlying area, you can take an interurban electric train operated by the Japan National Railway (JNR) or a private company. These trains connect with the subway system and with long-distance trains. Again, you will find that the ticket machines give the fare chart only in Japanese characters. You can choose one of the four schemes we just mentioned in connection with the subway.

You have to be careful about one thing while taking the interurban trains. In addition to locals, there are both express trains and limited-express trains (the latter having fewer stops than express trains). Since express trains don't make every stop, be sure you don't get on a train that whizzes past the stop you want. You have to learn the Japanese characters for "express" and "limited express" that are shown in window panels of these trains. They are also used for long-distance trains. (A JNR map of Tokyo and vicinity can be obtained from the JNTO.)

While riding either the subway or the interurban trains, it's a good idea to avoid rush hours, unless you enjoy having a briefcase slammed into your solar plexus. You may have seen pictures of Japanese station guards shoving passengers into the trains. They have to shove, because the train won't start until the doors are all shut tight. At least

ESSENTIALS

you're not being shoved by sweaty palms, but by hands elegantly encased in white gloves.

Getting into the train is half the battle. The other half comes when the passengers are spewed out. You may find yourself carried along, and your screams that this is not your station don't do any good, assuming you can scream Japanese in the first place. If you really have a masochistic desire to experience the rush hour, go to Shinjuku Station between eight and nine in the morning, or five and six in the evening. But before surrendering yourself to the maelstrom, make sure all your detachable parts, such as contact lenses, are firmly attached.

Lately there is a rumor going around that female passengers are getting pinched during the rush hour, when it's too crowded to spot the culprit. Since Japanese women pride themselves on their composure, they can't scream or make a fuss. This is one more reason to avoid (or choose) the rush-hour commuter trains.

Most of the remarks about the subway and interurban trains apply not only to Tokyo, but to other cities like Osaka, Nagoya, Kobe, Sapporo, and Yokohama. Kyoto has no subway as yet, but one is under construction.

LONG-DISTANCE TRANSPORTATION

Now that we have discussed how to get around in a city, let's make a long-distance trip.

FLYING

If you don't have much time and want to see the extreme ends of Japan, flying is the best way. Persons aged twelve to twenty-two can use the Skymate plan and go half fare on a stand-by basis. The departure lounges at many airports have a special lounge for Skymate customers, where they can watch TV, read magazines, or nap while they wait for word on space availability. (Most Japanese can nap at the drop of an eyelid.) To buy tickets at the Skymate rate, simply show your passport as proof of age.

There are three airlines operating domestic routes: Japan Airlines (JAL), All Nippon Airways (ANA), and Toa Domestic Airlines (TDA). The last operates only local routes and won't concern us much, since it is better to take the train for short trips. The service on JAL and ANA flights is comparable to that of domestic airlines in the West, except that they don't serve hot meals or alcoholic drinks. But the flights are so short that few passengers grumble (the flight from Tokyo to Sapporo takes only one and a half hours). You do get snacks, soft drinks, coffee, tea, and an *o-shibori*, or damp towel. You also have the free use of earphones for music or travelogues.

One inconvenience about the domestic service is that you can't check in too far in advance. At some airports, if you arrive much too early, you can't unload your luggage until about one-half to one hour before departure. The lockers at the airports, like lockers everywhere in Japan, don't accommodate large, Western suitcases, and there are usually not enough lockers to go around anyway. Many Japanese trustfully leave their luggage unattended while they go off to buy a magazine or a snack, but this is not advisable at an airport, where there are a lot of foreigners around.

Trains

It is a very time-consuming hassle to go to and from the airport. Unless the trip is quite long, you are better off taking the train, because Japan has the most advanced railway system in the world. When travelers talk about Japanese trains, they are usually thinking about the *Shinkansen* super-express bullet trains.

ESSENTIALS

Shinkansen means "New Trunk Line," and its famous bullet trains run along the densest arterial route of Japan, connecting Tokyo with cities on the southern coast of the left arm of the Honshu boomerang. The line goes to the western tip of Honshu, crosses the Kanmon Straits to Kyushu by an undersea tunnel, and ends at Hakata, a city in northern Kyushu. These trains are known the world over as a miracle of modern engineering. Here are some figures on the trains: maximum speed, 130 miles an hour; average speed from Tokyo to Hakata, 95 miles an hour, including stops! Every hour, eight of these bullet trains start from Tokyo, with the first train leaving at six in the morning and the last train at eleven at night. Even more impressive is the trains' punctuality. When a train is two minutes late, the station master calls up the previous stop to find out what is wrong. Then there is the trains' safety record: during more than fifteen years of service, 900 million passengers took the trains with not a single fatal accident.

There are two kinds of bullet trains, the *Hikari*, meaning "Light," and the *Kodama*, meaning "Echo." The Hikari is faster because it makes fewer stops. The stops are very brief — two to five minutes — and passengers getting out should be prepared to move smartly. Before reaching your destination, you should be standing at the door with all your luggage about you. And if the stop is not your destination, for heaven's sake don't get out of the train — it will be gone before you can get back on! (Other limited-express trains have similarly short stops.)

You may be tempted to get out, because the train platforms have stalls and vendors selling all kinds of goodies like food, magazines, and souvenirs. Too bad — you should have bought these at the start of the trip before you entered the train. But even if you didn't, don't fret. Carts are pushed up and down the aisles at regular intervals, from which you can buy drinks, ice cream, sandwiches, and lunch boxes (see Chapter 3, FOOD). The trains have dining cars, but you may not get immediate seating, and frankly, the food is not worth waiting in line for.

Fares In order of increasing speed, Japanese trains are classified as local, express, limited-express ("limited" means a limited number of stops), or super-express. There is a basic boarding fare that depends on the distance, and you pay extra express fare, the amount depending on how express it is. If you take the super-express Shinkansen from Tokyo to Kyoto, for example, it costs about twice as much as taking a local. On top of the express fare, you pay 200 yen if you want a reserved seat. You don't have to reserve a seat, and if you're not traveling at a busy time you can usually find a seat in the non-reserved section. Those who feel extravagant and want a wider seat can buy a first-class ticket for the so-called Green Car. On the Shinkansen the first-class ticket comes close to being twice as much as an ordinary ticket.

Reservations can be made at the Japan Travel Bureau or at the train station. Go to a ticket window with green lettering, and if you don't see it, ask for the *midori-no-madoguchi*.

After you have bought your ticket, look at it carefully and note the time, the number, and the name of your train. It is easy to get on the wrong bullet train, because there are so many identical-looking trains all going in the same direction at approximately the same time. I once got on a train that left five minutes later than scheduled. I was about to jeer at this failure of the famous Shinkansen punctuality when I realized I was on the wrong train. Since I forfeited my seat reservation and it was a busy time, I had to stand the whole way nose-to-nose with a little boy who had a bad cold. I could have been even unluckier: I might have been on a train that didn't stop at my station.

ESSENTIALS

The Shinkansen is the showpiece of the Japanese railway system and eventually a network of super-express trains will cover the whole country. But right now there are other crack trains only slightly inferior to the bullet trains in speed and comfort. Although there is nothing in Japan corresponding to Eurailpass or Britrailpass, there are various discounts available. The Japan Travel Bureau can tell you which ones fit your travel plans.

Sleepers Sleepers are available; they cost about 10,000 yen for the wide ones and 3000 yen for the narrow. But they are not really necessary if you are traveling west from Tokyo, since the Shinkansen takes you to your destination in just a few hours. As yet there is no super-express going north up the right arm of the Honshu boomerang. A train trip to the northern tip of Honshu from Tokyo takes about eleven hours by limited express, and you may want a sleeper if you make the whole journey non-stop. People in a hurry to go to Hokkaido may want to make a non-stop trip, but by the time you add the cost of the sleeper and the ferry, it will turn out to be cheaper to fly.

Baggage You are allowed to carry two pieces of luggage with you into the train, provided they are not too big. Besides the problem of fitting your luggage onto the overhead rack that we've talked about earlier, you have to do a certain amount of walking up and down stairs, through long corridors, and along train platforms. Burdened with heavy luggage, your arms will soon stretch to gorilla length. Think about this while you're buying all that beautiful folk pottery. If you can't arrange to have your souvenirs shipped, at least check your baggage before getting on the train. Japanese passengers are allowed to check two pieces weighing up to 30 kilograms (66 pounds) each, but foreign tourists, upon showing their passports, can check two pieces weighing up to 50 kg. (110 pounds) each.

Maybe the officials guessed that tourists can't resist buying folk pottery. Checked baggage is kept for you three days free of charge; after that you have to pay for storage.

Foreign tourists sometimes complain that there are not many porters, or redcaps, at Japanese stations. If you are a Japanese VIP and accustomed to comfort, you have a retinue of underlings to carry all the bags and stow them into place. Businessmen and government officials have eager subordinates to see them off, and professors have students. Plain folk learn to travel light.

Seeing people off is an institution in Japan, and it's fun to watch a wedding party seeing off a honeymoon couple at the train platform. You can recognize a wedding party by the formal black kimonos of the women and the identical parcels everyone is holding (at a Japanese wedding, the guests all receive a souvenir gift to take home). The newly married couple is wafted aboard on such a wave of good wishes that you feel tempted to join the cheering.

FERRIES

In the old days, the only way to get from one island to another of the Japanese archipelago was to take the ferry. Today there is an undersea tunnel connecting the main island of Honshu with the southern island of Kyushu, and another tunnel is under construction between Honshu and the northern island of Hokkaido. The eastern end of Shikoku is connected to Honshu by a bridge, which has a couple of intermediate islands as stepping stones.

At present, however, you go to Hokkaido by plane or by ferry. For the shortest ferry to Hokkaido, go to the city of Aomori near the northern tip of Honshu. There are many departures from Aomori for the city of Hakodate on Hokkaido, and the trip lasts about three and a half hours. The economy fare is about 1000 yen, and the first-class fare is twice that amount.

Although you can reach Shikoku by a bridge, there are

ESSENTIALS

many ferries across the Inland Sea from Honshu, too numerous to list here. One of the most frequent is the ferry starting from Uno, a port city south of Okayama (a city between Kobe and Hiroshima, which can be reached by Shinkansen from Tokyo), to Takamatsu on Shikoku. There are many hydrofoil services across the Inland Sea, most of them connecting Hiroshima with Matsuyama. You can also take a hydrofoil from Kobe to Tokushima on Shikoku, a trip lasting one hour and forty-five minutes. Your choice of ferry or hydrofoil depends on where you want to start and end.

The hydrofoil is three times faster than the conventional ferry, and flying is faster still. People who take the ferry do it because it is such a beautiful trip. A long ferry ride across the length of the Inland Sea is one of the most scenic rides in the world, going past thousands of tiny islands, some of them only large enough to support one twisted pine tree. The view is straight out of a landscape painting. There are a number of long ferry rides that start from the eastern end of the Inland Sea and finish at the island of Kyushu at the western end. A popular one starts from Osaka (or Kobe) and ends at Beppu (on Kyushu) thirteen hours later. This particular ferry carries only passengers, but some ferries carry cars as well.

It has become fashionable in Japan to take long ferry trips lasting a couple of days. Some of the ships are like ocean liners, with swimming pools, deck sports, restaurants, bars, and dance halls. Long ferry trips are especially popular with honeymoon couples, who can retire into their staterooms and emerge periodically for meals. A good example of a long ferry trip is the one from Tokyo to the city of Tomakomai in Hokkaido, starting at night in Tokyo and arriving early morning on the third day.

There are four classes of accommodations on the long-distance ferry boats: deluxe first class, first class, deluxe second class, and second class. The most expensive fare is about three times that of the cheapest, and the fare for an automobile is slightly higher than that of the deluxe first class. The fare does not include meals, which you eat in one of the restaurants or snack bars, but many economize by bringing their own food. There is one pleasant aspect to traveling on a Japanese ship: you don't have to tip anybody (this is true also for ocean liners).

The deluxe accommodations consist of staterooms with beds, large picture windows, easy chairs, and private bathroom and toilet. In the economy classes, you grab what chair you can in a public lounge and use a public bath (see Chapter 5, BATHS, BATHROOMS, AND TOILETS). Economy passengers sleep in a huge hall covered with tatami mats. The first thing you do when you go aboard is to make a dash for the big tatami room and stake out a little area for your party by putting down some clothing or parcels. Other passengers will then respect your right to the territory. The Japanese are used to living in crowded conditions, and the way they respect the privacy of others is by turning a blind eye. You can be in the tatami room crowded with hundreds of people, and yet each little family or party stays in its territory and ignores the chatter, laughter, or moans from adjacent groups.

For longer ferry trips, it is essential to make a reservation with your travel agent or the Japan Travel Bureau, especially during the busy season. One time of the year when the ferries are not crowded is September, during the typhoon season. At that time even cast-iron stomachs wobble.

BUSY SEASONS

In Japan there are four major travel seasons (besides weekends), and you would be wise to avoid major traveling at these times. One is spring vacation time in April and May, which reaches a climax during "Golden Week," a period that includes three national holidays: the Emperor's birthday on April 29, Constitution Day on May 3, and Children's Day on May 5. The second peak is in July and August, when schools are on summer vacation. Then there is the fall travel period in October and November, a favorite time for weddings and honeymoons. The last peak period is the year-end vacation period, the last week of December and the first week of January. If you can't avoid traveling during one of these busy seasons, make your reservations well in advance for train, plane, ferry, bus, or lodging.

2
LANGUAGE

The Japanese believe their language is too difficult for foreigners to learn. Most tourists have a mental block against Japanese writing, and anyway they soon decide that English is adequate for satisfying the usual tourist needs along the Ginza. Therefore they seldom take the trouble to learn any Japanese beyond *arigatō*, which they say when the waiter brings them a glass of water (the Japanese don't thank waiters). This confirms the belief that foreigners can't learn Japanese.

I know of an American who was born in Japan of missionary parents and lived there until college age. He spoke faultless Japanese. Once he managed — with some difficulty — to get into a conversation with an old farmer. After they had chatted in Japanese for a long time about this and that, the old man said, "You know, it's amazing. I never knew English was so easy to understand!" The farmer could not believe it was possible for Japanese to issue from the mouth of someone with blue eyes and red hair.

After all this, you begin to wonder whether it's worth

the trouble to learn any Japanese at all. It *is* worth the trouble, as those of you know who have traveled the byways of other countries. You don't have to know much of the language, just enough to communicate your basic needs to a helpful listener. You may find yourself tramping along in rural Japan, and the only person you meet may be a little boy carrying a butterfly net. Since you're famished, you want to say, "Where can I find a place to eat?" (It's *Shokudō wa doko?*).

DIFFICULTIES OF SPEAKING CORRECT JAPANESE

We are going to make an outrageous suggestion: speak uncouth Japanese. You can acquire a smattering easily enough, but for a number of reasons it's almost impossible for a foreigner to speak correct Japanese without serious study. There are social traps that even native speakers fall into. Certain verb forms are used while talking to your classmates, but if you use them to your teacher your grades may suffer. Being too polite is also hazardous. If you use too polite a form of speech to workmen, they'll think you're mocking them and give you a dirty look.

Women's Speech

Men and women speak differently. Shortly after World War II, some officers of the American occupation forces in Japan were given intensive courses in Japanese. They had all the latest language-lab techniques, and they received intensive drills in pronunciation with their teachers. But all the teachers were women! When the officers completed the course and were set at large among the Japanese population, they couldn't understand why, when they opened their mouths, people kept breaking down into unseemly giggles. Still smarting under defeat and oc-

LANGUAGE

cupation, the Japanese were enjoying the spectacle of their tall conquerors speaking like mincing women.

CLASS DISTINCTION

Most of the differences in the various modes of speech are in the verb forms. But there are also differences in the use of certain pronouns. For the first person singular "I," young boys and men in casual conversation use *boku*, while women and men speaking more formally use *watakushi* or *watashi*. The Emperor uses the form *chin* for the pronoun "I," which no other person in the world uses. In the old days noblemen used one form, samurai another, while commoners used still a third. In one adventure story, a young samurai tries to penetrate the headquarters of the enemy by pretending to be the rice delivery boy. But he gives himself away when he slips up on the pronoun.

Not only do we urge you to forget about social distinction, we recommend that you cut out all unnecessary frills, even at the cost of being ungrammatical. The reason is that Japanese has far fewer distinctive sounds (or phonemes) than English, and therefore requires many more syllables to say the same thing. (A mathematical analogy is that a number expressed in base 2 has more digits than a number in base 10. For example, 36 is 10100 in base 2.) When you have to catch a train, you don't want to trip over a lot of syllables. You just want to yell, "Tokyo Station, where?"

PHRASE BOOKS

No traveler should be without a phrase book. There are dozens of useful English-Japanese phrase books, and we can't begin to list them all. You can buy them at airports, major train stations, and bookstores, but many travel centers, such as the Tourist Information Centers in Tokyo and Kyoto, give them out free.

ESSENTIALS

The only objection to these phrase books is that they are too correct. As a result, many phrases for even simple everyday needs come out rather long, and tourists have trouble remembering them. It is best to dispense with non-essentials. By the way, our remarks here are not addressed to people already studying Japanese, but only to tourists trying to communicate basic needs without fretting about details like *wa* and *ga*, which overload your circuits. Why should you care if you speak pidgin Japanese? Everybody knows you're a foreigner.

Suppose you want to say that you can't speak Japanese. The phrase books, ever conscientious, tell you to say, "*Watakushi wa nihongo o hanasemasen.*" There are so many syllables to remember that the average tourist gets discouraged. It's better to forget the correct grammar and just say, "*Nihongo hanasemasen*," which means, "Japanese, can't." What about the things we left out? First, the pronoun *watakushi*, meaning "I," can be left out without ambiguity, because the person you are addressing knows perfectly well that *you* are the one who can't speak Japanese. We also omitted the particles *wa* and *o*, which indicated subject and object.

Many verbs can be safely omitted. Suppose you want to know where the toilet is. The phrase books tell you to say, "*O-benjo wa doko ni arimasu-ka?*" But you can get away with simply saying, "*Benjo doko?*" We have omitted the *o* in front of *benjo*. The *o* is only an honorific used for the sake of politeness, and we reduced the honorable toilet to a plain toilet. We also omitted the grammatical particles *wa* and *ni*, and we left out *arimasu*, "is" and "*ka*," the interrogative particle. So that instead of saying, "The honorable toilet, where is it?" we said, "Toilet, where?" Crude, but adequate.

Another word you can omit is *gozaimasu*. It has no meaning, but is liberally sprinkled around to make things more polite. *Arigatō* is a rather curt "thank you," but *arigatō gozaimasu* is more gracious. *Ohayō gozaimasu* is

28

much nicer than a blunt *ohayō* for "good morning." (Once an American traveler decided that the way to remember the Japanese for "good morning" was to think of the state of Ohio. When he finally got to Japan, he mystified everybody with *Iowa gozaimasu*.)

PRONUNCIATION

You can get away with sloppy grammar, but you do have to exercise care over pronunciation, because there is a very real danger of being misunderstood. (I once overheard a tourist trying to buy a ticket to Kyoto, and she was furious because the clerk, although claiming to speak English, couldn't understand what she wanted. The traveler was pronouncing *Kyoto* like *coyote*.) Fortunately, the pronunciation of Japanese is not too difficult.

Vowels
There are five vowels, *a*, *e*, *i*, *o* and *u*, and they are pronounced approximately as follows:
    a is like the *a* in "father"
    e is like the *e* in "pen"
    i is like the *i* in "machine"
    o is like the *o* in "horse"
    u is like the *u* in "full"

Long and Short Vowels
You do have to watch out for the distinction between long and short vowels. (A long vowel is one that is held longer than a short vowel, but the quality of which is unchanged.) In most of the phrase books and dictionaries, the long vowels are marked by a dash above them, as in *ohayō*, "good morning." If you neglect to lengthen the vowel, you can be misunderstood. In fact, you can say the opposite of what you intend. For example, *ō* is "big," as in *Ōno*, "Big Field." But *o* is "small," as in *Ono*, "Small

ESSENTIALS

Field." Both of these are common surnames, and by neglecting to lengthen the vowel, you may be asking for Mr. Small Field when you really want Mr. Big Field.

When the vowel *u* follows *t*, *s*, or *z*, it sounds a little different, and is more like a buzz. The name Suzuki sounds somewhat like the buzzing of a bee. Also, when either *u* or *i* is between or following consonants like *p*, *t*, *s*, *sh*, and *k*, the vowel is unvoiced, that is, whispered. A word like *sukiyaki* sounds like *skiyaki*.

CONSONANTS

There are seventeen consonants, usually rendered in the English alphabet by *b*, *ch*, *d*, *f*, *g*, *h*, *j*, *k*, *m*, *n*, *p*, *r*, *s*, *sh*, *t*, *ts*, and *z*. They are pronounced pretty much as you would expect, with only the following things to watch out for:

> *g* is hard, as in "go"
> *r* is flapped, like the way some British speakers pronounce the "r" in "very"
> *f* is not like the English *f*, with teeth against the lower lip, but is made between the lips, as if blowing out a candle. In some systems, this consonant is rendered by the letter *h*, but the consonant is neither the English *f* nor *h*.

DOUBLED CONSONANTS

In English, the doubled consonant, as in *apple*, is pronounced as if it were a single consonant. But in Japanese (as in languages like Italian), you have to give an extra moment — a pause — to indicate that the consonant is doubled. For example, *matta* means "wait!" but *mata* means "crotch" or "groin." It's important to remember this when you yell "Wait!" to a taxi driver.

STRESS AND PITCH

The hardest thing about pronouncing Japanese is the absence of stress. English speakers pronounce the name of the city that suffered the first atomic bomb as Hiro-SHIma. A few people, on learning that this is wrong, try to correct it by saying HiROshima. Both are incorrect. The proper way is to place equal stress on all four syllables.

Pitch is another factor often neglected by English speakers, since in English the meaning doesn't change when you change the melody. But in Japanese, you can actually be misunderstood. There is an example of a tourist who went into a confectionery shop and asked for *ame*, "candy." In Japanese, the word for candy has both syllables on the same pitch. But the tourist made the first syllable higher, the normal English practice. The startled clerk heard his customer demanding "rain."

We have gone into such detail about pronunciation while advising you to be negligent about grammar because many of the factors that seem like nit-picking — stress, long vowels, doubled consonants — are less important in English but crucial in Japanese. A large vocabulary and elegant grammar aren't going to help you if you put a lot of stress where it doesn't belong. Listening to the melody, the Japanese will think you are speaking English, and he will automatically tune you out.

But with even minimal trouble over pronunciation, your smattering of Japanese will go a long way, and you will acquire a gratifying reputation for linguistic genius. If you are worried about sounding too blunt or uncouth, you can always accompany your speech by a nice, friendly smile, and the Japanese will know that you're trying hard and they will readily forgive your grammatical lapses.

READING AND WRITING

You can impress people with your few phrases of spoken Japanese, but you'll really dazzle them if you can also read and write a little. It has been said that Japanese writing is the hardest in the world. The reason is that not one, but four systems of writing are used, and all of them actively.

Romaji

The system easiest for Westerners to learn is *Romaji*, literally "Roman letters," and it is simply the use of the roman alphabet to spell out Japanese sounds phonetically. In fact, we have been using it all along in this chapter.

Romaji began to be used widely after World War II, and you see a lot of it in the modern parts of Tokyo on street signs, stations, and store fronts. But once away from the big city, older forms of writing take over. Even in Tokyo, Romaji is not always there when you need it. You won't find it on the ticket-selling machines at train and subway stations, for example.

Kanji

The earliest form of writing to be adopted was the use of Chinese characters, called *kanji* by the Japanese. Before the sixth century, when Chinese writing was first introduced, there had been no writing at all in Japan. Chinese characters are not phonetic — that is, they do not represent units of sound. Instead, each character represents a unit of meaning. When the Japanese took over the characters, they used them for the corresponding Japanese object, and pronounced them in Japanese. To illustrate: the character 山 is read *shan* in Chinese, and *yama* in Japanese, and it means "mountain" in the two languages. You see it used in names like *Fuji-yama*, Mt. Fuji. To make things more complicated, the Japanese sometimes give the characters a Chinese pronunciation as well, except that the pronunciation is in the Chinese of the sixth century (when writing first came to Japan) and not in modern Chinese. Are you still with me? Therefore in Japanese 山 is sometimes pronounced *san*, and Mt. Fuji is called *Fuji-san* as well as *Fuji-yama*.

LANGUAGE

By now, many of you will say, "Let's forget about Chinese characters and go on to the next system of writing." But it does pay to learn a few kanji and recognize them on street signs, maps, and station platforms. About two thousand kanji are in common use, and school children are supposed to master them by the time they finish junior high. An exceedingly well-educated Japanese knows about six thousand kanji, but these days few people know more than about three or four thousand.

In the appendix is a list of characters tourists are likely to encounter often. Although some travelers and even foreign residents get along in Japan without learning any kanji at all, your life will be much richer if you make the effort to recognize at least the most common ones. There is a tremendous satisfaction in recognizing that a certain bunch of strokes you see in a subway station means "exit."

At first the list of kanji looks rather daunting, and some of you may balk when you see it. The first ten or so characters are the hardest to learn. But the second ten are easier, and the next ten easier yet. Perhaps this is because there are certain brain cells used for learning pictographs, and these are activated when you put them to work. It is more probable, though, that you grow cunning as you learn more and more characters. You start inventing little tricks to help yourself remember. These tricks may be based on the history of the characters, since in the beginning they were often actual pictures of objects.

Thus the character 川, *kawa*, "river," really looks like a flowing stream, and the character 山, *yama*, "mountain," does look mountainous. *Ta*, "cultivated field," is 田, and you can see the subdivided rice paddies in the character.

Another trick is to break the characters into bite-size pieces, instead of trying to swallow them whole. The kanji for "island," *shima* (in names like Hiroshima), is 島, and it has a little mountain underneath. After all, an island is

33

a mountain poking out of the sea. The character 田, *ta*, "cultivated field," occurs in many combinations. For instance, 男, *otoko*, is "male," and you can think of a male as someone who works in the fields. 馬, *uma*, means "horse" (you can see the mane and the four legs of the horse). It is part of the character 駅, *eki*, "station." Think of a station as a stop for post horses.

You can invent many more of these tricks as aids to learning the kanji. Soon you will find it a game that's fun for its own sake. The rewards of learning a few kanji are out of all proportion to the effort you put in. Some Japanese are convinced that the Western mind is incapable of learning characters. This, of course, is racist nonsense, and you'll feel great satisfaction when you confound them with your knowledge, even if it's meager.

You don't have to memorize these kanji completely before starting your trip. In fact, if you don't use them right away, you're likely to forget them after a few days. But once in Japan, you can keep a list of the most common kanji in a pocket so that you can refer to them constantly. You'll see them so often on street signs and advertisements that you will learn them painlessly. Remember: you don't have to be able to write them; you only have to recognize them. Japanese children learn about fifty kanji in the first grade, so there is no reason why you can't do it too. Even the laziest traveler should learn 日本, *Nihon* (Japan), 東京, Tokyo, and kanji like 駅, *eki*, "station." The time will come when it is convenient to know the characters that tell you the train station from which your train is leaving, and that the one for Tokyo is on Platform 5.

KANA

On any page of a Japanese newspaper, magazine, or book, however, the writing is not entirely in Chinese characters,

LANGUAGE

but is a mixture of kanji and phonetic symbols called *kana*. We now come to the third and fourth forms of writing, *hiragana* and *katakana*. These are phonetic systems with forty-six symbols each, in which the symbols represent syllables. People of average studiousness can learn one of the systems in a few days. (A table of hiragana and katakana is in the appendix.)

Hiragana

The symbols in hiragana look like Chinese characters that have been written in such a hurry that they have melted a little. This is probably how they were originally derived. Hiragana is the system school children learn first, and children's books are almost entirely written in this form. By learning hiragana, which is phonetic, you can pick up a children's book in Japanese and read it aloud. You may not understand what you are reading, but it will be an impressive performance all the same. In English, on the other hand, a foreigner can learn all twenty-six letters of the alphabet and still not be able to cope with words like "enough."

Katakana

The second syllabic system is katakana, whose symbols are parts of Chinese characters. For someone who is spending just a few weeks in Japan, this system is more rewarding. All foreign terms are written in katakana. In fact, the chances are good that any sign written in katakana is a Japanized form of English. It is estimated that ten percent of the vocabulary of everyday speech in Japan is derived from English, and in the modern parts of Tokyo and other large cities the percentage is undoubtedly much higher. By mastering katakana, you no longer feel like a complete illiterate, and much of the writing all around you, which looked so exotic, starts making sense. It is not an exaggeration to say that the single most useful thing

ESSENTIALS

you can do to prepare for your trip to Japan is to spend a couple of days learning katakana.

Once you reach Japan, you will be getting practice in katakana wherever you go. A big movie poster shows a familiar mustachioed hero carrying a fainting heroine in his arms, and underneath the picture the katakana caption says that the movie stars *Kurāku Gēburu* (Clark Gable) and *Bibian Rī* (Vivien Leigh). Or you walk into a place with a katakana sign that says *kōhī shoppu* (coffee shop) and you are handed a *ranchi menyu* (lunch menu). For *ranchi* you can't decide whether to have *chikin raisu* (chicken rice) or *omuretsu* (omelet), but you know that for *dezāto* (dessert) you're going to order *aisu kurīmu* (ice cream). (In this discussion of Japanized English, we are using Romaji to render the expressions which would actually be written in katakana in Japan. We do this for the sake of readers who have not yet learned katakana.)

JAPANIZED ENGLISH

You can become very proficient in Japanized English if you remember the following facts:

There is no short *u* (ŭ) sound in Japanese, and that's why lunch becomes *ranchi*.

There is nothing corresponding to the English sound *er* (as in words like "shirt"), and the vowel *a* is substituted. In the men's clothing section of a department store, white shirts are labeled *wai shatsu*.

There are no consonant clusters in Japanese, so that in words like *strike*, the Japanese have to break up the cluster *str* by inserting vowels. When the labor unions call for a strike (which they do regularly every spring), you keep hearing the word *sutoraiku* for "strike." Frequently it's shortened to *suto*.

Another thing to remember is that there is no *v* in Japanese, and the consonant *b* is substituted. That was why Vivien Leigh became *Bibian Rī*.

LANGUAGE

You probably know already about *l* changing into *r*, producing friendly greetings of *Harro* wherever you go.

Japanese words never end in a consonant, except for *n*. After other final consonants, a vowel is added, as in *hotto kēki*, "hot cakes."

There is no *ti* sound in Japanese, and it often becomes *tei*. So you might be invited to a friend's house for a *pātei* (party).

There is no *si* sound in Japanese, and *si* becomes *shi*, so brace yourself for a shock when a Japanese invites you to sit down.

There is no *tu* sound, and it becomes *tsu*. If you ever go past a school playground while the students are exercising, you will hear the teacher saying, "*Wan, tsu! Wan, tsu!*" for "One, two! One, two!"

After some weeks in Japan, many tourists fall into the habit of pronouncing all English like this. They are not doing it to mock the Japanese; it's just that they hear it all around them, and the habit is contagious.

You will also become addicted to the habit of reading signs aloud in the streets, the stores, the subways, and the trains. You can spend your whole trip muttering things like *Bazā: biggu sēru* (Bazaar: big sale).

I know of an American family who spent half a year in Japan. The parents didn't want to bother learning katakana, but the children picked it up in school. They were soon driving their parents insane by using katakana as a secret code. They would write messages to each other like *Ā yu gōyin tsu mūbi jisu ī beningu?* (Are you going to a movie this evening?)

BASIC PHRASES

As we have said, it's better to use a curt form of Japanese, even if it sounds uncouth. The Japanese will be so im-

ESSENTIALS

pressed by the fact that you're trying to speak their language at all that they'll forgive you.

But you should try to make an effort at correct pronunciation. We have mentioned the importance of doubled consonants, long vowels, and the absence of stress. If you neglect pronunciation, people will misunderstand you, or even think you are speaking English to them.

Below are some phrases you may find useful.

Social Phrases

How do you do? (When introduced to someone for the first time)	Hajime-mashite.
I'm an American.	Amerika-jin desu.
My name is John Smith.	John Smith desu.
Good morning.	Ohayō gozaimasu. (Used until mid-morning)
Hello.	Kon-nichi-wa. (Used from mid-morning till dusk)
Good evening.	Komban-wa.
Good night; rest well.	Oyasumi-nasai.
Good-by.	Sayōnara.
Yes (agreeing).	Hai; sō desu.
No.	Īe.

Needing Help

Help!	Tasukete!
Excuse me (to attract attention).	Gomen kudasai.
Excuse me (I'm sorry).	Sumimasen.
Do you understand English?	Eigo wakarimasu-ka?
I don't understand.	Wakarimasen.
Where?	Doko?
Where is the post office?	Yūbinkyoku doko?
Where is the police box?	Kōban doko?

LANGUAGE

policeman	junsa
doctor	isha
toilet	benjo; toire

Time

What time is it?	Ima nanji?
yesterday	kinō
today	kyō
tomorrow	ashita
now	ima
later	atode
quickly	hayaku
Wait a minute.	Chotto matte.

In a Restaurant

delicious	oishī
I want a little more.	Mō sukoshi.
I've had enough.	Mō takusan.
What is this?	Kore nani?
Please (asking someone to go ahead).	Dōzo.
(To attract the attention of the waiter; also used as "hello" by the caller on the telephone)	Moshi moshi.
Thank you.	Arigatō.
Fine; O.K.	Kekko desu.
bill; check	kanjō

Traveling

airport	hikōjō
station	eki
reservation	yoyaku
room	heya
baggage	nimotsu
map	chizu

ESSENTIALS

telephone | denwa
sightseeing bus | kanko basu
Is it far? | Tōi desu-ka?
Is it near? | Chikai desu-ka?
I'm leaving tomorrow. | Ashita tachimasu.

Shopping

I want some . . . | . . . o kudasai.
I want some cigarettes. | Tabako o kudasai.
souvenir | omiyage
How much is it? | Ikura?
It's expensive! | Takai nē!
big | ōkī
small | chīsai
too small | ammari chīsai
I'll take this. | Kore o kudasai.

3
FOOD

In Japan the ultimate in luxury dining is to retain your own bevy of geisha girls and eat in a private dining room that opens onto your own bit of landscaped garden. As you eat, the girls make music, play games, tell jokes, engage in witty conversation, and ply you with sake. This type of dinner is expensive. Besides, many people feel uncomfortable with the coy playfulness of a geisha, and in any case wouldn't have the faintest idea of how to hire one. You don't just look up "geisha" in the yellow pages. If you have some Japanese acquaintances or colleagues who have the right connections, they can arrange a geisha party for you. Otherwise it is very difficult for a foreigner to obtain an introduction to geishas.

It costs somewhat less to eat a Western-style meal at a deluxe hotel, but it is still expensive. In general, Western meals tend to be expensive in Japan because they involve a relatively large quantity of meat. You can get an idea of the price of meat by visiting a food market (the food basement of any department store is a good place). Meat is sold in grams, and by the time you've converted yen into dollars and grams into pounds, you come up with a price of meat that takes your breath away. After double-checking your arithmetic, you begin to understand why it pays the Japanese to airlift beef cattle into the country, and why Japanese tourists bring home packages of beefsteaks as souvenirs of their trip abroad.

A TRADITIONAL JAPANESE MEAL

How about eating at Japanese-style restaurants? In your search for authenticity, you may want to try a *ryoriya*, a high-class Japanese-style restaurant. These places look more like private homes than commercial establishments, and from the landscaped entryway to the private dining room with its tatami-matted floor, the décor of a ryoriya breathes quiet good taste. You sit on the floor Japanese fashion, and serving girls in silk kimonos bring an individual tray of food for each customer. There is no menu — you are served a complete dinner of whatever is the specialty of the day. A meal in an authentic ryoriya gives you a pretty good idea of how a prosperous Japanese traditionally eats.

Just as a full-course Western meal has several distinct components — appetizer, soup, salad, meat, potato, cooked vegetables, dessert — so a traditional Japanese meal has certain components. In the West, the meat, potatoes, and cooked vegetables are served on a large dinner plate, while the soup, salad, and dessert are served separately. In Japan, all the components are brought to you on a tray (formerly, elaborate dinners had several trays brought in succession), but they are in separate containers. These containers can be deep bowls, shallow bowls, concave rectangular plates, oval plates, or even triangular plates. Unlike a Western dinner service in which all the dishes are of the same pattern, the dishes on a Japanese dinner tray are chosen deliberately with contrasting colors and patterns.

Soup is in a lacquer bowl with a lid. There are two kinds of soup: bean paste and clear. The bean paste soup, made of lightly fermented soy beans, is nourishing and forms an essential part of a Japanese breakfast (taking the place of coffee, tea, or milk), but it can also appear at dinner. The stock for clear soup is made from fish or kelp, and just before serving, little morsels of food are added, such as sliced fish cake, mushrooms, aromatic leaves, or even a twist of citron peel. These are cut into various pleasing shapes, so that when you uncover your soup bowl, you find yourself looking at a work of art.

Rice is served in a china bowl, and serving maids go around refilling rice bowls whenever they see one getting low.

Charcoal-broiled fish is usually one of the main "meat courses," although the helping is smaller than the meat portion in a Western meal. The fish can be a slice of some large fish such as *tai* (usually translated as "sea bream") or salmon. A whole, small, fresh-water fish called *ayu* is considered very good.

Sashimi, or raw fish, is served with a dab of green horseradish and very, very thin shreds of white radish. The sashimi can be tai, tuna, or some shellfish, such as abalone.

The salad is served in a deep bowl, and it consists of thinly sliced raw vegetables, such as cucumber, and some kind of cooked fish, very often shellfish. There is no oil in the dressing, only vinegar, salt, sometimes a little sugar, and possibly sesame seeds or herbs.

In another deep bowl you will find boiled food seasoned with soy sauce, sugar, and wine. This consists of pieces of fowl, fish, or vegetables, either singly or in combination. The vegetables can be bamboo shoots, chestnuts, mushrooms, or root vegetables, but the most elegant vegetables are the kind called *sansai*, "mountain vegetables" — various fern tips, tender shoots, and young leaves collected wild.

Finally, in a very small dish you have the pickles. These are salty, and are used primarily as rice chasers. They are made from eggplant, radish, greens, seaweed, roots, or herbs, and they come in various colors such as beige, green, yellow, deep purple, or dark brown.

With all these different colors and different serving dishes, a Japanese meal appeals to the eye as well as to the palate. Another characteristic of an elegant dinner is that it is prepared to suit the season. The vegetables, especially, are seasonal, and the shorter their season, the more highly they are regarded.

Eating in an expensive ryoriya can cost even more than steak dinners in a deluxe hotel. What is frightening is that you don't find out what the charges are for a long time. Everything at a ryoriya is conducted with such discretion that something as vulgar as the bill is presented almost stealthily. The safe thing is to have a Japanese friend introduce you to a ryoriya and tell you what the approximate cost will be. You may have trouble even making a reservation without his help.

DINING TOWERS

Less risky is going to one of those dining towers found in all the large cities. Unlike the ryoriya, these towers are not famous for the quiet good taste of their décor, but their prices are posted openly and you won't get a nasty shock when presented with the check. On each floor of these multi-storied dining towers is a different restaurant. One floor may be a Chinese restaurant (the good Chinese restaurants in Japan offer a great variety of authentic regional dishes). Another floor may be a French restaurant, another one Italian, still another Japanese (furnished in the Western style, and not with tatami rooms as in a ryoriya), and often a coffee shop serving snacks and quick meals. You simply take the elevator to whichever floor you want.

MODEL DISHES ON DISPLAY

Many restaurants and snack bars of the less expensive sort have a custom that is a great boon to the tourist: glass display shelves containing plastic models of the dishes they serve, each one labeled with the name and the price. The models are very realistic. Restaurants never serve you less than what is depicted in the models, and very often they give you a little extra.

Budget-minded tourists would do well to eat most of their meals at places with display shelves, because they tend to be fairly inexpensive and you know before you enter how much you will have to pay. Since you don't tip the waiter or pay a service charge (there is a service charge at the expensive places, but not at cheap ones), you know to a yen what your bill is going to be. The labels for the dishes are mostly in *katakana* (see Chapter 2, LANGUAGE), and if you did your homework, you will be able to read the name of the dishes and tell the waiter what you want. If you can't read katakana, you can at least copy down the name on a little piece of paper and show it to the waiter. But if you can't even do that, take the waiter out to the display shelf and point at the dish you want.

SHOKUDŌ

The models can be seen outside of all sorts of eateries, from regular restaurants serving authentic Japanese food to ice cream parlors. The largest display shelves are to be seen in front of a type of restaurant known as a *shokudō*. This literally means "food hall," but it usually refers to a place that serves both Western and Japanese food. Every department store has a large shokudō. Train stations have them, as do airports, amusement parks, museums, and other public facilities. The display case of a shokudō shows Japanese rice and noodle dishes, as well as Western (or pseudo-Western) dishes. The usual procedure at a shokudō is to inspect the display case, decide what you want, and buy a ticket for your selection. You'll have to communicate your choice to the ticket seller, using one of the three means we mentioned earlier. Then you sit down at a table (in some places you share a long table with others) and when the waiter appears, you hand him your ticket. If it is not a busy time, you'll receive your food promptly.

The shokudō is an eating emporium equipped to handle masses of people efficiently. A meal at one of them is not a memorable dining experience, unless you happen to pick a department store shokudō on a Sunday during the hectic hour between noon and one. Then your experience will be memorable indeed. These department-store dining halls seat hundreds, and just the noise from people snapping apart the disposable chopsticks is deafening.

The food at all the cheaper restaurants tends to be fairly standardized. Of the typical inexpensive Japanese foods, the noodle dishes are the most numerous, but these require a full treatment and we'll come back to them later. The rice dishes can be divided into cold and hot varieties. *Sushi*, the most common and delicious way of eating cold rice, is taken up a little later. Of the hot rice dishes, *kare raisu*, "curry rice," is only borderline Japanese. It consists of hot rice covered with a thick curry-flavored sauce containing lumps of something. Since East Indians indignantly disown kare raisu, and since it has become the staple diet for millions of students, we shall have to consider it as native Japanese. *Chikin raisu*, "chicken rice," runs a poor second to kare raisu. It is fried rice with some vegetables and microscopic bits of chicken.

There is a group of delicious hot rice dishes called *donburi* — literally "bowl." The most expensive and elegant is *unagi donburi*, hot rice topped with broiled eel. *Tendon*, short for *tempura donburi*, is rice topped with tempura (more about tempura later) and sauce. Less expensive is *oyako donburi*, which has chicken and eggs; the name literally means "mother and child."

INEXPENSIVE WESTERN DISHES

There are a few Western dishes that have become a regular part of Japanese eating habits (like chop suey and pizza in America). While these dishes are not exactly the same as what mother used to make at home, they will at least taste more familiar to you than vinegared rice wrapped in seaweed. Probably the most common Western dish is *ton katsu*, a breaded pork cutlet. Ton katsu is a great favorite in Japan, and most people no longer think of it as foreign. Another favorite is *kaki furai*, where *kaki* is "oyster" and *furai* is "fry." You will often see *hambagu suteki*, "hamburger steak," but the meat pattie is adulterated with egg, starch, soy beans, and other meat stretchers. Very often you will get a fried egg on top. All of these — the pork cutlet, fried oysters, and hamburger pattie — are served with a small salad of lettuce, shredded cabbage, and tomato wedge. Rice is usually on a separate plate.

BIGGU MAKKU

By now most of you know that the twin golden arches of McDonald's is a familiar sight in Japan. The burgers taste pretty much the way they do at home (and not like the hambagu suteki), although the price is slightly higher. In general the Japanese McDonald's has only take-out service, but this doesn't prevent many young Americans from hanging around this home-away-from-home even after they've finished their hamburgers. In addition to

McDonald's, you can also find Kentucky Fried Chicken, Shakey's Pizza Parlors, and Dairy Queen.

AUTHENTIC JAPANESE FOOD

For good, authentic Japanese food that doesn't cost too much, you should try the small one-room establishments that specialize in a particular type of food. These places are often arranged like a lunch counter, but they may also have a small raised area covered with tatami mats, with one or two low tables for those who want to take off their shoes and eat in comfort. The majority of the customers, however, sit at the counter so they can be closer to the food.

SUKIYAKI

There are several major types of food served at these small establishments. Many Western tourists immediately think of *sukiyaki*, a dish where strips of beef and vegetables are cooked at the table in a flat pan over a charcoal grill. Eating sukiyaki in Japan is not really recommended. As we've said, beef is terribly expensive there, and you can get better and cheaper sukiyaki at home. Furthermore, sukiyaki isn't even a traditional Japanese dish. The Japanese didn't start eating beef until late in the nineteenth century, because of the Buddhist taboo against eating meat. One story has it that sukiyaki was invented when some farmers got so desperately hungry they slaughtered a cow and cooked its meat, using their plow share as a grill.

TEMPURA

More authentically Japanese is *tempura*. This was introduced into Japan by the Portuguese in the sixteenth century, but since it has been around for nearly four hundred years, it can claim to have gone native. Tempura consists of various seafoods and vegetables dipped in a thin batter and deep fried. The best way to eat tempura is to go to a little tempura bar and watch it being cooked in front of your eyes. Each time your turn comes, you point to what you want, and the chef cooks it then and there and deposits the sizzling morsel on your plate. It can be not only prawn or shrimp, but fish, mushroom, sweet potato, seaweed, green beans, or even a fern tip or maple leaf. You dip the morsel in sauce, pop it into your mouth, and greedily wait until your turn comes round again. The cost of a tempura meal (which includes rice, pickles, and tea) depends on the quantity you eat and the location of the restaurant. On the average you can probably get a delicious dinner for about $5.

SUSHI

A tempura bar is fun, but a sushi bar is even livelier. *Sushi*, sometimes called a "rice sandwich" by tourists, consists of a ball of cold rice flavored with vinegar and salt, topped off with a bit of seafood, usually raw. This may sound unappetizing to the uninitiated, but once you get used to the idea, you'll find it a great treat. It is one of the most popular forms of food in Japan. At a sushi bar, the chef stands behind the counter with his cutting boards and bowls of ice containing seafood. You tell him what kind of sushi you want (pointing, if necessary) and he shapes the ball of rice, trims a bit of seafood, puts it atop the rice, and places it before you with a flourish. Sometimes the rice is rolled in a flat sheet of seaweed, with some egg, vegetables, and other filling in the center. This is called *makizushi*, "rolled sushi." There are also less expensive varieties of sushi in which egg or fried bean curd is used in place of raw fish. Sushi chefs are very dashing. Wearing dazzling clean clothes and a special headband, they wield their wicked knives with flair. They always place the sushi before you as if they are offering you a work of art. Perhaps it is.

Just a word of warning: between the rice and its topping is a coating of green paste. This is Japanese horseradish (we mentioned it earlier as accompanying sashimi), and if you let a blob of this vicious stuff hit the roof of your mouth, you'll feel as if someone is drilling a hole in your head. (A friend of mine said it cleared his sinuses, which had been plugged up for months.)

The size of your bill at the sushi bar depends on how long you've been sitting there stuffing yourself. It is generally easier to run up a huge bill at a sushi bar than at a tempura bar. Tempura is oily, and you start feeling full sooner, but the smooth little pieces of sushi glide down your throat one after another, until you suddenly find yourself dangerously distended. The bill can come to $15 or more, especially if you've consumed a lot of expensive topping like caviar, sea urchin roe, or live prawns.

A cheaper type of sushi bar is found in many train stations and shopping centers. This kind has a moving counter. Little dishes of ready-made sushi pass in front of you and you reach for the one you want. Later your bill is calculated by adding up the number of saucers you've accumulated. But the sushi at these places are generally inferior to the ones made to your order.

Japanese Roulette

Fugu, or globe fish, is not a food for the timid. The liver of this fish contains a poison that paralyzes the central nervous system and kills the victim within a few hours. There is no known cure. Not too long ago a famous Kabuki actor died from eating globe fish, and after that incident restaurants specializing in the dish suffered a sharp drop in business. But there are still plenty of globe fish restaurants around. You can always recognize one by the plaster model hanging in front showing a gray fish with a huge, globular stomach. Before you go in, make sure the chef has a certificate proving he is qualified to prepare this dish. It's a good idea to go only to those globe fish restaurants personally recommended by a reliable friend. After all this, is the fish worth it? It does taste delicious, and maybe the knowledge that you're flirting with death gives it a very special flavor.

For tourists on a very tight budget, these small specialty restaurants have to be only occasional treats. You had better stick mostly to the sort of place that has a display case of model dishes, where a meal comes to around $2.50. These places are very popular with office workers, and you should avoid eating during their lunch hour, which is from noon to one. The idea of staggered lunch hours still has not caught on in Japan, and when the noon hour strikes, millions of office workers drain out of their buildings like water from a sieve. Best not to stand in the paths of these human streams pouring out in search of food. Crouch out of the way in some refuge and wait until after one before venturing forth to eat your lunch.

NOODLES

Not all office workers eat out during lunchtime. Some work fiends — and seven out of ten Japanese over the age of forty-five are likely to be work fiends — eat lunch at their desks. A very common practice is to have a bowl of soup noodles delivered to their office. Around lunchtime, you will see thousands of delivery men holding huge trays, or several tiers of trays, containing bowls brimming with soup noodles. Miraculously, they never seem to spill a drop.

Not everyone has his noodles delivered. There are tiny noodle shops where you can gulp down your bowl of noodles, pay your money, and rush out in a matter of minutes.

If you think hamburgers are fast food, you should see the way noodles go down in one gigantic gulp. Some noodle shops don't even have seats, and the customers stand at the counter as they eat. A curtain, called a *noren*, screens the upper part of the body, so that passers-by only see the customers' legs and hear slurps.

Three main types of noodles are popular in Japan. The first kind is made of buckwheat, called *soba*. Since buckwheat cannot be easily hulled, the whole grain is milled. As a result, soba has a nice, nutty flavor and is rich in vitamins. Japanese soba lovers claim that it is not only nutritious, but lowers blood pressure and prolongs life. Like whole-wheat bread, soba has a rough texture not to everyone's taste. In the old days, the inhabitants of eastern Japan were supposed to be comparatively uncouth and therefore liked the roughness of soba.

The emperor and the nobility, on the other hand, lived in the western part of the country. They were refined, and preferred smooth white noodles made of wheat. Even today, easterners generally favor buckwheat noodles, and the westerners wheat noodles. There are various kinds of wheat noodles. One is *udon*, a thick, fleshy noodle looking like a bleached earthworm. Another is *somen*, a very thin noodle, thinner than vermicelli. Then there is *ramen*, a narrow, crinkly noodle of Chinese origin. The word *ramen* comes from the Chinese *lamien*, which is noodles coated lightly with oil and baked into dry clumps for storage. When you are ready to eat the noodles, you simply boil a few of these clumps. The method comes from Szechwan, but has finally reached American supermarket shelves via Japan.

All these noodles — soba, udon, somen, and ramen — are served in a variety of ways. Most commonly they are served in a big bowl of broth with slivers of green onion, fried bean curd, sliced fish cake, hard-boiled egg, or even a whole raw egg. Sometimes the noodles are stir-fried with bits of meat and vegetables, and sometimes they are served cold on a bamboo rack called a *zaru*.

BENTO

A bowl of noodles does not make a substantial lunch, and many Japanese prefer to take a lunch box, called a *bento*. It is flat, oblong, or rectangular, and can be made of lacquer, wood, aluminum, or plastic. In the old days, most of the box was filled with cold, cooked rice, with a few rice chasers in a corner. These consist of salty bits of cold fish, vegetables, pickles, and the like. One rice chaser is *umeboshi*, pickled plum, which is about the size of a marble and is reddish in color. (A poor man's lunch is often called a *hinomaru bento*. It consists of white rice with a red sour plum in the center, so that it looks like the Japanese flag, which is called *Hinomaru*, "Sun Disk.") If you ever meet an umeboshi, treat it with respect, because it's so sour that it can take off the enamel of your teeth. People with aluminum lunch boxes are careful not to let the sour plum touch the sides, since it can eat its way through the aluminum. In recent years, the Japanese have become more affluent, and the rice chasers are gradually giving way to more nutritious foods such as chicken, fish, and sausages. The proportion of rice has steadily decreased, so that instead of nine-tenths rice, most lunch boxes now contain two-thirds rice or less.

The bento is so much a feature of daily life in Japan that every tourist should try one. Train stations are particularly good places to buy bento, and you can see vendors on station platforms wheeling carts piled with gaily wrapped flat boxes. The names on the lunch boxes don't always tell you much about their contents (you get things like "Great Edo"), but some vendors have pictures of the contents, and these can help you decide. The cheap bento, costing about $1, contain mostly rice, with a few chasers such as salted fish, pickles, and the formidable sour plum. The fancy bento can cost as much as $4 or $5, but they are such works of art that you can hardly bear to disturb the contents. The station bento, called *eki-bento*, feature regional specialties, and experienced travelers know which stations sell good ones.

The types of lunch boxes sold to travelers are disposable, made of cardboard, thin wood, or plastic. They are very convenient, but present a litter problem. You can see many places of natural beauty marred by discarded lunch boxes strewn all over the grounds. If the Grand Canyon is in danger of being filled with empty beer cans, Mt. Fuji is in the process of being covered by bento boxes.

Snacks Whether lunch is a bowl of noodles or some cold rice with sour plums, after a couple of hours comes an urge to fill the void. Many Japanese eat an afternoon snack at three, called *osanji*, "the honorable three o'clock." Others prefer a snack at four, called *oyattsu*, "the honorable four o'clock." Traditional Japanese snacks consist mainly of sweetened bean paste and glutinous rice, but nowadays people eat many Western-style snacks like cake, ice cream, custard, and fruit. Snack shops have display cases showing dishes of fruit cut and arranged attractively. When the fruit is topped with ice cream, the dish is called *furūtsu kurīmu*, "fruits cream." There is a Japanese sweet dessert called *mitsu-mame*, which consists of jelly cubes made of agar-agar (a seaweed derivative and tasteless) and sweetened whole beans. This is frequently served with slices of fruit, and then it is called *furūtsu mitsu-mame*.

KISSATEN

This literally means "shop for drinking tea," but you can also eat some of the sweets described above, and drink coffee and soft drinks in addition to tea. If you read katakana, you will enjoy reading out names on the menu such as *Koka Kora, aisu kōhī* ("ice coffee"), or *gurēpu jūsu* ("grape juice"). The kissaten are extremely popular with shoppers and students.

COFFEE HOUSES

Most students, however, prefer coffee shops. These vary, not so much in the quality of the coffee, but in the atmosphere. Some of them are like the kissaten and serve coffee and sweets accompanied with light popular music. Some are more like European coffee houses, where you meet all your friends and discuss the vital issues of the day. The music in the background (or foreground) can be jazz, rock, or Beethoven's late quartets. Many students go to coffee houses to get away from their homes or noisy dormitories. They sit in a quiet corner and study or read comics.

The coffee is very good but expensive, usually about $1 a cup, and even more in places that go in for fancy blends. But you can nurse one cup of coffee for hours without being pressured to buy more. The coffee shops all serve snacks such as *kare raisu* ("curry rice") and *hamu tōsuto* ("ham toast"). In some coffee shops you can get breakfast, which is called *mōningu sābisu*, "morning service." This usually consists of coffee (or juice), toast, and a soft-boiled egg, and it costs about $1.25.

BEER HALLS

If you want something a little stronger than coffee, tea, or kora, you can try a beer hall. In atmosphere these vary as much as do the coffee houses. Some are big, smoke-filled, and raucous. Some have vaguely Bavarian décor and aim at *Gemütlichkeit*. Some are just quiet little cafés where tired shoppers can put down their parcels. All these beer halls serve beer and light snacks. Japanese *bīru*, or beer, is very good. Most Westerners seem to prefer Kirin Biru, although Asahi Biru is the brand most widely sold.

The snacks can be familiar things like cheese and salami, but they can also be startling: boiled green soy beans, pickles, or a vegetable salad. Or you can have *yakitori*, literally "grilled bird." Yakitori consists of pieces of chicken broiled on little skewers, and they are delicious. But the pieces of chicken are not always muscle meat. Sometimes you can order chicken livers (acceptable to Westerners) or skin (tasty, actually) or gizzards (okay if you don't know what you're eating), or intestines (for chitterling lovers). In Japan organ meat is called *horumon*, "hormone," so that you often see *horumon yaki*, "grilled hormones," on the menu.

Beer gardens are beer halls set up in summer on the roofs of tall buildings, where you can get a good view and cool breezes. Shaded with awnings and decorated with lanterns, they are very pleasant places to spend a couple of relaxing hours.

NOMIYA

You can usually identify these by a big red paper lantern outside. *Nomiya* is literally "drinking place." It is sometimes just a counter with a row of stools, and sometimes it has a few small wooden tables in addition. Here you can drink and eat snacks, such as yakitori. In addition to beer, a nomiya serves sake and Western drinks like whisky. (Japanese domestic whisky is quite good, especially the premium brands. But Scotch whisky carries a lot of prestige, and a fine gift for a Japanese friend is a bottle of Johnny

Walker Black Label.) The nomiya are popular with salaried men (called *sararimen*), who want a few drinks after work to help them unwind before they get home.

For those unwilling to spend a lot of time in a coffee house, kissaten, beer hall, or nomiya, there are thousands of little shops where you can grab a bun, a sweet roll, a glass bottle of milk, or a fruit drink. The bun is usually filled with sweet bean paste and the milk is reconstituted from dried milk, but they provide cheap, wholesome food and quick energy when you need it.

VENDING MACHINES

But if you're really in a hurry, you can buy food and drink at vending machines found in the streets, stations, and even lobbies of hotels. Japan has the largest number of vending machines per capita in the world. Most of these sell drinks, usually fruit juice, soda pop, and sweet coffee drinks. But you can also get beer and sake at vending machines (in spite of this, alcoholism is not a serious problem in Japan). There is food for sale, too, from the machines. You can buy sweet buns or instant *ramen*, but more often a cup of dried noodles to which you add boiling water. Yogurt is another food you can buy from a vending machine. The Japanese have taken to yogurt, but when you buy it, don't get the sweetened, fruit-flavored yogurt, which is like cheap custard. Get a brand called Bulgarian Yogurt. It's wonderfully creamy, and tastes better than yogurt has any right to taste.

YAKIMONO

Vending machines may be modern and efficient, but the old-fashioned food stalls and carts are more picturesque.

ESSENTIALS

Before we discuss these, however, we should take up a category of food known as *yakimono*, where *mono* is just "thing," (as in *kimono*, "a thing to wear"). We have already said that *yaki* means "grilled," as in *yakitori*, "grilled bird." But *yaki* can also mean "baked," "broiled," or even "stir-fried." *Yaki soba* is the Japanese version of chow mein. On the other hand, *Rondon yaki*, "London bake," turns out to be crumpets.

Many of the yakimono can be described as some form of pancake. Pancakes are very versatile in Japan. The sweet *hotto kēki*, "hot cakes," make an elegant snack for the honorable three o'clock. But most pancakes have things added to the batter, and are baked in a variety of interesting ways. *Tai* being a kind of fish, *tai yaki* is pancake batter baked in little fish-shaped molds, with a lump of sweet bean paste inside each fish. *Tako* is octopus, and when you see *tako yaki*, you say "Aha! This must be pancake batter baked in octopus-shaped molds." Wrong. Tako yaki is made by adding chopped octopus feet and seasoning into the batter, which is baked in little round molds. The fanciest pancake of all is *okonomi yaki*, a large pancake baked on a flat grill, and you add whatever your heart desires, such as shredded meat, vegetables, fish, bits of seaweed, chopped hormones — anything. This pancake is not served with maple syrup, but with a sauce whose main ingredient tastes like Worcestershire sauce. "Pancake" is not really a good description. It's the Japanese equivalent of pizza.

STREET VENDORS

These pancakes, as well as many other types of inexpensive food, are sold in street stalls or carts called *yatai*. The street-vendor institution dates back to feudal times, and the vendors still retain their old style. Your trip to Japan is not complete unless you patronize a few. In fact, you may have to hurry, since the dangers from auto traffic are driving them off the streets. They are to be found only in small side streets or the residential parts of the city, away from the modern thoroughfares.

Try to find a roasted-sweet-potato vendor if you can. He pushes a cart containing a small oven, and he calls out his wares in a long, drawn-out plaintive voice. The roasted sweet potato is called *yaki imo*, and as a snack it is not only cheap and filling, but really delicious — like an American roasted sweet potato. It's especially welcome in winter to students studying late at night in unheated rooms, because it warms their cramped fingers.

Most of the noodles we discussed earlier are sold by street vendors. The noodle carts have a tiny counter, where you slurp down your bowl of noodles while standing. Another hot snack you can get from a street vendor is *oden*, a stew containing bean curd, hard-boiled eggs, fish cakes, bamboo shoots; *konyaku* (a gelatinous cake made of root starch); and various kinds of vegetables all boiled together in a huge pot. Oden can come on skewers, in which case you buy a certain number of skewers but have no choice over what you get. Sometimes the various kinds of foods are still swimming around in the cauldron, and you can point to what you want. Served with mustard, a plate of oden is both tasty and nutritious.

TABLE MANNERS

At the beginning of this chapter we talked about first-class Japanese restaurants called ryoriya, and described the food in a typical dinner. But we did not mention table manners. Etiquette being so important in Japan, table manners are naturally elaborate and rigid.

Fortunately, as a foreigner you're not expected to have

ESSENTIALS

any table manners. Anything you do is excusable. Of course you should avoid obvious crudities like putting out a cigarette in a dish of raw fish. Most of you, however, have a spark of vanity and want to show that you are not totally ignorant.

The best thing to do at a formal dinner is take a peek at a Japanese member of your party and copy every move he makes. But in case you can't remember everything he does, or get distracted so that you skip a few steps, we will describe the correct procedure for taking a meal.

First, let's take a look at the individual tray set down on the floor in front of you. Elaborate dinners in the old days used to have several courses, with a new tray of food brought in for each course, but nowadays formal dinners seldom involve more than one or two courses. If the dinner involves drinking, you may have a preliminary tray of food that accompanies the sake, with the tray for the main course coming later. We will, however, just look at the tray for the main course.

Diagram of an individual place setting

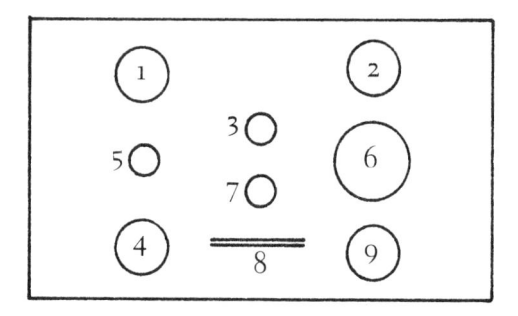

1. Broiled fish.
2. Sashimi.
3. Salad.
4. Rice bowl.
5. Sauce for sashimi.
6. Boiled food.
7. Pickles.
8. Chopsticks.
9. Soup bowl.

And now, this is what you do:
1. Say *Itadakimasu*, which means "I receive."
2. Uncover the lid of the empty rice bowl with your left hand and place it to the left of the bowl, stem down. A maid will come around to fill it for you.
3. Uncover the soup bowl with your right hand and place the lid to the right of the bowl, stem down.
4. Pick up your chopsticks with your right hand.
5. Pick up the soup bowl with your left hand, take one small sip, and then put it down.
6. Pick up the rice bowl with the left hand and eat one mouthful of rice with your chopsticks. (Don't put the bowl to your mouth and shovel in the rice; that's only done with tea-soaked rice or gruel.) Put the bowl down again.
7. Take another sip of soup and, with your chopsticks, pick up a tidbit of solid food from the soup bowl and eat it. Then put the soup bowl down.
8. After that, you sample the various dishes one at a time, except for the pickle dish, which you leave alone for the time being. The rice bowl should remain in the left hand, unless you put it down to pick up the soup bowl.
9. Don't finish the soup at the start of the meal, since it's supposed to accompany the whole meal.
10. The serving girl will refill your rice bowl when it gets down to one mouthful. If you empty the rice bowl, it is a signal that you've finished the meal.
11. It is not good manners to eat only one bowl of rice, and therefore you should let the serving girl refill your bowl at least once before emptying it.
12. You can start eating pickles when you've finished the other dishes on your tray.
13. Don't leave any food uneaten. (This rule is not observed strictly these days, especially with children.)
14. The meal should end with rice and pickles, so don't finish your rice before finishing the other dishes.

15. Green tea is often poured into the rice bowl when you're at the pickles stage. Many Japanese like to end the meal with rice soaked in green tea, because it leaves the mouth with a clean feeling.
16. At the end of the meal you say *Gochisōsama deshita*, which means, "That was a feast."

There are certain things considered bad manners in the West that you should also avoid in Japan, such as talking with your mouth full. You should also avoid picking up a big piece of food, such as fish, and taking a bite from it. Instead, break up the piece with your chopsticks and pick up only bite-size morsels. (Something difficult to break, such as a piece of steak, is not served at a formal Japanese meal.)

Japanese table manners and etiquette began taking their present form during the fifteenth century, and became more or less codified in the seventeenth century. The procedure here for eating a formal dinner largely follows the dictates of the fifth Tokugawa shogun, set down in 1682. (How many Frenchmen still eat like King Louis XIV?) With the breakdown of the traditional Japanese family, table manners are changing. Instead of individual trays of food, the whole family is grouped around a low dining table. Each person still has his own array of little dishes, but much of the food is brought to the table on a large platter and distributed by the mother. Although the rules about seconds on rice, holding the soup bowl in the left hand, and so forth, are still observed by many, table manners have become much more relaxed. Japanese children are pretty boisterous at home, and when they are present at the dinner table, formality is impossible. Maybe that's why the father ate alone in the old days.

In recent years many parents have become worried about their children's table manners. Elementary schoolchildren used to bring lunch boxes, but now most schools serve hot lunches. The food is served on a platter, and the eating utensil is a spoon. Children find it hard to convey the food to their mouths, and most of them have developed the unfortunate habit of bending their heads down to the platter and shoveling the food into their mouths. After six years of school lunches, this habit has become ingrained. Parents are horrified, and call this manner "dog-style eating." As one mother moaned, "My parents used to be so particular about my manners. I had to pick up my chopsticks in a certain way, and the cover of my soup bowl had to be placed exactly right. And now my daughter gulps her food like a dog!"

Nobody expects a foreigner to go through the sixteen correct steps for eating a formal dinner. On the other hand, neither do you have to descend to dog-style eating. Try to practice until you can eat neatly with chopsticks (it doesn't really take long to become pretty proficient, and the food seems to taste better with chopsticks). Finally, your Japanese hosts will be perfectly delighted if you remember to say *Itadakimasu* at the beginning of the meal and *Gochisōsama deshita* at the end.

4
HOUSING

If you are lucky enough to be invited to stay with a Japanese family, you have the opportunity for a firsthand look at everyday life in Japan. The experience will be a particularly fascinating one if the family lives in a traditional house. Because of the structure of the traditional house, however, there are certain do's and don't's you should observe in order to behave decently and be comfortable. We shall therefore describe a typical old-fashioned Japanese house.

ENTRANCE

In a simple, unpretentious city house, the front entrance is close to the street. But the better homes are set back from the street and surrounded by gardens and a wall. To reach the house, you pass through the gate, cross a small front garden or courtyard, and come up to the front door. Whether the house is humble or grand, the front door opens into a small vestibule, or entrance hall. Here you take off your shoes, which are stowed away in a cupboard, and go up one or two steps to the main part of the house.

SHOES AND SLIPPERS

You don't have to remove your shoes when you enter a public building such as a store, a restaurant, a school, or a theater, but it is absolutely *de rigueur* when you step into a private house or an inn. Except for modern thoroughfares, streets and roads in Japan are dusty in dry weather and muddy in wet weather. By taking off your shoes, you leave the dirt outside. Since the floor is used for sitting and sleeping, it must be kept spotlessly clean, and therefore no street shoes are allowed past the vestibule. Inside the house, the halls and stairs are of polished wood. As they feel rather chilly to bare or stockinged feet, the Japanese normally wear soft slippers on these wooden surfaces. If you are a guest in a house or an inn, you are provided with a pair of slippers as soon as you enter.

TATAMI

In rooms covered with tatami mats, however, you are not supposed to wear even slippers. The feel of the tatami mat is so pleasant underfoot that it's a joy to take off your slippers when you enter a matted room. It has been said that the tatami mat is the loveliest thing invented by the Japanese. Besides being springy, soft, and fragrant, it is cool in summer and warm in winter. A tatami mat is constructed of a two-inch-thick base of rice straw with a finely woven rush cover. In an ordinary mat, the edges are bound by a border of black cloth, but elegant mats have a brocade border. All tatami mats are of the same dimensions, approximately three feet by six feet, and in a traditional house the rooms have floors entirely covered by closely-fitting tatami mats. Not only that, there is a standard way of arranging the mats in a three-mat room, a four-and-a-half-mat room (there is rarely a four-mat room, since the word for "four" is *shi*, which sounds the same as the word for "death"), and so on. Therefore, rooms in Japanese houses are modular — that is, they come in standard sizes, and any two rooms with the same floor space are identical in shape.

FURNITURE

The tatami is so comfortable that you don't mind the absence of furniture. You don't need a chair because you sit on the floor, and you don't need a bed because a thin mattress, called a *futon*, is spread on the tatami and makes it soft enough for sleepers. Traditional covers consist of quilts with removable cotton cases, and during the day the futon and quilts are folded and put away into cupboards. When the day is sunny, you can see rows of gaily colored futon and quilts hung out to air along balcony railings or over the walls. Except for a clothes rack (there is no clothes closet), a chest or two, a lamp, and a few flat cushions, the room looks bare. Nowadays, an additional piece of furniture in many of the rooms is a television set.

FLEXIBLE USE OF ROOMS

Since there is no heavy furniture, the bedroom, living room, dining room, and guest room are not distinguishable. Every room is a living room to start with. It becomes a bedroom when a futon is spread on the floor, and a dining room when a few trays of food are brought in or a portable dining table is set up. In a Japanese inn, the maid places a table in your room and serves the meal, but afterward the table is removed and beds are spread out on the floor.

Pillows

Most Westerners have no trouble adjusting to sleeping on the floor, but they find Japanese pillows another matter. Pillows used to be little stands made of wood or porcelain, and they supported the neck without disturbing one's elaborate hair-do. These days the pillows in a Japanese inn or an old-fashioned house are likely to be small bags firmly stuffed with bran. Western tourists find Japanese pillows literally a pain in the neck.

Tokonoma

It is easy to accommodate a guest in a Japanese house: a futon is spread for him wherever there is space. Usually an honored guest is put into a room with a *tokonoma*, or alcove, with a slightly raised platform on which are displayed a few prized items such as a painting, a scroll, a vase, or a flower arrangement. The tokonoma looks like a convenient shelf for knickknacks, but if you are staying as a guest in the room, you should resist the temptation to put your toilet articles, sweater, or soft-drink bottle on it. It is for treasured articles only. When a party is held in the room, the guest of honor is always seated nearest the tokonoma. Therefore don't plunk yourself down in front of it, but make some polite attempt to sit farthest away from it and take the honored seat only when your host insists.

IMPERMANENCE

The scroll, flower arrangement, or other exhibit in the tokonoma is changed from time to time, and is always chosen to fit the season. It would be unthinkable for a Japanese to hang a painting permanently in one place, even if it is the portrait of an honored ancestor. The only exception would be a photograph of a dead relative, such

ESSENTIALS

as a father or a husband. In that case the picture is a memento, not a work of art. For the rest, Japanese décor tends to emphasize the impermanence of things. Indeed, to Western eyes the houses look very flimsy. They are. The Japanese deliberately make their houses flimsy not only because they lack the natural resources to build more solid structures, but because flimsiness can actually be an advantage, such as during an earthquake, when the houses break down into their components instead of crashing down like a ton of bricks. Repair is much easier afterward. Another reason for the flexibility is that few nails are used in the construction; instead, the parts fit together like a wooden puzzle.

SLIDING SCREENS

The walls are among the most impermanent aspects of a Japanese house. They slide on runners and can even be lifted out entirely. With the bedding folded away and a few wall panels lifted out, a four-bedroom house is transformed into a zero-bedroom house. This is a tremendous advantage when one is throwing a huge party.

There are several kinds of sliding wall panels. The panels called *amado* are made of wood, and when in place they form part of the exterior wall of the house. They are put up at night to make the house secure and taken down every morning and stored away to let in air and light. They are also put up in case of a heavy storm. For interior walls, there are panels called *fusuma*, made of thick, opaque paper with wooden frames. In elegant houses these are painted by famous artists, and some outstanding examples can be seen at Nijo Castle and at the Katsura Imperial Villa in Kyoto.

SHOJI

A second kind of interior wall panel is called *shoji*. Western decorators have discovered shoji, and you may already be familiar with these panels, which have wooden grid-like frames covered by thin white paper. Light passing through shoji is soft and diffuse, creating a very agreeable effect. The disadvantage of a shoji panel is its fragility. It is all too easy to poke a hole in one with the sharp corner of a book, a tray, or even an elbow. These days some shoji panels are covered by white plastic, but in old Japanese houses they are always covered by thin white paper.

Not all the walls are made of sliding panels. There are some permanent wall sections, but even these are flimsy, being made of a latticed bamboo skeleton covered with mud and plaster. Therefore you have to avoid any rowdiness in a Japanese house. It has been said that Japanese behavior is so quiet and subdued because if you bump against a wall, it may fall down. During the fight scenes in samurai movies, a house is sometimes literally torn to pieces. Remember to tuck your elbows in when you are a guest in a Japanese house, and also keep your hands clean, since a smudge really shows on the paper of the fusuma or shoji. You can always tell when a family has young children, because the shoji will be full of patches and smudges.

CLOTHING

You will feel a lot more comfortable in a Japanese house when you are wearing suitable clothes. The best thing to wear, of course, is a kimono. Many Japanese men wear a Western-style suit to work, but as soon as they come home they take it off and slip on a comfortable kimono. Women's kimonos are not nearly so comfortable, especially the stiff, costly silk ones with the wide sash. *Yukata*, the informal cotton kimono worn by both men and women, is the perfect thing to wear for lounging or sitting

ESSENTIALS

on the tatami during the summer. All Japanese inns and many hotels provide you with a crisp, clean yukata when you arrive. Hotel guests lose no time in throwing off their own clothes and getting into it. The yukata is used as a nightgown, but it is quite acceptable to wear in public. During warm weather, guests at inns and resorts walk around the corridors and gardens wearing the cotton hotel yukata. With the change of clothes, people's very behavior seems to change. Some Japanese seem nervous and strained in Western clothes, but as soon as they slip into a kimono, especially the informal yukata, they look more cheerful and relaxed.

Tight trousers are uncomfortable to wear when you have to sit on your legs Japanese fashion, because there is a strain on the fabric at the knees. That is why many Japanese youngsters, who wear jeans, prefer to sit on chairs rather than on the floor. Tight skirts are also awkward. A long, loose skirt, or better yet, a caftan, is much more comfortable and graceful when you are sitting on the tatami.

Dress for Warmth

In winter, traditional Japanese houses are cold and drafty. Foreigners who are spoiled by centrally-heated houses (often overheated) dress very lightly in their own homes and seldom wear undershirts. In Japan undershirts are really necessary if you want to be comfortable during winter. It's a good idea to bring a supply of thermal underwear, turtleneck shirts, thick sweaters, down vests, and very thick socks or booties.

What did the Japanese do in the old days before they had thick sweaters? Paintings show court ladies wearing as many as a dozen kimonos, one on top of another. The amazing thing is that their feet are shown as bare. No chilblains are visible in the paintings, but perhaps after so many generations of exposure to the cold, people with specially insulated feet were bred. During the cold weather hotels and inns provide you with a heavy warm kimono called a *tanzen*. Although the tanzen doesn't protect your feet, you feel cozy and sybaritic when you're wrapped in its thick, generous folds.

Hibachi

During winter, a feeble warmth is traditionally provided by a *hibachi*, although nowadays most Japanese use a portable kerosene or electric heater even in the older houses. There is a certain amount of misunderstanding in America about a hibachi. For some reason, a hibachi in America has come to mean a small, portable charcoal grill. In Japan this charcoal grill is called a *konro*, while a hibachi is a huge ceramic pot or, more rarely, a metal pot set in a wooden box. It contains mainly ashes, with some burning charcoal on top. Although water is sometimes heated in it, the hibachi is not used for cooking purposes. Occasionally it is used to burn incense. I still remember a Japanese friend's look of horror as he listened to his American host boasting at length about his backyard barbecue, in which a hibachi was used to broil salmon and steaks. A hibachi — not a grill — is beautiful to look at, but it is not very efficient for heating a room. You have to be almost plastered against its sides to get any warmth. Many Japanese spend a lot of time idly stirring the hot ashes in a hibachi with a pair of iron chopsticks. This doesn't help the fire much, but it is a good excuse for hugging the hibachi.

Kotatsu

You get a lot more warmth from a *kotatsu*, a very ingenious contraption using only a tiny amount of fuel. It consists of a low table with a large quilt spread over the top and covering the sides. Under the table is a small box containing a few pieces of burning charcoal. People sit around the table with their legs tucked under the quilt and read, study, play games, chat, or tell stories. The heat from just a few pieces of charcoal can keep four or more people warm for hours. It is hard to imagine any invention that provides so much warmth using so little energy. One of the dangers of a kotatsu is that you get so comfortable you can't tear yourself away. At night, children refuse to leave the kotatsu and go to their cold beds, often falling asleep at the kotatsu and having to be carried to bed. The modern kotatsu uses a low wattage infrared bulb instead of charcoal to provide the heat, and instead of telling stories, you watch TV as you sit with your hands and legs tucked cozily under the quilt. The TV sponsors have a perfect captive audience — people are too comfortable to get up and leave during breaks for commercials.

OPENNESS

Japanese houses are less of a problem in summer because they are built to provide maximum shade and ventilation. The Japanese always take great care to have their houses face the proper direction so they have the least exposure to the summer sun. They can also get relief from the heat (which can be stifling) by pushing aside some of the walls and opening the house to the garden. The best rooms of the house are always in the back facing the main garden, and a long veranda usually runs all the way across that side of the house. When the wall panels are open, the indoors and outdoors merge, and you have the comforts of the living room with the delights of the patio.

Mosquitoes   Leaving the house open during the summer brings in swarms of mosquitoes. One solution used in Japan and other Asian countries is to burn a coil made from a certain kind of chrysanthemum, called *katori senko*. It produces a pungent but not unpleasant odor, and burning two or three coils will keep the mosquitoes away from a fairly large area. At night mosquito netting is also hung up inside the house. A Japanese mosquito net consists of four sides and a top, and when hung by hooks at the four corners, it forms a square box about the size of a room. When entering a mosquito net, crawl under it quickly so that you don't bring in a few mosquitoes with you. At night there are often fierce whispers of "Who let in that mosquito?" "You did!" "I didn't!" "Yes, you did!"

KITCHEN

As a guest in a Japanese family, you won't have anything to do with the cooking. It is not the custom for guests to enter the kitchen and offer to help with the meals or the washing up. Old farmhouses have an open hearth in the main room of the house, and some of the cooking is done over the charcoal fire in the pit of the hearth. An iron kettle is hung over the pit from a hook attached to the ceiling by a chain. (These hooks and pots are picturesque antiques and are fast becoming collectors' pieces.) In the city, however, the kitchen is a separate room and is not an attractive place. Dark and cluttered, it is considered fit only for women and servants. The kitchen has a split-level floor. Half of it is on the same level as the ground outside, and this is where you find tubs for washing vegetables and the charcoal grill (konro, not hibachi). Tradesmen delivering their goods stop here without stepping up to the higher level. This higher level has a wooden floor, and a wood stove is placed here for the main cooking chores — nowadays the wood stove is replaced by a gas one. In most Japanese families now the food is brought out in large bowls or platters and distributed at the dining table. But in the old days the maid or housewife arranged dishes on individual little trays in the kitchen, and then brought in the complete dinners to the dining room, somewhat like an airline stewardess bringing in a dinner tray to a passenger. Even with modern stoves, refrigerators, and sinks, the kitchen in a Japanese house is not the cozy family room we have in the West, but a rather dreary place you enter only when you have to.

The only other rooms are the bathroom and toilet. These require a separate discussion, which we will take up in the next chapter.

GARDENS

Japan is famous for its gardens, and many tourists regard their visits to some of the outstanding ones the highlights of their trip. The gardens of Kyoto alone are the subject of many coffee-table books. Walking through the residential districts of Kyoto, however, you see mainly high walls and seldom do you get any hint of the beautiful gardens within. The Japanese almost seem to enjoy hiding away this precious part of their home. The main garden is always in the back of the house, farthest from the entrance, and the more opulent the garden, the more completely is it screened from outside view.

When you are a house guest, don't treat the garden as a yard. You don't play games, sun bathe, or even read a book in the garden. It is usually too small for much anyway. A garden is about the size of the living room, and all you can do is admire it as a piece of art, which it really is. If the house is a mansion with spacious grounds, the garden may be large enough to have foot paths, a pond, and a bridge or two. In this case it is called a "stroll garden." But only the very wealthy or temples and shrines can afford something like this.

PRESENT-DAY HOUSING

A genuine, old-fashioned Japanese house is now a rare luxury. The materials for their construction are becoming scarce, and the craftsmen capable of doing the work are a vanishing breed. Only the very rich and the very conservative now live in a completely Japanese house. Many of those owning an old house cannot afford to maintain it in its original condition, and are forced to repair it using modern materials. The result is often an ugly hybrid. Owners are glad to modernize the bath, toilet, and kitchen, but it is financial necessity that forces them to replace the wooden latticed windows with aluminum sash windows and the fragrant tatami mats with nylon carpeting.

When Japan first opened its doors to the West, it was a status symbol to have one room of the house furnished in the Western style, with rugs, overstuffed chairs, sofas, tables, kerosine lamps, and a piano. Nowadays many Japanese live in homes where most of the rooms have Western-style furnishing, and only one room is preserved in traditional Japanese style.

APARTMENTS

Because of the land shortage, more and more Japanese live in apartment-house complexes. An apartment house is called an *apāto*, but the newer, more luxurious ones are now called *manshon* ("mansion"). Those who think a *manshon* doesn't have enough snob appeal will move to a still newer, taller, and more luxurious type of apartment house called *haitsu* ("heights").

In most of the newer apartments, the rooms are completely Western, except for possibly one tatami room. A typical middle-class apartment has a kitchen-dining room combination (no longer is the housewife working alone in the dank kitchen), a living room with chairs, and a bedroom or two. The bedrooms are likely to have real beds and a study desk for the school-age child. The toilet is probably Western-style, but the bath remains Japanese-style.

If you are staying with a Japanese family in a modern apartment, you still have to pay attention to the slipper etiquette. You keep your street shoes on in the corridors of the apartment house, but right inside the front door of your friend's apartment is a tiny vestibule where you remove your shoes and put on slippers. Now, in the traditional house, you wear slippers on wooden floors but take them off on the tatami. In a modern apartment, the kitchen-dining area has linoleum or wooden floors, and you keep your slippers on. But what about the living room and bedroom, which have carpeting? Do you treat the carpets as tatami? No national policy has been laid down so far, and individual families differ. Some keep their slippers on when they are in the carpeted living room but take them off in the bedroom. Some keep them on everywhere, and some remove them on all carpeted areas. You just have to follow the example of your hosts.

JAPANESE-STYLE LODGING

INNS, OR RYOKAN

Unless you have the good fortune to be invited by a friend living in an old house, your best chance of sampling a traditional house is to stay at a Japanese inn, or *ryokan*. Oliver Statler's book, *Japanese Inn*, gives an excellent idea of the whole institution of Japanese innkeeping, as well as fascinating dollops of history.

In a ryokan you have tatami floors, a tokonoma decorated with a flower arrangement or painting, futon unfolded to make beds, shining wooden floors in the corridors, beautifully landscaped gardens — in short, all the beauty and comforts of a traditional Japanese house, plus extraordinary maid service. This service includes having your meals served in your room. At a ryokan you always pay for room, breakfast, and dinner, and you have no choice over the menu, but accept what is served. Some ryokan are so famous for their cooking that customers go there especially for the food. Breakfast tends to be more standardized than dinner. A typical Japanese breakfast consists of hot rice, pickles, seaweed, raw egg, bean paste soup, and green tea, plus a few specialties of the region. An innkeeper may decide that his Western guests won't be able to face raw egg and seaweed first thing in the morning, and he will serve ham and eggs — sometimes in addition to the regular breakfast.

Extreme personal attention to the needs of the guest is the mark of a ryokan. The innkeeper finds out what hour you prefer for your bath, and will come to call you when the water is ready. If you go out, the innkeeper, his wife, or a maid (sometimes all of them) will appear at the entrance to put out your street shoes and wish you a good excursion. Language permitting, they will question you on your sightseeing plans for the day and offer suggestions. This personal interest is too friendly to be regarded as nosiness. You are treated as a family guest whose welfare is the host's main concern.

Sometimes Westerners find the low bows and solicitous attention oppressive. If you are used to informality and privacy, you may not enjoy the formal farewell ceremony at the front entrance every time you step out for a stroll.

Another disconcerting thing about a ryokan is that the rooms have no locks. Theft is so uncommon that the idea of putting locks on the doors is insulting — to both the host and the guests. If you are really worried about your valuables, you may leave them with the innkeeper.

Leaving your door unlocked makes it possible for the innkeeper and maids to walk in on you unannounced, and this they frequently do. Perhaps they show slightly more discretion toward a honeymoon couple, but they seem to think that a single person should have nothing to hide.

They feel no embarrassment whatever if they catch their guest in his underwear or even totally naked, and the guest is equally nonchalant. Embarrassment is a cultural thing. A Japanese woman may be terribly embarrassed if a single strand of hair is out of place while she is calling on her son's teacher, but when traveling she feels nothing at all if the innkeeper walks into her room while she is in her panties and bra.

A luxury inn is expensive. It is not uncommon for it to cost more than a deluxe hotel. But, as in hotels, restaurants, and taxis, you don't have to tip. If a maid has performed some unusual service, such as emergency babysitting, you may give her some money wrapped up in a gift envelope, but otherwise you pay a ten to twenty percent service charge, which is added to your bill. Some two thousand of the better ryokan belong to the Japan Inn Operators' Union, and you can get a list from the JNTO (see appendix for the addresses). Reservations are necessary.

There are some eighty thousand less expensive ryokan, charging on the average $25 per person, double occupancy, for room and two meals. These inns provide the same friendly attention and service, but they are less impressive aesthetically. Instead of looking like a traditional Japanese house, they may look Western on the outside, although inside they have tatami rooms and mattresses on the floor. The maids will probably not be wearing silk kimonos, but slacks or short skirts and bobby socks. The food varies from adequate to very good. Reservations for one of these smaller inns won't be necessary unless it is the busy season (see Chapter 1, GETTING AROUND, on the busy seasons).

MINSHUKU

A cut below the economy inns are places known as *minshuku*, "people's lodging." These vary widely in comfort, but on the whole the mattresses are thinner and the décor less attractive than what you have at an inn. But they are considerably cheaper, averaging about $15 for bed, breakfast, and dinner. The distinction between a minshuku and a ryokan is that in the "people's lodging" you don't take your meals in your room, but eat in a dining room with other guests. Some of the minshuku are quite large, accommodating forty or more, and at these places you eat at long tables. Other minshuku are Ma and Pa establishments that take in four or five guests, and there you eat at the family dining table, although the family usually eats only when the guests have finished.

Gregarious people, bored by the isolation at a ryokan (inns don't have lobbies or public lounges), actually prefer the togetherness of a minshuku. If he wishes, a lone traveler can share his room with several others. He not only saves money this way; he can make friends and find companions for his sightseeing.

The minshuku are particularly plentiful near places of historical or scenic interest, but you really have to make reservations in advance during the busy seasons, because they are very popular not only with young people, but also with budget-minded families. At major train stations, such as Shinjuku Station, there are minshuku centers, little offices where you can make reservations and get brochures. Unfortunately the staff at these places on the whole speak only Japanese. If your Japanese is inadequate for describing your reservation needs, you had better go to the old reliable Japan Travel Bureau or some other travel agency with English-speaking staff. Sometimes travel agents may not want to reserve a room for you at a minshuku. They are afraid a foreigner will have a miserable time because he won't know how to use a Japanese bath or toilet, or enjoy the food, or understand the language.

It is true that in a minshuku you need a smattering of Japanese — not much, but a few key phrases. At a ryokan you can take a bath any time in the afternoon or evening. But at a minshuku you are usually more restricted about both bath and meal times. Therefore you must know enough Japanese to find out when you should show up in the dining room for meals. You certainly have to know the Japanese characters for "men" and "women" so you won't wander into the wrong bathroom or toilet. Most of all, you won't even be able to find your minshuku unless you can recognize its name in Japanese.

There are more than sixteen thousand minshuku all over the country, in cities, towns, and scenic spots. They are inexpensive, pleasant, and friendly, but you do have to know some basics about Japanese customs and language in order to enjoy your stay.

Kokumin Shukusha

It is easy to confuse the minshuku with the *kokumin shukusha*, which are also called "people's lodging" in English. The latter are subsidized and run by the government or by non-profit organizations like the National Park Commission. There are only about three hundred of these kokumin shukusha, situated in or near parks and other areas of outstanding scenic beauty. Because they are subsidized, the cost is low, around $12 for bed, breakfast, and dinner. They are clean and comfortable, although neither the food nor the accommodations are luxurious. If you are traveling as a family, you can have your own room, but if you are alone you are generally asked to share the room with several others. The food and sleeping arrangements are Japanese style.

Kokumin Kyuka-mura

In addition there are some twenty "vacation villages," called *kokumin kyuka-mura*, run by non-profit organizations. These are inexpensive resorts located in national parks and quasi-national parks. You can either camp or stay at their lodges, which are clean and wholesome, but not luxurious. The charges are about $12 to $20 for bed, breakfast, and dinner.

Reservations are absolutely necessary for both the kokumin shukusha and the kokumin kyuka-mura. In fact, these places are so popular during summer vacation that you have to make your reservations six months in advance if you want to stay there during that time.

HOSTELS

If you are prepared to rough it, you can stay at one of nearly six hundred youth hostels scattered throughout the country. About seventy-five of them are managed by the government, and the rest by the Japan Youth Hostels, Inc. (JYH). To stay at a government hostel, you need only an ID card, such as your passport. But if you want to stay at one of the JYH hostels, you have to belong to the Youth Hostel Association of your own country. You must also make reservations well in advance, and your stay is limited to three nights, unless there is an unexpected vacancy.

The youth hostels are the least expensive form of accommodations, charging about $1.50 for bed at the government hostels, and about $3 at the JYH hostels. Meals are extra, usually around $1 for breakfast and $2 for dinner, but you can use the community kitchen to cook your own meals if you want. There is a small extra charge for heat and for a sheet, if you need them. Sleeping accommodations consist of mattresses unfolded in large dormitory rooms (separate ones for men and women).

The JNTO can send you a list of youth hostels in Japan. To make reservations, write directly to the hostel you want, enclosing return postage for the reply (enclose international postal coupons if you are writing from outside Japan). You have to give your name, address, occupation, age, sex, and dates of arrival and departure.

ESSENTIALS

WESTERN-STYLE LODGING

You may feel that after a day of strenuous sightseeing you need the comforts of a solid bed for a good night's sleep. Actually, the springy tatami is more comfortable to stretch out on than a Western-style bed or sofa. But when you've just arrived in Japan, suffering from jet lag and a nerve-wracking taxi ride, the exotic elegance of a Japanese inn may be too much of a culture shock. Your weary bones need familiar Western furnishings.

Luxury Hotels

It is not necessary for us to say much about luxury hotels, because travel agents can book you into one easily. In comfort these hotels compare with luxury hotels in other countries, with a few extra Japanese touches like clean cotton kimonos to use as nightgowns, rice crackers, and hot tea in a thermos. You also get a free toothbrush. but this you get even in the cheapest hotels and inns. Tourists complain that these toothbrushes are good for only one use, and sometimes not even that. If you brush too vigorously, the brush is worn out before you finish your uppers. Toothbrush aside, the luxury hotels are wonderful — if you can afford them. Tokyo has been called the most expensive city in the world, and the high cost of hotels is certainly a contributing factor. Moreover, meals are extra at a hotel, unlike the arrangement at an inn, where breakfast and dinner are included. A service charge of 10% to 15% is added, but at least you don't have to tip (service charge is also added at luxury inns, but not at cheaper inns or people's lodgings).

Business Hotels and Hoteru

For ordinary mortals, there are cheaper Western-style hotels that are not so attractive. One category of hotels, called *bijinesu hoteru*, "business hotel," costs far less, averaging perhaps half of what the deluxe hotels charge. As is the rule with Western-style hotels, meals are not included.

The deluxe hotels are situated at the choicest scenic spots or at the most central part of a major city. The lesser hotels are often found at railway stations or suburban centers. Architecturally, they are not distinguished. You won't find it a joyous adventure to stay at one of these hotels, but neither will you find it sordid. Most of these places have a large proportion of single rooms for businessmen on trips, and hence their name, "business hotel." Refer to them by this at the travel agency when you want reservations.

Many establishments are called *hoteru*, and the tourist concludes that they are hotels. To be sure, a *hoteru* usually offers Western-style accommodations, but often the same building has Japanese-style tatami rooms as well. The plumbing at such a place can be a mixture of Western and Japanese styles. Occasionally a *hoteru* can refer to a Japanese-style inn of the poorer sort. You just can't tell by the word *hoteru* alone.

"Bring-Along" Hotels

There is one type of *hoteru* that posts a special rate for a daytime stay of a few hours. Apparently some married couples, who live in a tiny apartment with children and in-laws, come to these for a few hours of privacy during the day. But another reason for a daytime rate leaps to our dirty minds. The Japanese themselves often refer to these hotels as "bring-along hotels." They have poetic names like "Lily," "Chrysanthemum," or "Twilight," and what you bring along is not your own bottle, but your own roommate. (Fortunately, all Western-style hotels have locks on the doors.)

Motels

A number of hotels are now calling themselves motels. Except for the fact that they provide parking space for their customers (parking is very scarce and expensive in Japanese cities), they are not like Western motels at all, but more like the business hotels. Along highways there are so-called motels that don't offer lodging at all, but are more like rest stops, with toilets and gasoline.

Pensions (called PANSHION by the Japanese).

Recently, European-style pensions have begun to spring up in Japan, offering room and two meals for a modest price. The service and facilities are usually Western-style, although the price puts them in the minshuku bracket. So far there are only about four hundred of them, mostly at resorts and scenic areas, but they are very popular among budget travelers, and undoubtedly there will be more of them. Ask the Tourist Information Centers if you are interested.

Except for the deluxe hotels, Western-style lodging in Japan is no great treat. You will have a much more interesting time at a ryokan, or inn. If your budget doesn't permit a luxury inn, try a less expensive type of inn, or even one of the minshuku.

5
BATHS, BATHROOMS, AND TOILETS

TOILETS

The first time you enter a public toilet in Japan — say at an airport — you will see a long row of cubicles, with one or two at the end having a sign "Western-style" on the door. (The sign can be in English or in Japanese characters 洋式 .) Inside the cubicle is a perfectly normal toilet. But on one of the side walls is a little diagram, showing human figures involved in various ways with the plumbing. You don't have to understand the Japanese words under the picture to realize they are instructions on how to use the toilet. Translated, the instructions say, "For ladies and for gentlemen's large use, lift cover of toilet, sit down on seat. For gentlemen's small use, lift seat, stand facing toilet bowl." (Incidentally, a lot of these signs are now disappearing, because unscrupulous tourists peel them off and collect them as souvenirs.)

腰掛便器の使い方

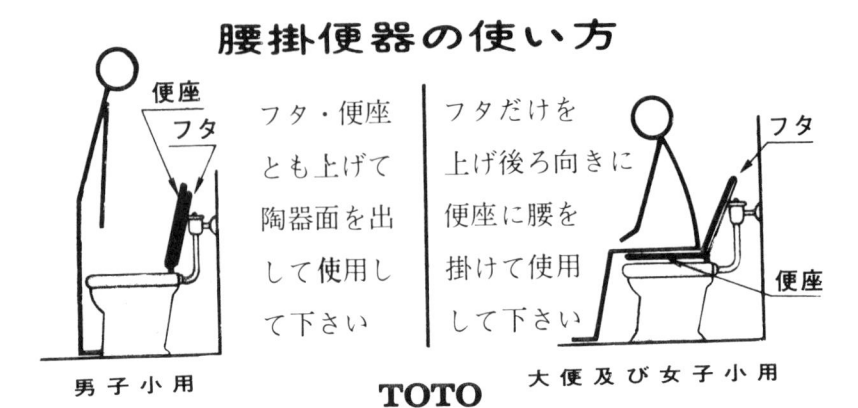

便座
フタ

フタ・便座
とも上げて
陶器面を出
して使用し
て下さい

フタだけを
上げ後ろ向きに
便座に腰を
掛けて使用
して下さい

フタ
便座

男子小用　　　　**TOTO**　　　大便及び女子小用

This is the diagram peeled from a public Western-style toilet by an unscrupulous tourist (me).

You can draw two conclusions, both disquieting. The first is that since only a few of the cubicles have the "Western-style" sign on them, the great majority must be non-Western. The second is that the non-Western toilets must be drastically different if the Japanese need diagrams on how to use the Western-style ones.

Once away from major airports, stations, and hotels, the likelihood of finding Western-style toilets decreases further. What do you do, then, during that panic-filled moment when you are alone in a little cubicle with a totally unfamiliar piece of plumbing? We should like to describe the pitfalls of using a Japanese toilet, because that's what a Japanese toilet is: a pit. Of course modern toilets are no longer open pits in the ground. Most of the ones you encounter will be indoor, flush toilets that are no worse than any Western-style ones back home. Some of the more recent ones are even on a raised platform about a foot high. But essentially a Japanese toilet, called a *benjo*, is still a hole in the floor.

POSTURE

The correct posture for using a hole in the floor is to squat. Squatting is tiring for muscles unaccustomed to it, and many Westerners rashly try to use a Japanese toilet standing up. Since this increases the distance between the source of the projectile and the receptacle, the chances of missing the target are increased. One end of the hole has a shield-wall around the rim, and it is imperative to face this shield while using the toilet.

The problem is aggravated in a moving train. If the train gives a lurch while you are in the middle of using a Japanese-style toilet, inertia will spoil your aim. This effect of Newton's First Law can sometimes be seen on the floor, showing that in a moving train Japanese themselves are not always bang on target. Fortunately, the better trains, like the super-express Shinkansen, all have at least one Western-style toilet. It is worth walking the length of the train to find it.

SLIPPERS

The floor around the toilet being liable to be less than spotless in some cases, special slippers marked W.C. are placed in the cubicle to prevent tracks going beyond it. This is especially true of inns and private homes. You must not fail to use the W.C. slippers. Equally, you must remember not to wear the W.C. slippers *anywhere* beyond the cubicle. Japanese hosts or innkeepers flinch and turn pale at the sight of their Western guests padding around the house in W.C. slippers.

Advantages of a Japanese toilet   Once you get used to Japanese toilets, you may actually prefer them to Western-style ones. They are more hygienic, because you don't come in contact with the seat. In winter, it is more comfortable than sitting on a cold toilet seat. Since the toilet room is never heated in most Japanese homes, the seat is like a ring of ice. Thoughtful housewives often put a stockinette cover of stretch nylon over a Western-style toilet seat. One company manufactures an electrically heated toilet seat, but this is a luxury item and not for hoi polloi. In an average home, therefore, a Japanese toilet is considered an advantage.

An authentic Japanese toilet is something to describe to the folks back home. At the Katsura Imperial Villa in Kyoto, one of the feature attractions is an elegant toilet. It is no longer in use, and many Western sightseers look at it without knowing what it is, because the guide's fluent English often falters at this point. Fastidious Japanese in the old days built their toilets over a flowing stream so that the waste was immediately carried away. There would be a window overlooking a breathtaking view. Besides the view, the room would be decorated with flowers, and even today, the tiny modern toilet in a private house always features a bunch of flowers (even if they are plastic).

TOILET PAPER

Those of you who have traveled in England know that it's a good idea to carry your own toilet paper, since the English variety is about as absorbent as Saran Wrap. Japanese toilet paper suffers a different problem: it is so flimsy that it starts to bio-degrade before it leaves your hand. Many people make a point of using local products when they travel, but American toilet paper can be truly a comfort. You don't have to stuff your luggage with rolls and rolls before leaving the States, however, because you can get American-style toilet paper in any Japanese department store or corner drugstore. It's a good idea to take a wad wherever you go, since many public toilets don't provide any, even the flimsy kind. (A note to female readers: you can easily buy the familiar brands of sanitary napkins and tampons in Japan, so don't bring a huge package of these with you.)

BATHS

The benjo, or Japanese toilet, is also called *toire*, from "toilet." If you forget, write "W.C." on a piece of paper, since that term is now universal. But don't ask for a bathroom when you want the toilet. As in many European countries, the W.C. and the room used for bathing are distinct. An American friend told the following story. Soon after arriving at the house in which he was staying, he asked for the bathroom. His host looked dismayed and promptly dashed out. After a moment he returned and said there would be a slight delay, but it wouldn't be too long. More than half an hour passed, during which the guest grew increasingly fidgety and the conversation became strained. Finally the hostess came in, bowed, and said the bath was ready. They led the guest into a room with a large steaming tub and apologized profusely for the delay: it had taken them so long because the family took their baths at night, and they normally didn't start heating the bath water so early.

A Japanese-style bath, called a *furo*, can be a delightful experience once you know the proper moves. Many tourists become so enthusiastic about the furo that they dream of having a Japanese-style bath built in their own home. That this is more than a pipe dream is shown by the number of firms in America specializing in building wooden Japanese bathtubs.

Wash First

The most important thing to remember about a furo is that you should be clean before stepping into the tub.

First you soap, scrub, and rinse yourself outside the tub. Modern bathrooms have faucets and shower heads outside the tub for rinsing, but in an old-fashioned bathroom you scoop water out of the tub. The floor in an older bathroom is made of wooden slats spaced apart so the water can drain away. A modern bathroom has a tiled floor, with grooves around the edge of the room and a drain. Only when you are completely washed do you step into the tub for a long soak, which is not for cleansing purposes but for warming up and relaxing tension. One of the worst social blunders you can commit is to soap and wash yourself right in the tub. The water has to remain clear because it is used by a number of people in the course of the afternoon and evening.

Some people may feel slightly squeamish at the thought of stepping into a tub of water that has already soaked other bodies. But these bodies have all been scrubbed, and the water in the tub is probably cleaner than that used in a public swimming pool. The Japanese method of bathing saves fuel, and if the worldwide energy shortage gets worse, we may all find ourselves taking Japanese-style baths. Already there is talk in America about taking showers together. As we shall see, in Japan we have three men in a tub, or even a dozen.

In a private home, the tub is rarely large enough for more than two people at a time. With an old-fashioned Japanese family of several generations, the members bathe in a strict order, beginning with the grandfather, and followed by the father. They may or may not be accompanied by their wives. Then the sons take their turns in order of seniority. After that the female members who haven't already bathed will follow. The mother bathes with children too young to do it by themselves.

WATER TEMPERATURE

If you are staying with a family, out of courtesy you will be invited to bathe first, whatever your sex. Try to wriggle

BATHS, BATHROOMS, AND TOILETS

out of being first if you possibly can, and offer to go after everyone else. Since the Japanese are ruthlessly polite, you may not succeed, but try anyway. This advice is given to save the unwary from a shock. The Japanese like their bath water very hot, the average being 109°F but sometimes going to the limit of human endurance, or even a bit beyond. Therefore when you enter a Japanese bath for the first time, you think you're stepping into a vat of boiling oil, and need only batter to turn into a giant piece of tempura.

Some tubs have a cold-water tap, and you're tempted to turn it on and make the temperature more tolerable. If you're first in line to take a bath, this would be an inconsiderate thing to do, because in many Japanese households there is no hot water running into the tub (in fact, there is sometimes no running hot water at all). Instead, the bath water is heated by a separate heater either under the tub or next to it. Bath water needs time to heat, and if you've made the water pleasantly cool for yourself, it is probably much too cold for the rest of the household. They will have to light the heater again and wait a long time before the water gets hot enough for them. That's why it's a good idea to insist on bathing last — not only can you add all the cold water you want, but you can impress your hosts by outdoing them in Oriental politeness. In any battle of politeness, however, you will probably be the loser, and reluctantly find yourself first into the bathroom.

To avoid being parboiled, wash yourself and rinse with buckets of water. Then step into the tub for two seconds of agony, to find out what it's like. It helps to stir the water before entering. Since hot water rises to the top, stirring makes the temperature more even and reduces the searing agony when you step in. You can impress your hosts further by remembering to replace the boards that cover the top of the bathtub. This will keep the water nice and scalding for the others.

Types of Bathtubs

In a private home the bathtub can be barrel-shaped, but it's more likely to be cubicle. Modern tubs are made of tile or plastic, such as fiber glass. But bathing in a traditional tub of cedarwood, with its fragrance, warmth, and velvety smoothness, is a wonderful experience. You may also run across old bathtubs made of iron, which look uncomfortably like a cannibal's cooking pot. What makes it worse is that sometimes a fire is kept going even when the bather is right in the pot. This arrangement is now rare, but you may still come across it in certain rural areas. If you ever find yourself in the soup, don't remove the round piece of wood at the bottom of the cauldron! It's there to protect you from getting scorched.

In the old days a family bathroom was often detached from the rest of the house and was a hut hardly larger than a closet. There was just room for the tub and space for the bather to wash himself. People with nasty minds could cook up all sorts of murderous plots. In one instance, a treacherous host locked his guest in the tiny bathroom and proceeded to murder him by lighting a roaring fire under the tub. In another story a warrior was assassinated in the bath when spearmen surrounded the hut and thrust their spears through the cracks in the wooden walls. People were often attacked in the bath, because they were particularly vulnerable there.

Sento

Most homes now have their own bathrooms, but until a few years ago, the majority of Japanese went to public bathhouses, or *sento*. In many older parts of Tokyo and other cities you still find people walking in the street wearing a cotton kimono and carrying a bowl containing towel, sponge, and soap. By the steamy aura around them you know they are coming out of a public bath. Even in winter

BATHS, BATHROOMS, AND TOILETS

they look flushed, relaxed, and comfortable in their thin kimonos, because the heat from the bath keeps them warm until they get home.

Even if the hotel or the people you're staying with have their own bathroom, it will be an interesting experience for you to try a public bathhouse. You can recognize a sento by a sign that says 湯, which literally means "hot water." The bathhouse has two sliding doors of frosted glass. One of them is marked by the character 男, "male," and the other one 女, "female." Even if you have no intention of learning a single Japanese character, you should still know these two, since they are used for public toilets as well. By now you've realized that despite all the spicy stories, men and women bathe separately at the public baths. Only at certain hot springs in the country do you still have coed bathing.

Having passed through the proper door (we hope), you buy a ticket from the attendant, for around 50¢. In public bathhouses, cheap hotels, and inns, you are expected to provide your own towel. These are about 75¢ in the stores, and you can also buy one from the bath attendant. A Japanese bath towel is not very large, being only about 2½ feet long, 1 foot wide, and thin. It looks more like a hand towel, and is used as a washcloth as well as for drying. Because the bath water is so hot, you will have no trouble drying yourself on this scrap. The large, thick towels in which Westerners luxuriate are quite impractical in Japan. The summer humidity there is so high that the thick towels become mouldy instead of drying.

After paying for the ticket, you take off your shoes and enter the dressing room. Now comes the moment of truth: you are expected to undress in a room full of strangers and under the eyes of the ticket seller, who is as likely as not a member of the opposite sex. If you have lived in a dorm, especially a coed dorm, you won't think anything of stripping in public. Many of you have also taken Physical Education in school and have used public showers. On the other hand, if you like privacy and lock the bathroom door to keep out other members of the family even at home, you may gulp a bit at the prospect of undressing and bathing with strangers. But the shock wears off quickly. It's like going to a nudist beach or public sauna for the first time. In the beginning you don't know where to look; then you look, but have to remember not to stare; and finally you get blasé about the whole thing and wonder why you ever worried.

One interesting fact is that although the Japanese look quite unembarrassed walking around nude in a public bath, they always manage to hold their bath towel casually in front of them. But don't expect to be able to wrap your skimpy little bath towel around yourself sarong fashion.

Most bathhouses provide lockers, but some carefree establishments hand you a plastic or rattan basket for your clothes, and you just put the basket on the open shelf. Again, theft is so rare that nobody worries about leaving his clothes unwatched. If you have valuables, however, such as an expensive watch, ring, or money belt, it may relieve your mind to leave them with the ticket seller.

Naked and clutching a towel in front of you, you slide open another glass door and enter the steamy bathing room. In the men's section, people may be shaving as well as scrubbing away and soaping. In the women's section, you often see young children being washed by their mothers, especially during the early afternoon. Older children show up later in the afternoon, when they are out of school. Adults prefer bathing in the evenings. In the mornings, the bathhouses get mostly people who have to work very late, such as bar hostesses and other ladies of the night. They go to the bathhouse on their way home.

Most of the area in the washing room consists of tiled floor, where you scrub and rinse yourself. Along the lower part of the walls are many hot and cold faucets, and you

BATHS, BATHROOMS, AND TOILETS

can use them to fill plastic basins for washing. Higher up on the walls are shower heads as well. Actually, if cleanliness is your sole purpose, you can simply take a shower and leave. But that is not the reason why the Japanese take a bath. For them the best part is climbing into the big pool for a long soak.

The soaking pool in a sento comes in various shapes, such as rectangular, oval, kidney, or even free form. On the average it holds about ten to twelve people. The water is not quite so deep as in a swimming pool — perhaps chest deep for the average Japanese. Many pools have a section roped off where the bottom is raised, so that the water is shallow and safe for young children. At one end of the pool is a faucet slowly dripping cold water, and the temperature of the water under this faucet is more tolerable than is that in the rest of the pool. If you are the faint-hearted sort, you can do your soaking huddled under the cold faucet, but don't turn it on fully, or the rest of the bathers will be more than annoyed. Scalding hot water is continuously gushing out from a pipe at the bottom of the pool (at a public bath the water is constantly changing all day long) and it is at that end of the pool where you will find the masochists.

A wall separates the rooms for men and women, but in many bathhouses an attendant sits on a high chair overlooking both sections (no, I don't know how you go about applying for the job). The attendant functions pretty much as a lifeguard, keeping an eye on rowdiness and making sure that no one gets an attack of giddiness and drowns.

Although we don't hear of people getting heart attacks from the extreme heat of the bath water, you can get a little dizzy, especially if you bathe right after a heavy meal. That's why most Japanese prefer to take a bath just before dinner. They claim the bath helps them relax and unwind, acting much like a pre-dinner cocktail.

We have gone into such detail about a public bath because youth hostels, dormitories, and the cheaper hotels and inns have shared baths on their premises, and the procedure is the same as that in a sento. Again, our advice is to go late in the evening, when most people have already washed. Then you can add lots of cold water without making the bath too cool for others.

WASH BASINS

Another characteristic of hostels and cheaper hotels is that they have no wash basins in the bedrooms. The guests brush their teeth, comb their hair, pluck their eyebrows, or whatever at a big row of wash basins in the community washroom used by men and women together. (In some places the wash basins are right in the corridors.) After walking around naked in a public bath, gargling in public is no big deal, but what *will* interest you is the sight of the other guests walking around in their underwear. The sort of Japanese who appear publicly in their underwear are not girls in their scanty briefs and bras, but mostly middle-aged men in their long johns. Because of the lack of central heating, people keep warm with underwear that is thick and hairy. If you take your time brushing your teeth, you can watch a perfectly fascinating assortment of underwear parading past. The most interesting accessory is a thick, knitted woolen band that many men wear around their waists to keep their stomachs cozy. Think what you are missing if you stay at a deluxe Western-style hotel with a private bath!

HOT SPRINGS, OR ONSEN

No discussion of bathing is complete without mentioning hot springs, or *onsen*. In Japan, a volcanic country, there are thousands of onsen. The Japanese love of bathing is sometimes attributed to this abundance of naturally hot water. People have been going to hot springs since prehistoric times, and some of the more famous hot-spring resorts can boast of patronage by emperors as far back as the seventh century. The Dōgo Spa near Matsuyama on the island of Shikoku had a monument erected by Crown Prince Shotoku (see Chapter 10, RELIGION) attesting to the curative powers of this hot spring.

MEDICINAL SPRINGS

More than eighteen hundred onsen are officially recognized as having medicinal value. In the middle of the nineteenth century Europeans discovered the delights of the Japanese onsen, and some of them became enthusiastic patrons of the Hakone spas. One Frenchman, a General Le Bon, praised the onsen at Kiga (one of twelve famous Hakone onsen) so highly that the grateful villagers raised a monument to him.

Thermal springs (heated water with little chemical content) are supposed to be good for rheumatism and skin diseases. Carbon dioxide springs help digestion. The sulphur springs smell like rotten eggs but are supposed to help gout and lumbago. There are even radioactive springs, and they supposedly help respiratory problems. The Japanese consider practically all the hot springs good for nervous disorders. Those who suffer from anxiety, depression, and other ills of modern society find that a trip to a hot-spring resort works better than pills.

The benefits of an onsen are not only in its medicinal waters. The whole atmosphere of the place makes for relaxation. The hot springs are usually found in areas of outstanding natural beauty, since they are connected with volcanic activity. Hotels, inns, restaurants, souvenir shops, and recreational facilities soon develop. When they are not taking a bath, customers spend their time lolling about in their hotel kimonos playing card games, chess, or watching entertainers. The more active can go fishing or hiking. Some of the onsen are operated in conjunction with ski resorts.

The hot-spring resorts are not just for the rich. Farmers regularly go to the onsen in the winter, during their slack period. No matter how poor you are, there is an inn with its own mineral pool to suit your pocketbook. In the old days, thousands of natural, open-air mineral springs were patronized by rich and poor alike. But these pools are so picturesque that nowadays many of them are roped off and run as luxury resorts.

Health Centers

In contrast to the inns and their small pools, you have big modern establishments with pools that accommodate hundreds. These places are called *herusu sentā*, "health center," because in addition to the mineral baths, you can get massaged. It's fun to try one of the coin-operated chairs that pummel you gently on the back.

You can also hire a masseur. Much has been written about scantily clad girls who walk up and down your spine, in addition to performing other services. Traditionally, a Japanese masseur is a blind man, called an *amma*. At inns and hot-spring resorts you can ask for an amma to be sent to your room. He also practices acupuncture as a sideline, in case the massage alone doesn't cure your aches and pains.

Jungle Baths

Some of the health centers call themselves "jungle baths," because they have giant halls decorated with palm trees and other tropical plants to lend an exotic atmosphere. But don't expect any me-Tarzan-you-Jane business, because men and women are kept in separate jungles. Inside the big hall are many pools of various sizes, temperatures, and odors. You take your choice depending on whether your affliction is gout, falling hair, or melancholy. Some pools are hot even by Japanese standards, and probably do an adequate job of poaching eggs. Others contain ice-cold water. Jumping from a hot-hot pool right into an icy one is the Japanese equivalent to the Finnish practice of dashing out of the sauna for a roll in the snow.

FAMOUS SPAS
There are far too many onsen to make even a representative list. Here are just a few:
In the Hakone district are twelve famous onsen, all popular with Westerners, especially Miyanoshita, Gōra, and Kowakidani. This area is outstanding for its views of Mt. Fuji and for its cherry trees in the spring. It is easily accessible from Tokyo.
The Atami area is also easy to reach from Tokyo. The name *Atami* means "Hot Sea," and the whole area is said to be part of an extinct volcano that gave rise to the numerous hot springs.
In Hokkaido, the most popular onsen is Noboribetsu, which is situated near boiling mud holes and geysers. Jozankei Spa, only twenty miles from Sapporo, is also very popular.
The city of Beppu in Kyushu has hot springs gushing from nearly thirty-eight hundred openings. Day and night the gutters of the city run with hot water. Besides the numerous inns and hotels with their own pools, you can take a hot sand-bath on the Beppu beaches. Unzen, also on Kyushu, is another famous hot-spring resort and a favorite with honeymoon couples.
Among the oldest of the existing onsen once patronized by early emperors and aristocrats are Shirahama on the Kii Peninsula, Dōgo on the island of Shikoku (which we mentioned earlier), and Arima near Kobe.
The hottest hot spring is probably at Kusatsu, in the mountainous part of central Japan close to a famous ski

resort (see Chapter 7, SPORTS). In the town square is the notorious Netsunoyu, or "Heat Bath." The water there is about 136°F, and bathers submit to a militaristic discipline called a "time bath." Under the direction of a bathmaster, the bathers enter the water and remain completely still (if they move, they feel twice as hot). As the sufferers poach away, the bathmaster calls out the time remaining of their ordeal. Usually the bathing period is fixed for four minutes, and at intervals the bathmaster calls, "Three minutes remaining," "Two minutes remaining," and "Just a little longer." About a million years later comes the announcement, "Time to get out."

The Kusatsu hot spring was highly praised by a German physician, Dr. Erwin von Baelz. He must have been a Prussian.

ENTERTAINMENTS

6
AMUSEMENTS

NIGHT LIFE

In the larger Japanese cities things are pretty lively at night. In Chapter 3, FOOD, we've already mentioned coffee houses and beer halls where you sit nursing your drink and listening to a variety of music, from the most cerebral classical to the loudest rock. We also talked about the *nomiya*, or small drinking places where you sit over a counter, sip your drink, munch on little plates of food, and unburden yourself to the sympathetic bartender (who is often a woman and a very good listener). All these places are relatively inexpensive. For a few dollars you can spend some very pleasant hours relaxing from your daytime sightseeing.

But if you want more excitement and are prepared to pay for it, you won't be short of opportunities. Tokyo has the most, with more than fifteen thousand bars, night clubs, and cabarets, but other large cities are also well supplied. We won't go into detail about night spots, because the type of entertainment they offer is pretty much the same as you find in the West. In fact, a number of cabarets particularly feature foreign girls.

You may discover that some night clubs are not too eager to have foreigners — they may refuse to admit you at all. Many are private clubs open only to members, but some may refuse you because they've had unpleasant incidents in the past with foreigners who argued about their bill. There are all kinds of unexpected charges, such as paying for "charms," a dish of food you are obliged to buy whether you want to eat or not. To prevent screams from their foreign customers caught unaware by their bill, a number of places now make a flat charge of about $50 for cover, show, hostess, and two drinks. For anything else you pay extra.

The bar or club hostess is a specialty of Japanese night spots. She lights a man's cigarette, pours his drink, and nods understandingly at his remarks (whether she understands his language or not). You pay for her services by the hour, and if you're lulled by her soothing presence, your bill may climb alarmingly before you know it. Therefore, it's safer to go to a place with a flat charge.

THEATERS

Movies

If you are a Japanese movie fan, you probably know the works of directors like Ozu, Mizoguchi, and Kurosawa. You may even have seen *Seven Samurai* more than once. It is sad that Ozu and Mizoguchi are both dead, and Kurosawa has not made a samurai movie in years. Moreover, television has stolen most of the movie audience. The Japanese movie industry is in trouble, although there are signs that it may pick up again, as it did in America after the initial competition from television.

Young people in Japan are very interested in movies

made abroad. In smaller towns and neighborhood theaters, the movies are frequently dubbed into Japanese, and if you don't care for the spectacle of Robert Redford spouting Japanese, you can go to a first-run theater where the movies are shown in their original languages, with Japanese side-titles. These theaters are expensive, with tickets from $4 to $6. There are some second-run theaters that charge as little as $1.50, but check first to see if the movies are dubbed.

Those of you interested in Japanese costume movies may enjoy visiting the Movie Village, a movie museum in Kyoto run by the Toei Movie Studios. Among other exhibits, the Movie Village features whole streets of complete feudal-period houses. You can strut down the main street of the village, snarl out of the corner of your mouth, and pretend you are Toshiro Mifune.

KABUKI

Among the types of traditional theater, the one most familiar to Westerners is Kabuki. The black-green-vermilion curtain, the gorgeous costumes of the actors, the complicated revolving stage, the trap doors — all these make Kabuki an extravagant spectacle. Although many theaters provide English program notes, you don't need them to enjoy the show.

A Kabuki play is a musical, with an orchestra, chorus, and dancing. The orchestra, sitting right on the stage, consists of various drums, flutes, and the *samisen*, a three-stringed banjo-like instrument. In addition, there is an instrument — if you can call it that — that consists of two short sticks of wood called *hyoshigi*. The crisp, sharp staccato sound of the hyoshigi being beaten together signals the opening and closing of the curtain. They are also beaten during moments of great emotional intensity. To the ever faster beat of the hyoshigi, the actor works himself into a frenzy — his teeth gnash, his eyes dilate or cross themselves, and his face revolves seemingly independent of his neck. Then, suddenly, he freezes. This climax, this motionless tableau, is called a *mie*. The woodblock artist, Sharaku, in many of his prints catches a Kabuki actor in the moment of his mie.

The actors do all the dancing, but not the singing, which is performed by the chorus. One characteristic of Kabuki is the *hanamichi*, or "flower path," a gangway leading from the stage, through the auditorium, to the rear of the auditorium. Some of the most dramatic moments take place on the hanamichi, and it is there that the actor often strikes a mie.

There are two main types of Kabuki plays. One is the *jidaimono*, or historical drama, full of heroics. The other is *sewamono*, a more intimate type of drama about commoners. In both kinds, the underlying theme is usually the conflict between one's duty and one's natural feelings. In the historical plays, parents sacrifice their children and husbands divorce their wives out of duty to their feudal lord, while in the intimate plays shopkeepers and courtesans commit double suicide because their sense of duty and their love for each other cannot be reconciled.

Kabuki owes much to *Noh*, which we shall discuss later, but the beginning of Kabuki as a separate form is attributed to a woman called O-Kuni, who danced on the banks of the Kamo River in Kyoto around 1600. O-Kuni was a smash hit, and after her came women Kabuki troupes that became wildly popular. The government finally banned them for having a bad effect on public morals. Next, young men took the place of the girls. It wasn't long before the government decided that the beautiful young male actors were even more of a threat to public morals than the women actors. The actors were ordered to shave the front part of their heads to lessen their seductiveness. But they continued to attract devoted admirers, until the government banned the young men's Kabuki theater as well. Kabuki was later allowed to reopen with adult male actors, and instead of relying on physical beauty alone, they began to develop their acting and dancing skills.

Kabuki actors still attract fanatically devoted fans. At one time women of fashion copied the hair styles and kimonos of the leading Kabuki female impersonators. Called *onnagata*, these actors are considered by fans to be more feminine than real women, although Westerners find their heavily made-up features harsh and their falsetto voices rather grotesque.

A matinee Kabuki performance lasts from about 11:00 in the morning until 4:30 in the afternoon, and the evening performance from about 6:00 to 10:00. Many plays are so long that the usual practice is to put on segments of several plays instead of one complete play. *Chushingura*, one of the most famous Kabuki plays ever written (for the story, see the section on the Forty-seven Ronin in Chapter 9, CASTLES AND SAMURAI), has eleven acts, and would last all day and all evening, even with cuts.

With such long performances, audiences at Kabuki bring food and drink into their boxes. Since most of the seats in the modern theaters are arranged in rows, it is more common these days for people to get refreshments at one of the restaurants or bars in the theater. Eating, drinking, and socializing are important parts of attending Kabuki.

In Tokyo, you can see Kabuki at the Kabukiza Theater near the Higashi-Ginza Subway Station, or at the Main Hall of the National Theater near the Nagatachi Subway Station. The National Theater puts on not only Kabuki, but also other types of traditional theater like *Bunraku* (see below) and dance. The theater is also a museum of Japanese drama, with valuable archives. It is worth visiting for its architecture alone, being in the style of a huge log cabin, in imitation of the *Shosoin*, an eighth-century imperial treasure house (see Chapter 8 ARTS AND CRAFTS).

ENTERTAINMENTS

In Kyoto, you can see Kabuki at the Minamiza Theater at Shijo-Ohashi. Tickets for Kabuki are fairly high, starting at around $6 and going as high as $35. A trick of foreign tourists is to buy one ticket and share it among several persons by taking turns going into the theater.

Puppet Theater, or Bunraku

Bunraku, the Japanese Puppet Theater, is less familiar to Westerners. When a famous Bunraku troupe toured the States, many people brought their children to the theater under the impression that they would be seeing fairy tales. Instead, they saw plays about merchants and prostitutes committing love suicides. Bunraku is adult drama, and some of the greatest Japanese playwrights, such as Chikamatsu (1653–1724), wrote serious plays intended to be performed by puppets.

It takes years of training to become a skilled puppeteer, and some of the puppet masters have been designated as Living National Treasures (more about Living National Treasures in Chapter 8). The puppets are about two-thirds life size, and those that depict important characters require three manipulators, one for the head and right arm, one for the left arm, and one for the body and legs (or skirt, if the puppet represents a woman). The puppeteers work in full view of the audience, but you become so engrossed in the drama that you forget their presence after a few minutes. The narrators are as important as the puppeteers, and some of them are also Living National Treasures. They have to tell the whole story as well as project the emotions, sometimes very intense, of all the characters.

The curious thing is that at one time Bunraku was more popular than Kabuki. In order to keep up with the competition, some Kabuki actors even began to imitate puppets. You can see traces of the stiffness and jerkiness of a puppet in some of the Kabuki movements.

The Small Hall of the National Theater in Tokyo,

which we have mentioned, shows Bunraku, but Osaka is even better for the puppet theater. Try the Osaka Asahiza Theater, at Yaguracho.

Noh

Both Kabuki and Bunraku were intended as entertainment for commoners. They were considered rather lowbrow, and members of the samurai class were not supposed to enjoy them. (This didn't prevent many samurai from sneaking off to the Kabuki theaters anyway.) The theater considered suitable for the samurai class was *Noh*. Unlike the extravagant staging for Kabuki and Bunraku, the Noh stage is almost bare and the imagination of the audience supplies the rest. There are usually only two main characters in a Noh play, and they deliver long, uninterrupted declamations. Since they use the language of the fourteenth and fifteenth centuries (when most of the great Noh plays were written), they are hard to understand even for people fluent in Japanese. The acting is slow and stately, and the sentiments lofty. It has been said that Noh, like English madrigal singing, is more fun for the participants than for the audience. Some of the famous warlords in the feudal period were said to have been creditable amateur Noh performers.

Even today there are numerous amateur Noh groups, and they sometimes give free public performances. Many women are enthusiastic amateur performers of Noh, although traditionally the Noh actors were all male. By asking around, you may be able to see an amateur performance of Noh without paying for expensive tickets. You won't be seeing the polished style, elegant costumes, and priceless masks of the professional troupes, of course, but you get an idea of what Noh looks and sounds like.

Kyogen

Several hours of loftiness are hard to take, even for the most masochistic samurai. A performance of Noh is made more endurable by breaking up the serious plays with comic interludes called *Kyogen*, or "wild speech." Kyogen are short, comic plays with colloquial, understandable dialogue. They poke fun at the samurai class for which they are intended to be performed, and a typical play shows a noble master being outwitted by his rascally servants.

Tickets for Noh and Kyogen cost around $6 to $25, and in Tokyo you can attend the plays at the Kanze Nohgakudo near the Shibuya JNR or Subway Station. In Kyoto, the Kanze Kaidan at Okazaki presents Noh-Kyogen. Incidentally, the Mibu Temple in Kyoto puts on a Kyogen festival every year. The actors wear marvelous wooden masks that have been treasured by the temple for hundreds of years. The plays presented here are extremely bawdy. English summaries of the plays are available, but you don't have to read them to enjoy the low comedy.

All-Girl Revues

In contrast to the all-male Kabuki and Noh casts are the all-girl troupes. The most famous are the Takarazuka Girls' Opera and the Shochiku Kageki-dan. Many teenage girls develop terrible crushes on the girls who play the male roles. The programs of the all-girl revues are as mixed as their sexuality is confusing. There is classical Japanese dancing, with a hint of a Western beat in the music, as well as Western dancing such as ballet, ballroom, and modern dance. The quality of the dancing is very high, and you can easily believe the stories about the harsh, rigorous training the girls must undergo. There are also bits of Kabuki-like drama on the program. Since Kabuki is performed entirely by men, what we have is a woman impersonating a man impersonating a woman.

You can see the Takarazuka girls at their Tokyo theater in the Hibiya district or at their home base in the town of Takarazuka, a forty-five-minute train ride from Osaka on the Hankyu Electric Railway. The Shochiku girls perform at the Kokusai Theater in the Asakusa district of Tokyo. Tickets for the revues are about $6 to $15.

GEISHA PARTIES

In Chapter 3, FOOD, we have already said that geisha parties are prohibitively expensive and hard to arrange. But many tourists feel their trip to Japan is not complete unless they attend one. If you insist on going to one, there are certain things to remember.

First of all, a geisha is trained to entertain at a party of male guests. When faced with married couples, and foreign ones at that, the geisha is too well-trained to show her dismay, but her performance of her duties will probably be lackluster. Secondly, the aim of a geisha is to make her male guests forget they are important executives or government big shots, and make them act like little boys again. That's why at many geisha parties the men wind up playing children's games. But in the case of a foreign male, whose wife is coldly looking on, the geisha has her work cut out for her.

READING

The Japanese are voracious readers. The country has one of the highest literacy rates in the world, and both weekly and monthly periodicals have readership in the millions. Most families have morning *and* evening papers delivered to them. Paperback books are well-bound and reasonable. But some readers are too stingy to buy even paperbacks; what they do is read the books right in the bookstore. It's an unwritten rule that you can read in the store as long as you like, provided you don't sit down. Therefore a standard form of amusement for people who are broke is to go to a bookstore and read standing up.

ENTERTAINMENTS

Bookstores are very plentiful, but their greatest concentration is in the area of the universities. Near the Ochanomizu Station in Tokyo is a famous street where you can find more than a hundred secondhand bookstores, one next to another. Most of the books are in Japanese, of course, but there are many books in European languages and English as well.

If you want books about Japan written in English, go to one of the bookstores that sell foreign books. The following have a very comprehensive selection of the books written in English:

> In Tokyo, *Maruzen*, near the Nihonbashi Subway Station;
> *Kinokuniya*, near the Shinjuku JNR Station, and a second branch in the Toho Twin Tower Building;
> *Kyobunkwan* and the *Jena* bookstores, both near the Ginza Subway Station.
> In Kyoto, *Maruzen* on Kawaramachi near Sanjo.

These stores are wonderful for foreign browsers, but remember, if you read sitting down, you are supposed to buy the book.

As you ride commuter trains and buses, you can't help being impressed by the literacy of the Japanese. Even in rush-hour trains, when breathing itself is difficult, you can see commuters reading books. But you may get a surprise when you peer over the shoulder of a pale, studious youth with thick glasses. Instead of a book on Existentialism or thermodynamics, he may be reading a comic book. There are comics and comics in Japan, and their readership is enormous — something like twenty-five million. The ones selling best are comics aimed at teen-age girls. The stories in these are incredibly saccharine, and the drawings depict long-legged girls with huge, square eyes filled with tears of disappointed love. Then there are adult comics full of sex and violence. These are the ones a commuter leaves behind on the train so his kids back home won't see them. Comics sell so well that there are entire bookstores selling nothing else. If you are too embarrassed to buy an X-rated comic in a bookstore, you can get one at a vending machine. There is a campaign by some mothers to prohibit the vending machine sale of adult comics to children.

TELEVISION

The Japanese spend a lot of their leisure time watching television, averaging some three and a half hours a day — not so long as in some countries, but still pretty long. The quality of Japanese television is exceedingly good — its color is probably the best in the world, and the camera work is superb. NHK, the public television network, commands the same prestige as does the BBC in Britain, and its scope is equally wide. You may enjoy tuning in on some of the English lessons presented on NHK. The big show on NHK is the Sunday-evening historical drama in serial form. It lasts precisely one year, starting on the first Sunday of January and ending on the last one in December. It receives the same fierce audience loyalty given to such British serial dramas as *Upstairs, Downstairs*. Commercial TV in Japan, like commercial television elsewhere, is criticized for its excessive violence and the inane content of its programs. At least the commercials tend to be lumped together, so that you have fewer annoying breaks. Many American TV programs have been imported and dubbed into Japanese. Even if you don't understand a word, it can be fun to watch *Kojak* in Japanese.

ENTERTAINMENTS

INDOOR GAMES

Pachinko

The most popular pastime in Japan, next to watching television, is playing *pachinko*, a kind of vertical pinball machine. All ages, sexes, and income groups play pachinko. Many attempts have been made to explain the extraordinary popularity of the game; sociologists say that modern urban life is full of frustrations, and sending the little ball zinging on its way releases pent-up frustrations. Others claim it's a form of gambling and is thus addictive. But there is a certain amount of skill involved, since the more experienced players win frequently, while beginners seldom get anywhere. Veteran pachinko players somehow snap the lever of the machine in just the right way.

It costs about four yen per ball, which you feed into the machine, and if you send the ball successfully into one of the winning slots, you get some balls back, usually fifteen. You can shoot the balls again or take them to the cashier and exchange them for items such as cigarettes, candy, drinks, fruit, or toys. Professional pachinko players can be spotted by the basin of little balls they've won. They exchange the balls for prizes, which they sell for money. Approximately twenty-five million people a year play pachinko, many of them spending as much as $400 a year on the game. It is easy to see why pachinko is a multi-trillion-yen business.

Mahjong

Close behind pachinko in popularity is the game of *mahjong*. University students play it a lot when they should be studying, but its appeal is not confined to one age group, economic class, or sex. There are many mahjong parlors, small, privately-owned establishments where people play for money.

The game originated in China, but its popularity there is nowhere near what it is in Japan. The pieces of a mahjong set are small flat tiles about one and a quarter inch long. A really elegant set has pieces made of ivory backed with bamboo, but most of them are now made of plastic. When shuffled, the pieces make an agreeable clicking sound that is music to the ears of an addict.

Although the stakes are not usually high in mahjong, some people play it so often that they lose as much as a thousand dollars annually. Mahjong takes a combination of skill and luck, and the less skillful players are always hoping their luck will turn in the next game. That's why mahjong is a major industry in Japan, although the earnings of each little mahjong parlor may not be great. Every large city has hundreds of mahjong parlors. You can drop in for a quick peek to see what they are like, but unless you know the game, don't get roped into playing. You can lose money without trying.

Go

Unlike mahjong, the game of Go is all skill. The interest in Go is increasing rapidly in America, but Europeans have played it for years, especially Germans and Austrians. More and more Westerners are visiting Japan each year for the sole purpose of playing Go. The game originated in China about 4000 years ago, although the size of the board was smaller at first. It is interesting that the Chinese have always regarded chess as a game for the common man, while they have regarded Go as a game for highbrows. (Chess is called *shōgi* in Japan. Like Chinese chess, it is a weaker game than either Western chess or Go.) Those who are strong players in both Western chess and Go claim that Go is more interesting. The number of configurations in Go is astronomical, and a good player must extract general principles from observing thousands of situations. That is why the game appeals to people with logical minds, especially mathematicians.

ENTERTAINMENTS

But Go is not just mathematics. It resembles modern warfare, whereas chess is like medieval warfare. In Go, all the men are of equal rank, so it's like massing infantry. The players must also worry about extending supply lines, digging foxholes, and sometimes invading enemy territory by parachuting. Because Go requires a high order of strategic thinking, it is still considered an essential part of military education in Japan. During the feudal period, special Go academies were set up for the samurai.

Worldwide, there are some ten million Go players, of whom seven million are Japanese. If you want to play, ask the Tourist Information Center for the address of a nearby Go club. The fees for membership are low and it isn't necessary to speak Japanese if you already know something about the game. The only Japanese word you need is *atari*, which, like "check," tells your opponent you are about to take his men.

AMUSEMENT PARKS AND ZOOS

Going to an amusement park in Japan is a waste of time and energy, since there are many amusements that are much more interesting and more easily at hand. But if you're overcome by a desire to ride a Ferris wheel, here is a list of major amusement parks:

    Tokyo: Kōrakuen Yuenshi, near Suidōbashi JNR Station;
    Yomiuriland, near Yomiuri Station of the Keito-Teito Ofura JNR Station.
    Nara: Nara Dreamland.
    Takarazuka: Takarazuka Familyland. This is the home of the Takarazuka Girls' Opera, and time is better spent attending the musical.

Japan has its zoos, but it seems a bit pointless to seek far and wide for a Japanese zoo in order to look at African lions. But if you adore zoos, you'll be interested to know that the Ueno Zoo, near the Ueno JNR Station in Tokyo, has a pair of giant pandas. Recently the two pandas mated, and excitement reached fever pitch to see if the female would produce the first baby panda born outside China. Department stores sold millions of stuffed baby pandas. Alas, hopes were dashed when the female turned out not to be pregnant. But zoo goers haven't given up hope for the future, and long lines of people still file past the panda cage every day.

STORES

Department Stores

Instead of spending what may be hours trying to find your way to an amusement park or zoo, you are better off taking advantage of the free entertainment offered by department stores. The Japanese department store, called a *depāto*, is an institution that covers a slightly wider range of activities than do Western department stores. It offers more services, engages in overseas trading, and sells a wider range of products. In a depāto you can buy real estate or cemetery lots. You can even get married in one.

The stores are closed on one week day, different stores closing on different days. But they are all open on Sundays, which is their liveliest day. You don't go to a depāto merely to shop. You go to its dental clinic, photo studio, theaters, art gallery, or even its small zoo. There are fashion shows and demonstrations on how to put on a kimono. (Putting on a kimono is such a complicated procedure that many young Japanese women need instructions on how to do it properly. Department stores often give demonstrations, and watching one is like attending a performance of traditional dance.)

The depāto has a restaurant or even several (see Chapter 3, FOOD), and the roof garden is always an amusement park where children can get rides while their parents shop. During summer a part of the roof is transformed into a beer garden with awnings and lanterns. The bargain basement is not in the basement, but on one of the upper floors. Instead, the basement is always the food department. This is one of the most fascinating parts of the store. Fresh vegetables, fish, and meat are sold here, as well as a very complete line of groceries. But the real fun is watching ready-to-eat foods being prepared. You can spend hours watching cakes being decorated, pastries fashioned, fish cakes fried, and *obento* arranged (see Chapter 3, FOOD). Many counters have plates of free samples, and customers (not only the destitute) have been known to eat a free lunch by going from one plate of samples to another.

SHOPPING ARCADES

Department stores are fascinating, but shopping centers are even more fun. Japanese shopping arcades cater to the pedestrian, and like the sooks in the Arab countries, they are a maze of narrow alleys lined with tiny shops of every description. Since shoplifting is virtually unknown, the goods lie in open bins, sometimes literally spilling out at your feet. The shopping arcades are a heady mixture of primitive stalls selling exotic Oriental curios and ultra-modern shops selling the latest in electronics.

UNDERGROUND SHOPPING CENTERS

A type of shopping center not too common in other countries is the underground shopping center. Since land is so scarce in Japan, there is no way for cities to expand except up or down. A number of skyscrapers are being built in Tokyo, notably in the Shinjuku area, but with earthquakes always a possibility, many Japanese feel nervous about tall buildings. Therefore cities have started burrowing underground.

The underground shopping centers are found at major train stations of large cities. Tokyo has several, Osaka has a mammoth one, as does Nagoya. Sapporo's is particularly extensive, because the winters are very severe there, and shoppers love the warm, sheltered underground centers. Complete with restaurants, bars, massage parlors, barbershops and theaters, these underground centers are like cities, only cities without climate, without day or night. They are especially convenient for the millions of commuters who can shop on their way home from work.

STREET ENTERTAINMENT

CHINDONYA

You don't have to go into a store for amusement, for there is plenty right in the streets. One of the quaintest forms of free entertainment is the *chindonya*, a glorified version of the sandwich man. Its purpose is to advertise, but instead of one man wearing a placard, *chindonya* consists of a team of three or four. They carry a placard, pass out leaflets, and play musical instruments. One instrument is always a big drum, but the others can be almost anything: a Japanese flute, hand bells, a clarinet, or even an accordion.

KOMUSO

If you are lucky, you may catch sight of another street musician, an itinerant priest called a *komuso*. He wears a deep basket that covers his head completely, and he plays a long, vertical flute called a *shakuhachi*. Don't expect to

ENTERTAINMENTS

find these priests on the Ginza; they are to be found on quiet, back streets. They date back to the tenth century or earlier, and if you are a Japanese movie fan, you may have seen spies disguised as these itinerant priests. Certainly the big basket hat and the dark notes of the flute make them seem rather sinister.

Vendors

There is fascination even in the street vendors. Every morning, the tofu (bean curd) seller makes his rounds. In many households fresh tofu is delivered daily, like milk. The tofu vendor announces his arrival by playing a horn with a double reed that sounds like an oboe. In some localities the tofu seller plays a set of bells. Another kind of vendor announces his arrival by a horn — the roasted-sweet-potato vendor. And don't miss the fish vendor as he skins an eel. He drives a nail through the eel's head to hold it steady, slits its back with a sharp knife, and pulls the whole skin off in one rip. These vendors never go on the modern, downtown streets. To see them you have to go to the older, residential parts of town.

Yomise

Twice a month during the summer, many business districts hold something called a *yomise*, which is a combination of a fair, a downtown night, and a sidewalk sale. The street is gaily lit with lanterns, temporary stalls are set up, and, in the pleasant coolness of evening, people come out in their cotton kimonos and have a good time. They buy flavored shaved ice to eat and wander from stall to stall, succumbing to a little impulse-buying. They also watch craftsmen at work making traditional implements such as wooden buckets and paper fans. Mixed with the sales pitch and the chatter of the customers is the chirping of crickets for sale in little bamboo cages.

MATSURI

No one should leave Japan without going to at least one *matsuri*, or festival (see Chapter 10, SHRINES, CHURCHES, AND TEMPLES). Some festivals, like Kyoto's *Gion Matsuri*, are major events attended by thousands and televised. It's especially fun to attend a festival with audience participation, like the *Bon Odori* festivals held in many parts of Japan around July and August. *Odori* is "dance," and the *Awa Odori* (August 15-18) held in Tokushima on Shikoku Island is the most famous of the mass-dancing-in-the-streets festivals. You can obtain a list of famous Japanese festivals from the Tourist Information Center.

But in addition to attending one of the famous festivals, you should also go to a neighborhood matsuri. Thousands of little Shinto shrines have festivals financed and put on by local merchants and residents. These have a gay, friendly atmosphere missing from the more famous festivals. The smaller ones have dances performed by amateurs, but at least you can get close enough to have a good look. There are little stalls where you can try a game of skill. At one stall you try to catch goldfish with little scoopers made of rice paste. If you catch the fish before the scoop disintegrates, you keep the fish. At another stall you can shoot at round targets with a little bow. There are fortunetellers, and if you don't like your fortune, you can tie the slip of paper on a tree to get rid of the bad fortune. Masks are for sale — some space-age helmets from current science-fiction TV shows, and some from designs at least a thousand years old. All sorts of food are on sale — the familiar roasted corn, the less familiar Japanese pancakes, and the downright bizarre, such as roasted sparrows.

HANAMI, OR FLOWER VIEWING

Being particularly sensitive to nature and seasonal changes, Japanese of all stations, from emperor to peasant, have always enjoyed flower viewing, or *hanami*. Many old paintings show people on an outing enjoying themselves as they celebrate the blossoms. Among the flowers traditionally admired are the iris, hollyhock, morning glory, peony, and chrysanthemum. A few imported flowers have also found favor, like the rose. But the greatest enthusiasm is reserved for the flowering trees, such as the plum, peach, and cherry. We should stretch a point and include the Japanese maple as a flowering tree, because the celebration during its fall foliage season is similar to those for the spring blossoming trees.

When the trees are at the height of their glory, many expeditions are made to famous scenic spots, shrines or temples noted for their blossoms. Spreading out red blankets under the trees, the participants eat, drink, and make merry. The more aristocratic write poetry to the beauty of the blossoms, while the uncouth drink themselves into a stupor. Singing and dancing are an important part of any flower-viewing party. The rich bring geishas and the poor bring their wives. Even today, some theaters in such cities as Kyoto put on special seasonal programs of traditional dance: spring dances during the cherry season, and autumn dances during the maple season.

The tree that flowers earliest is the plum. A sprig of plum blossom dusted with snow is a favorite motif for painters. January is the time to view plum blossoms, and a good place to see them is a Tenmangu shrine (see chapter 10). The Tenmangu shrines are dedicated to Sugawara Michizane, a noted scholar (845–903), whose favorite flower was the plum. These shrines are crowded with students at this time of the year, because they are studying for entrance examinations which soon take place, and the scholarly Sugawara would look kindly on the studious.

The peach is the next tree to blossom. Since the peach blooms around the time of the *Hina Matsuri*, or Doll Festival (March 3), this festival is sometimes called the Peach Festival. The soft pink of the peach blossoms is supposed to be particularly suited to little girls and their dolls. There is an unusual kind of peach tree, highly prized by connoisseurs, which has blossoms both of pure white and of pure pink on the same branch. This kind of tree is called *gempei momo*, named after the medieval warring families of Genji and Heike, whose banners were white and red respectively.

The cherry is of course the climax of the spring blossoming season. First to flower is the single-petal cherry, whose flower is pale pink, almost white. The most famous place to view this kind of cherry is Mt. Yoshino in the Kii Peninsula. To reach Yoshino, take the Kinki Nippon Railway from Abenobashi in Osaka, a trip of about an hour by limited-express. At Yoshino Station the cable car takes you up the mountain to the cherry groves. Mt. Yoshino contains four groves, with some hundred thousand cherry trees altogether.

The single-petal cherry is the most highly prized, because it falls so quickly. The Japanese believe that beauty is more precious if it doesn't last. There is a variety of single-petal cherry called Yoshino, after the mountain — this is the kind planted at the Tidal Basin in Washington, D.C. The double-petal cherry blooms somewhat later in the month. The blossoms stay on the tree more tenaciously, and are therefore not so highly prized, although the weeping variety of double-petal trees has its admirers. Daigoji, a temple south of Kyoto, is famous for its weeping cherry trees.

It is impossible to say when cherry trees are at their

ENTERTAINMENTS

peak — so many factors such as the weather, the variety, the exposure, the soil, and so on contribute to their blooming. The trees always bloom first in the southern island of Kyushu, and then move gradually up until, nearly two months later, they bloom in the northern island of Hokkaido. The Japanese follow the advance of the blossoming with keen interest, anxious to plan their traveling so they are at the right spot at the right time to view the trees at their best. Newspapers and television stations put out bulletins on the progress of the cherry trees, such as "The middle grove on Mt. Yoshino is sixty percent in bloom." On TV, maps show the advance of the floral fronts, and at railway stations posters proclaim the names of the famous scenic spots and the current conditions of their blossoms.

A similar kind of fever hits the country in the fall, when the maple trees are aflame with color. Many national parks are wonderful for maple viewing, but the most famous spot is Arashiyama, in the western part of Kyoto. For a thousand years it has been the favorite place for courtiers and commoners alike to view the fall foliage. Again, the occasion brings its singing, dancing, and drinking, but with the celebration there is also a feeling of poignancy at the approach of winter.

The Japanese spend a prodigious amount of energy and money to view flowering trees at their best, to attend the famous festivals, to see a leading Kabuki actor perform, to hear a famous violinist give a recital — in short, they take their amusements very seriously.

The foreign tourist in Japan may find it hard to compete with the hordes. Instead of joining the frenzy at the famous scenic spots or lining up for tickets for the hit shows, you may prefer to stroll through a morning market, go to a neighborhood festival, see a kimono demonstration, look at some old women combing the moss in a temple garden, or simply watch a housewife buying eel from a fishmonger. For the tourist, the greatest enjoyment may be found in scenes which are part of ordinary life in Japan.

7

SPORTS

WESTERN SPORTS

What is the most popular sport in Japan? Surprisingly, it is not one of the sports we traditionally associate with the Japanese, like judo or karate. By far the most popular sport in Japan is baseball.

Introduced to Japan from America in 1873, it instantly became popular. As in the American system, there are two professional leagues, the Central and the Pacific, with six teams each. The season lasts from April to October, and the top teams in each league play each other for the Japan Series, the equivalent of the World Series in America. But instead of teams associated with cities, the Japanese teams are sponsored by companies. For instance, the Yomiuri, a national newspaper, sponsors the Yomiuri Giants, and Hankyu, a private railway company, sponsors the Hankyu Braves.

Schools and universities also have baseball teams, which arouse the same rah-rah school spirit in students and alumni as do football teams in America. Japanese

SPORTS

cheerleaders are not coeds in miniskirts, however, but boys wearing kimono, hakama (a wide, divided skirt), and wooden clogs. Instead of waving pompoms or leaping into the air, they wave fans and long cloth banners, and bang on a big Japanese drum. At one time the baseball teams of the two universities, Waseda and Keio, were such keen rivals that their fans regularly got into bloody street fights in Tokyo.

High school baseball attracts as much, if not more, attention than college baseball. The top high-school teams compete in two series of tournaments at the Kōshien Stadium in Osaka, once in spring and once in summer. These are events that are nationally televised and watched by millions of people who have no connection with the schools involved.

If you are a baseball fan, you should attend at least one Japanese baseball game for comparison's sake. The Tourist Information Centers can help you with information on tickets.

Another popular sport in Japan is volleyball. Most of the good volleyball teams are organized by company employees, and these teams practice with grim determination under fanatical coaches. There is so much pressure on the players to win that occasionally we hear of players having nervous breakdowns. Housewives also organize volleyball teams — the game has become so popular that the term *barē mama*, "volley mama," has been coined to describe the social phenomenon of a mother leaving the children home with daddy while she goes off to play.

ACTIVE SPORTS

The Japanese are also very keen on active sports like tennis. This sport has become fashionable ever since the Crown Prince met his future wife on a tennis court. Some cities, such as Tokyo, have municipal courts open to the public for a token fee, but they are so crowded that you

ENTERTAINMENTS

have to make reservations as much as two weeks in advance. To keep up with the demand, tennis courts have even been constructed on downtown roof tops and on the grounds of some Shinto shrines.

Golf is also very popular in Japan, but it is a rich man's game. What with the astronomical price of land and the difficulties of growing turf in the Japanese climate, it may soon be cheaper to play in a huge, indoor golf course with wall-to-wall carpeting. In many cities you may notice here and there an open green field with an immensely tall green net at one end. This is a driving range, for those who want to practice without paying the high fees of golf courses. Important business deals are sometimes concluded on the golf course, and membership in a private golf club is so essential to the career of a rising Japanese businessman that there are long waiting lists for vacancies. Memberships are bought and sold like real estate. If you want to play golf, call the Japan Golf Association for information, but it is best to know someone with a membership in a private club. The golf links at Kawana on the Izu Peninsula are supposed to be the best in Japan.

Although Japan is a maritime nation and also abundantly supplied with rivers and lakes, the Japanese have not always stressed swimming as a sport. True, they enjoy trips to the beach, but, in the old days, so many drowned that stories arose about mythical creatures called *kappa* who liked to pull unsuspecting victims into the water and keep them there. In recent years the Ministry of Education has been pushing to make swimming a required subject in school, and public schools in many of the large cities now have their own pools. But pools for the general public are in short supply. Tokyo has several large outdoor pools that charge a very reasonable fee (about 50¢ an hour), but they are terribly crowded when the weather is good. If you really want to swim, it is best to pick a rainy day. Surfing has become popular with swimmers, who learned the sport in Hawaii. It was discovered that the waves in Sagami Bay and on the Izu Peninsula are suitable for surfing, and some of the beaches there, such as the one at Ito, have been promoted as surfing resorts.

Ping-pong is very widely played in Japan, and until the Chinese entered the scene, the Japanese table-tennis teams dominated the international tournaments. Schools, universities, and factories all have their ping-pong teams. The high school National Ping-Pong Championship Tournament draws thousands of spectators. If you are a keen ping-pong player and want to try out your skill against some good Japanese players, visit Senshu University, whose ping-pong team is famous internationally. To reach Senshu University, take the Tozai Subway Line and get off at the Kudanshita stop. You will find the campus near Marunouchi Park.

Like ping-pong, bowling is a sport that makes very efficient use of land and requires little in the way of expensive equipment. There was a boom in bowling a few years ago, and thousands of "bowling palaces" were built, some with hundreds of lanes. The boom has burst, because the Japanese have become more affluent and now prefer "classier" sports, such as golf and tennis. But some of the bowling palaces still remain, and you may be interested in visiting one to look at its sheer size. Be quick, because by the time you get there, it may already be a supermarket.

RUNNING, WALKING, HIKING, AND BICYCLING

Although most Japanese feel a little self-conscious about individual jogging, organized running has become a fad. It is estimated that of a population of 111,000,000, three to five million do some long-distance running. Marathons are very popular, and a mammoth one is held just outside Tokyo in the fall. People of all ages and abilities take part, including many foreigners. If you are a distance runner, you will enjoy it — it's a great way to make friends.

ENTERTAINMENTS

The Japanese have always been good walkers. The country's mountainous terrain made vehicular traffic difficult, and people walked from one end of the country to the other. And how they loved to walk! They were always finding excuses for traveling, such as making pilgrimages to shrines and temples — at least that was what they told the family they left behind. (See Chapter 10, CHURCHES, SHRINES, AND TEMPLES.) During the Edo Period (1603–1867), the feudal lords were required to spend part of the time in Edo, the shogun's capital. Making these periodic trips between their own province and Edo was such an expensive undertaking that it drained the resources of the feudal lords and checked their power to revolt. Up and down the highways were the elaborate processions of these feudal lords and their retinues, all on foot except the lords themselves, who were carried in sedan chairs.

The most famous of the old highways in Japan was the Tōkaidō, linking Tokyo to Kyoto. You have probably seen reproductions of Hiroshige's woodblock prints, which show the fifty-four stations along the route. These prints give a vivid picture of the old highway, with its processions of feudal lords and throngs of ordinary pedestrians. Today most of the old highway is paved over by expressways, but here and there small sections of the highway are carefully preserved. One stretch is at Hakone, near a replica of the old Hakone Barrier (this was a checking station used in feudal days, which we mentioned in Chapter 1, GETTING AROUND). Today there are walking clubs whose members make a point of seeking out stretches of historical highways such as this. The Tourist Information Center can put you in touch with one of the clubs.

It is hard to draw the line between walking and hiking — perhaps it is hiking when you wear hiking boots. In addition to spectacular scenery, hiking will take you to back roads and small villages, and you can get a close look at country life you would never see on regular tourist circuits. You will see thatched farmhouses and rows of radishes hanging in the sun. If the season is right, you can see farmers transplanting rice seedlings in the paddies, or watch them harvesting and hanging the rice stalks on racks. You will also learn more than you really want to know about old-fashioned fertilizing methods.

Hiking is wonderful in the national parks. There are twenty-seven national parks, run by the central government, and forty-seven quasi-national parks, run by prefectural governments. These parks abound with hot springs, where weary hikers can soak away their aches and pains. The government has embarked on an ambitious program to build a long-distance hiking trail, called the Tōkai Nature Trail. So far, some 850 miles have been completed; you can find out where they are from the Tourist Information Centers.

In Chapter 1 we mentioned the hazards of cycling in the large cities. The Japanese still cycle, of course, and at train stations you can see thousands of bicycles left there by commuters. It is all part of a movement the Japanese call "Bikology," a word combining "bicycle" and "ecology." The commuters bike to the station from their homes in the morning, leave their bikes, and take the train into the city. Then they pick up their bikes on their way home in the evening. Incidentally, most of the bikes are left unattended and unlocked all day. Naturally, nobody steals them.

For a foreign tourist unfamiliar with the streets and the traffic patterns, cycling in a crowded city — for whatever purpose — is too dangerous. It is not all that safe even for people who live in the area, as you can see from looking at the traffic casualty lists in the daily paper. The Japanese have always believed that heroes should die young.

But cycling for pleasure outside the city is a different story. A nationwide system of bike routes is under construction, where cyclists can ride free of the menace of

131

ENTERTAINMENTS

automobiles. Again, the Tourist Informaton Centers have the latest information on which sections have been completed. In general, cycling on country roads is pleasant and safe. Like hikers, you can get a close look at rural scenery.

Bicycles are available for rent in many areas where the roads, scenery, and topography are particularly suited to cycling. At these places you can usually find bicycle rental shops near the train station. For example, you can rent bikes in Nara and Kyoto (not the central part of Kyoto, which is too crowded, but the suburban areas like Ohara and Arashiyama). The charge is about 50¢ an hour and $4 a day.

Some cities have a number of bicycles available to the public for no fee at all, or just a token fee. Sapporo, for example, has municipal bikes you can ride at no cost along certain designated bike routes in the city. In Tokyo, you can borrow bikes near the Imperial Palace Police Station and ride them in the Palace Gardens. Borrowers leave their names and addresses and return the bikes after an hour. And everyone returns the bikes!

Cycling is very actively promoted in Japan, a country so vulnerable to any energy crisis. More special bicycle lanes and routes will undoubtedly be constructed on a large scale.

MOUNTAINEERING AND SKIING

Mountaineering is a natural for Japan, where four-fifths of the nation is mountainous. For some good, challenging climbing, try the Japan Alps, a mountain range cutting across the middle, thickest part of Honshu. Although not as high as the European Alps (Mt. Fuji, the highest peak in Japan, is only 12,389 feet), these mountains were named the Japan Alps by an Englishman for their ruggedness as well as their alpine plant and animal life. A number of the peaks are no-nonsense climbs for experienced climbers only. Mt. Tanigawa, with its steep, almost vertical sides, is a notorious killer. Another especially vicious one is Mt. Kaerazui: its name means "Point of No Return," because of the many avalanches. The most famous peak in the Japan Alps is probably Mt. Yari — *yari* means "spear," and the mountain is spear-shaped, like the Matterhorn. The easiest peak to tackle is Mt. Norikura, since a bus takes you nearly to the top, leaving a climb of only two and a half hours to the summit.

A good starting point for exploring the Japan Alps is the town of Kamikochi. To reach Kamikochi from Tokyo, take the Chuo Line from Shinjuku Station and get off at Matsumoto (an interesting city, incidentally: it has a noteworthy castle and is also the home of the Suzuki Method for teaching the violin). From there take the Matsumoto Electric Railway.

When we talk about mountain climbing in Japan, we are usually thinking about Mt. Fuji. Climbing Mt. Fuji is a totally different matter from hiking or climbing in the Japan Alps. The Alps are quiet, remote areas far from the beaten path, while the paths up to Mt. Fuji are among the most beaten in Japan. There is a saying that everyone should climb Mt. Fuji at least once in his life. (There is another saying that anyone who climbs it twice is a fool. The reason for this saying will soon become clear.)

For most of the year, Mt. Fuji is covered with snow. The experienced climber with suitable clothing and equipment prefers to climb it in the spring, when the snow lies still and the scenery is breathtaking. Most people, however, climb the mountain during July and August, when the trails are clear. The mountain becomes so crowded that you may as well be on the Ginza. Your eyes and nose soon get clogged with dust kicked up by the heavy traffic. Worse, you are continually being overtaken by elderly climbers who look as if they are too feeble to get up from their TV sets. Many Japanese train for months before making this once-in-a-lifetime climb. So as you huff and puff your way up the mountain, don't feel too bad if you're overtaken by a stringy old lady carrying a cane.

There are five major trails to the summit: each trail is divided into ten sections, with a station marking the end of each section. Some stations are merely signposts, and some are stone huts in which you can rest and buy refreshments. If you want to take it easy, you can spend a night at one of these huts, but the accommodations are pretty poor. A popular way to climb Mt. Fuji is to start late in the afternoon and climb during the night, when it is cooler. You can reach the summit in time for sunrise, a really spectacular sight well worth all the dust and sweat. You can also cheat by taking a bus to the fifth station and climbing the rest of the way.

Skiing

Most of the mountain-climbing areas we mentioned have skiing in the vicinity. There are more than a hundred and twenty ski resorts in Japan, with excellent facilities, the most famous being Zao Spa in Tohoku, northeastern Japan. This part of Tohoku, which faces the Sea of Japan, has some of the heaviest snowfall in the world. The Zao grounds are known for the silvery ice-covered foliage of the trees, but the Kusatsu Ski Grounds are closer to Tokyo — about three and a half hours away by train. If you go to Sapporo on the northern island of Hokkaido, you will find ski grounds in the city's western suburbs. Sapporo was the site of the 1972 Winter Olympics, and the Teine Olympic Ski Grounds are forty-five minutes away by bus. (The city also has very good facilities for other winter sports, such as ice skating.) Skiing is good in the Sapporo area from December to late April. Some of the mountains in Japan are active volcanoes, and you may enjoy the thrill of whooshing by a steamy crater on your skis. At the end of a day of spills, you can soak your bruises in one of the numerous hot springs close to the ski resorts.

Skis and boots can be rented, but since there aren't too many pairs of large-sized boots available, you should avoid very crowded days, such as weekends and the New Year holidays. At these times trains going to ski resorts are packed, even with the addition of extra cars.

TRADITIONAL SPORTS

Although the facilities for hiking, skiing, mountaineering, and other Western sports are good in Japan, most foreign visitors are more interested in traditional Japanese sports.

SUMO

The most traditional sport of all is *sumo*, Japanese-style wrestling. Many Westerners have taken up judo, karate, and aikido, but sumo is still confined almost exclusively to the Japanese.

Sumo is a sport of great antiquity. It is said that a match took place before the emperor in 23 B.C. The sport was rougher in those days — in this match one of the wrestlers kicked his opponent, fracturing his ribs, knocked him to the ground, and stomped on him until he died. By the eighth century, however, sumo evolved into a more refined sport, and kicking, fist jabs, and striking with clenched fists were prohibited.

The size of the wrestling ring became standardized by the seventeenth century, and is still the same today: a circle about twelve feet in diameter, with the perimeter marked by bundled rice straw. The rules of sumo became fixed at about the same time. The loser of the bout is the one who touches the ground with any part of his body (except the soles of his feet) or is pushed or thrown out of the ring.

During the feudal period, sumo was so popular that feudal lords competed with one another in hiring the cham-

ENTERTAINMENTS

pion wrestlers into their service. The sumo wrestlers were also great heroes to the common people, and the woodblock prints of the day, which showed popular actors and courtesans, also depicted leading wrestlers.

Today the sumo wrestlers still wear a feudal-age hair style—long hair tied into a topknot. The referee of the sumo match also wears a costume and carries a lacquered fan dating back to the feudal period. Modern sumo matches preserve the ancient rites associated with the sport. In the old days, many sumo matches were staged at Shinto shrines as offerings to the gods. Today, sumo matches are held in huge, modern indoor auditoriums seating ten thousand people, but suspended over the ring is a canopy shaped like the roof of a Shinto shrine. As the wrestlers enter the arena, they perform the Shinto rites of purification by washing their hands, rinsing their mouths, and scattering salt. Between bouts there is a picturesque ceremony in which the champion wrestlers, wearing elaborately decorated aprons, clap their hands and stamp their feet.

The ceremony surrounding sumo matches lasts much longer than the bouts themselves, which average around fifteen seconds. When the bout lasts too long — stretching to two minutes or more — the referee may stop the fight to let the wrestlers rest. The impact of the two human mountains rushing at each other is momentous, and the bout is too violent to last long.

Sumo wrestlers are big men, being well over six feet in height and weighing sometimes over three hundred pounds. During the no-holds-barred matches of the old days, the bigger and stronger wrestler usually won. But now, with the small wrestling ring, speed and cunning can occasionally overcome size. Still, being big and fast is better than being merely fast, and having a huge stomach makes for a low center of gravity and therefore more stability. The wrestlers gain weight by eating as much as ten bowls of rice a meal. They also fatten up on a special stew called *chanko-nabe*, which contains meat, fish, and vegetables all cooked together. Restaurants located near sumo training schools sometimes serve chanko-nabe, if you are curious to try it.

There are six sumo tournaments a year, three of them in Tokyo and one each in Osaka, Nagoya, and Fukuoka. The first tournament of the year begins on January 8 at the Kurame Kokugi Kan sports arena in Tokyo, and this is a festive occasion that many women attend in their elegant New Year kimonos. Each tournament lasts fifteen days, and each wrestler fights one bout a day.

The wrestlers are ranked according to their number of wins. There is a special high rank, called *yokozuna*, which becomes permanent until the wrestler retires. At present, there are only two yokozuna holders, Wajima and Kitanoumi. Below this rank are four championship grades: *ozeki* (champion), *sekiwake* (junior champion), *komusubi* (third rank), and *maegashira* (senior rank). The rank of a sumo wrestler moves up or down according to how well he is currently doing.

The atmosphere of a sumo training school is traditional, and very few foreigners have managed to break into the sport. One notable exception is Jesse Kuhaulua, a Hawaiian of Polynesian descent. He is very popular with Japanese fans, and he wrestles under the ring name of Takamiyama. Although there are almost no foreign wrestlers, many foreign residents in Japan have become avid sumo fans because they love the color and excitement of the sport. In a gathering of foreign businessmen, teachers, scholars, and missionaries, you can often hear the company comparing the exploits of their favorite wrestlers.

Tickets to sumo matches are not cheap, but the highlights of the tournaments are televised. In fact, the popularity of sumo rose sharply when the matches became televised. Since the bouts are over so quickly, the close-ups and slow-motion replays on TV are particularly interesting to watch.

ENTERTAINMENTS

JUDO

The sport people think of first in connection with Japan is, of course, judo. *Ju* means "supple" or "pliant," and *do* means "way." In other words, *judo* is the "supple way." Before we go on, we should explain the difference between judo and jujitsu.

Jitsu means "martial skill" or "technique," and therefore *jujitsu* is the "technique of suppleness." In jujitsu you don't meet your opponent by brute force, but give way to him and use his own force to defeat him. Jujitsu has a long history. It derived originally from sumo wrestling, and then later developed as a combat technique. Many schools of jujitsu were established, but these degenerated after the beginning of the Meiji Era (1868) when the country turned to Western skills and techniques.

In 1882, Kano Jigoro gathered together the best techniques from various jujitsu schools and used them to form a new system he called *judo*. He wanted his system to be not only a combat technique, but also training for both body and spirit. The center for Kano's school of judo is the Kodokan Judo Hall in Tokyo, near the Kasuga Subway Station. It is a mecca for judo fans from all over the world, and many foreigners sign up for training sessions there or to watch some of the exhibitions. The biggest exhibition is held on January 12, but there are many others throughout the year. You can also watch practice sessions of judo and other martial arts between five and nine in the evening at the Budokan Hall near the Kudanshita Subway Station.

Incidentally, you may notice that in judo, attacks are often accompanied by a blood-curdling yell, called a *kiai*. The purpose of the yell is twofold: to frighten one's opponent, and to focus one's energy. You can hear the kiai not only during judo bouts, but also during bouts of other martial arts.

Aikido

There is a growing interest among Westerners in *aikido*, a system of self-defense. *Ai* means "harmony," *ki* means "spirit," and *do* means "way." Therefore *aikido* is the "way of harmonious spirit." The name emphasizes its non-violent, defensive nature.

The techniques of aikido have been known since early times, and for centuries they have been the specialty of the Takeda family of Aizu province. Ueshiba Morihei learned the skills from a member of the Takeda family, added some techniques from various jujitsu schools, and in 1925 organized them into a system, giving it the name of aikido. Ueshiba investigated not only jujitsu, but many different martial arts and even went to China to study kung fu techniques. Like Kano, the inventor of judo, Ueshiba believed in training character and developing mental composure as well as teaching physical skills.

Aikido resembles judo superficially, but it places more emphasis on wrist throws, whereas judo uses a great variety of throws. During judo bouts, the opponents are often standing close, with their hands on each other's collar. The opponents of an aikido bout, however, stand apart until the actual attack.

Aikido trainees spend a long time twisting, bending, and stretching their limbs to strengthen them. With its emphasis on blocking and neutralizing attacks, it is becoming very popular in the West, especially among women looking for self-defense against molesters.

If you are interested in watching or practicing aikido in Tokyo, get in touch with the *Aikikai*, near the Shinjuku JNR Station.

Karate

When Okinawa was occupied by the Japanese in the sixteenth century, the natives were deprived of their arms.

So the Okinawans began to study Chinese empty-hand techniques in secret. They were especially interested in attacks that used jabbing or kicking. After adding some modifications of their own, they called the resulting system *karate*. *Kara* means Tang, the name of a Chinese dynasty, but it was used in Japan and Southeast Asia to denote anything Chinese. *Te* means "hand," and therefore *karate* is "Chinese hand." Later, when karate was introduced into Japan, a different character was used for writing *kara*. This character is also pronounced *kara*, but it means "empty," and *karate* became "empty hand."

Karate was introduced into Japan during the 1920s. When Japanese officials were visiting Okinawa, they were impressed by the superb coordination and physical condition of some Okinawan youths. They were told that these youths were karate trainees, and after watching some demonstrations, the Japanese became convinced karate would be excellent for developing the physiques of Japanese students. Before long, several universities adopted karate as part of the physical education curriculum.

The worldwide spread of karate needs no discussion here. If you want to watch practice sessions in Tokyo, a good place is the Japan Karate Association near the Ebisu JNR Station. For those interested in signing up at a particular school, try the Federation of All Japan Karate Organization, whose headquarters are near the Toranomon Subway Station.

ARCHERY, OR KYUDO

Until about the fourteenth century, the bow was the warrior's principal weapon. One of the most famous archers in Japanese history was Minamoto Tametomo (1139–1170), reputed to be a giant seven feet tall. He once cut a man's leg off at the knee with an arrow, and legend has it that he used a turnip-shaped arrowhead. This arrowhead, which made a loud humming noise in flight, was normally

SPORTS

used to give signals or to frighten the enemy with its noise. Tametomo's feat would have been less incredible if he had used a sickle-shaped arrowhead. The latter was frequently used to shoot down the banner of the opposing army, thus shaming and demoralizing the enemy. Other arrowheads included a needle-sharp one for deep penetration, and one called "bowel raker," which requires no explanation.

In medieval Europe, the knights fought on horseback, while the base-born archers fought on foot. But in Japan the high-born warriors were the archers, and they shot both from horseback and on foot. If you want to see some shooting on horseback, go to an exhibition of *yabusame* (there is one at the Hachiman Shrine in Kamakura on September 16), when galloping horsemen shoot at three or five targets in rapid succession.

Robin Hood was famous for his pinpoint accuracy. Japanese archers, on the other hand, were more concerned with range and rapid fire. In the old days, the samurai were required to train by sustaining a flight of arrows for a twenty-four-hour period at a target seventy to a hundred yards away. The standard during such a session was to shoot a thousand arrows on target (though not necessarily bull's-eye). Very few go through such severe training today, and modern archers can no longer sustain the flights or reach the range of the old archers.

The Japanese bow is very long — averaging about seven feet — and some of them take several men to string. The strength of an archer is measured by the number of men it takes to bend and string his bow. Since the bow is so long, it is grasped not at midpoint but at a point two-thirds of the way down for easier handling while shooting on horseback.

Archery continues to be a popular sport, and the All Japan Kyudo Federation boasts a large membership. It is interesting that many women have taken up the sport. If you want to see a display of Japanese archery, go to the Sanjusangendo Temple in Kyoto on January 15 for a contest known as *Toshiya*. Archers line up to shoot arrows across the outer corridor of the temple, a range of about 120 yards. The archer who shoots the greatest number across is the winner. The all-time record is held by a seventeenth-century samurai, who shot 13,053 arrows in a twenty-four-hour period, of which 8,153 went the full length. Modern archers feel they are doing well if they get a few hundred across.

KENDO

Ken means "sword" and *do* means "way," and therefore *kendo* is the "way of the sword." A samurai regarded his sword as his soul, and it was the privilege of wearing two swords that distinguished him most visibly from a commoner. In 1588 Hideyoshi (see Chapter 9, CASTLES AND SAMURAI) made commoners give up the sword, thus drawing a clear line between the warrior class and the other classes. (In history this incident is called the "Sword Hunt.")

An elaborate etiquette surrounded the sword, and anyone guilty of a lapse in sword manners received more than a slap on the wrist. An irritable samurai whose scabbard was bumped might draw his sword and cut down the offender. A more lenient samurai might simply sever the man's leg tendons. The samurai wore two swords, the longer one a little over two feet, and the shorter one a little over one foot. The shorter one he kept in his sash (this is the one used for *seppuku*, or *hara-kiri*), but he took the longer one out when he entered the house. If he was visiting a trusted friend, he left the sword outside the room. During a visit to someone he knew less well but still trusted, he placed the long sword on the floor to his right. Since it takes a fraction of a second longer to draw your sword when it is on your right, placing it there was a friendly sign. Placing it on your left told your host you had some doubts about the quality of his hospitality. It was even more insulting to place your sword with the hilt close to the host's hand. It told the host you had such a low opinion of his skill that you had no fear he could snatch at your sword.

Swordsmanship was more than just etiquette. Those of you who go to samurai movies have seen master swordsmen cutting down opponents with the efficiency of a power mower. Of course you don't believe everything you see in the movies, but it is a documented fact that Miyamoto Musashi (1584–1645), Japan's most famous swordsman, once successfully extricated himself from a fight in which he was attacked by over a hundred men.

Kenjitsu, or swordsmanship, was so important to the training of a samurai that more than two hundred schools arose. To prevent class size from dwindling too fast, instructors used wooden practice swords. But these wooden swords could still inflict a serious injury (Musashi, in his most famous duel, killed his opponent with a wooden sword). A less lethal and more flexible practice sword was developed, made of pieces of bamboo bound together, and this is the one still in use today. The casualty rate is further reduced by the use of a face mask, breastplate, padded aprons, and gauntlets.

Kendo developed out of kenjitsu, in the same way that judo developed out of jujitsu. Trainees had to practice concentration and spiritual values as well as skill in the use of the bamboo sword. Today kendo is still regarded as important for building character. Both kendo and judo are taught at junior high and senior high schools. In buses and subways you often see a boy carrying mask, armor, and practice stick on his way to a kendo lesson. Since Japanese police are not armed with guns, they undergo a very rigorous training in both kendo and judo. In fact, a police station is a very good place to watch kendo exhibition bouts — not at a tiny police box called a *kōban*, but at a major police station called a *keisatsu-sho*. In Tokyo, try the Metropolitan Police Department near the Kyobashi Subway Station.

FOOTBALL, OR KEMARI

When tourists first hear of Japanese football, they expect a game played by bruisers built like sumo wrestlers. Japanese football, or *kemari*, is played by gently nurtured aristocrats, who stand in a circle wearing their court costumes (including formal hat). The purpose of the game is to keep a round leather ball in the air by kicking it. There is no opposing team to defeat, no goals to be made. The aim of each player is to kick the ball when it comes his way, and to do it gracefully, elegantly, and without losing his cool. This is not as easy as it sounds.

A demonstration of *kemari* is part of certain festivals in Kyoto. One such festival is the *Momiji Matsuri*, held at Arashiyama on the second Sunday of November, when the participants dress in tenth-century costumes and engage in elegant pastimes suitable to the imperial court.

Japanese football, or kemari, remains an esoteric sport of aristocrats. American football, on the other hand, is attracting a certain amount of interest in Japan. Already, professional teams have been formed, although it is not certain whether, with their slighter physiques, the Japanese teams will ever be able to compete with American teams. European football, or soccer, is another sport taken up by many Japanese youngsters. At the same time that a growing number of Westerners are showing interest in traditional Japanese sports like judo, karate, aikido, and even kendo, the Japanese themselves are attracted to more and more Western sports. It probably reflects a general internationalization of sports, and the day may come when people no longer think of judo as particularly Japanese, just as golf is no longer considered Scottish.

8
ARTS AND CRAFTS

There are times in Japan when you get the impression that the country has surrendered to Western culture. Fashion, entertainment, music, sports — all seem to be profoundly affected by Western influence. The trend is especially evident in art. Young Japanese art students take up oil painting and sketch plaster models of Praxiteles. If you go sightseeing at some scenic spot, you trip over students sketching with pencil or Western water colors. An exhibition of Western art in Tokyo brings in traffic-stopping crowds.

Ironically, some of the traditional arts and crafts became appreciated by the Japanese themselves only after they were discovered by Westerners. Woodblock prints were considered not much more than handbills until they were admired by the French Impressionists. The British potter Bernard Leach was influential in bringing Japanese folk pottery to the attention of the public. The Katsura Imperial Villa (we shall come back to it later) was falling into neglect at the beginning of this century until it was discovered by the German architect Bruno Taut. Many of

145

the museums and wealthy individuals in Japan are now belatedly buying back art works that had been allowed to fall into the hands of Western collectors.

NATIONAL TREASURES AND IMPORTANT CULTURAL PROPERTIES

To help preserve the country's cultural heritage, the Japanese government in 1929 enacted a law under which a number of art masterpieces were singled out as National Treasures. In 1950, a more extensive act was passed. Under the new law more than one thousand items were named National Treasures, and more than ten thousand works, less important but also worthy of mention, were named Important Cultural Properties. These works include pictures, sculpture, handicrafts, calligraphy, antiques, and architecture. (The Japanese do not make a real distinction between the fine and decorative arts. Famous artists, such as Kōrin (1658-1716), not only painted pictures, but also made lacquer ware and ceramics.)

LIVING NATIONAL TREASURES

In addition to these tangible National Treasures and Important Cultural Properties, the government in 1953 began to designate a number of persons as "Holders of Important Intangible Cultural Properties." They are popularly known by the less pompous title of "Living National Treasures." There are some seventy persons in this category, some of them named singly, some of them whole troupes. Periodically, new names are added, but the total has not increased greatly because many of them have died (most were not named until they were quite old). Included among the Living National Treasures are performing artists in dance, Noh, Kabuki, and Bunraku (see Chapter 6, AMUSEMENTS), but the majority are dedicated masters of traditional arts or crafts. They are given an annual allowance of about $1000 to help with the cost of training young people eager to learn their skills. The government also pays for the expense of exhibiting their works and makes movies recording their techniques so they will not be lost.

The Living National Treasures include sculptors and potters, dyers and weavers, printmakers and designers, metal and bamboo workers. Several are dollmakers. Some of them produce highly refined pieces fit for an aristocrat's display shelf, such as gold-inlay lacquer boxes too precious to serve as containers, and dolls of the look-but-do-not-touch variety. But some of them produce sturdy, rustic wares fit for everyday use. A few are internationally famous, like the late potter Hamada Shoji, whose influence can be seen in pottery workshops from San Diego, California, to Edinburgh, Scotland. Others were unknown outside their village until they were designated by the government. One was an old woman living in a remote village of northern Japan. She had been named a Living National Treasure because she was a walking museum of handicrafts. She grew her own flax and indigo, made the dye, spun the flax into thread, and wove it into stout cloth worn by farmers of the region (by now her cloth has become a collector's item and is much too expensive for farmers).

FOLK ART

To most Westerners, all Japanese art looks exotic and therefore "ethnic." Though they make no distinction between fine and decorative arts, the Japanese do distinguish between fine art and folk art. Fine art is signed work by a noted artist, often the descendant of a long line of artists the field. Folk art is the work of an unknown and is functional rather than decorative. These days folk art has come to be deeply appreciated in Japan, so much so that a potter like Hamada deliberately cultivated the style of village potters and refused to sign his work. The folk-art movement is a fairly recent phenomenon and was started in the 1920's by Yanagi Soetsu, who coined the word *Mingei*, "People's Art." An exception is the tea ceremony bowl. Hundreds of years before folk art became fashionable, the tea bowls were treasured, although they were plain and functional and made by unknown artists. Some of them have become family heirlooms and are priced at thousands of dollars.

BUYING FOLK ART

The price of a good tea ceremony bowl is steep for most tourists, but in general folk art, or Mingei, is inexpensive and makes good souvenirs. To buy authentic folk art, the purist goes to the region where it is produced. Otsu, a small city on Lake Biwa, is noted for *Otsu-e* (*e* is "picture"), a kind of primitive woodblock print full of vigor and humor. Morioka, an old-fashioned city in northern Japan, produces cast-iron ware, especially kettles, that has strength and dignity. If you want to make an impression on the after-ski crowd, startle them with a pair of straw snow boots from Yamagata, a prefecture in the Snow Country. Takayama (more on this city later) is noted for plain, unadorned lacquer ware in which the wood grain is visible. Unlike the heavily decorated lacquer ware, these plain utensils can be used every day. Ina, in central Japan, produces rough, hand-spun, hand-woven silk, so different from the glossy, brightly colored silk you usually see. The village of Uda is famous for *washi*, hand-made paper, and many of you may have heard of Mashiko, the pottery village. We could make a long list of places and their specialties. Folk art is reasonably priced and, best of all, you

ARTS AND CRAFTS

can actually find a use for it when you get home. Long after you've put away that brocade-dressed geisha doll that tips over every time you sneeze, you will be filling your plain lacquer bowls with salad.

It is romantic to visit a remote village, watch the local craftsmen at work, and buy a piece of their work right on the premises. But most travelers don't have time to seek out these places. Sightseeing and shopping don't mix anyway. There is nothing more annoying than having to untangle your parcels from your camera straps all the time.

Fortunately, you don't have to buy your folk craft from the horse's mouth. Many department stores have a section set aside for Mingei, People's Art. In the underground shopping centers, like the one under Tokyo Station, you can find stalls selling regional crafts, and the salesclerk will even have your purchase wrapped with paper printed in that region. It is a standard Japanese joke that a husband who is having an affair with his secretary at a downtown hotel can tell his wife a story about making a business trip to a distant province by producing a souvenir gift from that locality to back up his story.

Because of the boom in folk art, some souvenir shops are selling products that have a vaguely artsy-craftsy look but are actually shoddy, mass-produced stuff. Be careful when you pick up items claiming to be Mingei. The best folk art is plain, well-made, and practical. Before you buy, therefore, remember the Japanese saying, "If you can't use it today, you won't use it tomorrow."

If you have a serious interest in folk art, you should visit the Japan Folkcrafts Museum, founded by Yanagi Soetsu, who was the leader of the Mingei movement mentioned earlier. This museum is near the Komaba Todai-mae Station on the Inokashira Line of the Keio-Teito Electric Railway. Another museum is the Kurashiki Folkcraft Museum. Kurashiki is a city in western Japan, and the folkart museum is in a building created out of four feudalᴀd rice granaries. Their stunning white walls and ᴋ-tiled roofs are famous, and you may have seen pictures of the museum on travel posters. Close to the folk-art museum are an archaeological museum, a historical museum, and the Ōhara gallery of Western art (built like a Greek temple!). Osaka has a good open-air museum, the Toyonaka Folk Museum, which is in Hattori-Ryokuchi Park, twenty minutes away from the city by electric train.

Fɪɴᴇ Aʀᴛs

For fine art, as opposed to folk art, the most outstanding museum is the Tokyo National Museum in Ueno Park. Its vast and rich collection includes not only paintings and sculpture, but also metal work, lacquer, silk weaving, as well as priceless archaeological treasures. Close to the National Museum is the Tokyo Metropolitan Fine Arts Gallery, used for temporary art exhibits, the National Museum of Western Art, and the Japan Art Academy. In addition to art, Ueno Park also contains a Gallery of Eastern Antiquities, the National Science Museum, the Tokyo Metropolitan Festival Hall, and the Ueno Zoo. You can spend a whole day — or several days — in the area. Since Tokyo is not an easy city in which to find your way about, it is of small value to look all over town for a certain minor museum — especially when it turns out that its collection of Japanese art is not so good as the one in the Boston Museum of Fine Arts. Therefore, unless you are looking for a particular work, or you are a student of Japanese art and have several months in Japan, the museum group in Ueno Park is good enough, especially the Tokyo National Museum, with its rich collection of National Treasures.

If you are planning to spend the day in the Ueno vicinity, you may want to visit the area known as Yanaka, just northwest of Ueno Park. Yanaka has always been an old artisans' quarter and today many master craftsmen still live and work there. Since this area escaped bombing during World War II, the old houses and streets are intact. With its dozens of small Buddhist temples and its narrow, crooked streets, the district preserves the atmosphere of old feudal-age Edo.

MUSEUM CITIES

NARA

In Japan the best museums are not the institutional ones, but parts of living cities, or even a whole city and its surrounding countryside. An example of this is Nara, the capital of Japan from 710 to 784 A.D. Nara contains the most perfect examples of early Japanese Buddhist architecture in Todaiji Temple and Horyuji Temple. These wooden structures have been preserved unchanged for twelve hundred years, and are the oldest wooden structures in the world (Todaiji is also the largest wooden structure in the world). Nara has sculpture — the colossal bronze Buddha, dedicated in 752, and the pair of huge thirteenth-century wooden Niō, or Deva Kings, which guard the gate at Todaiji Temple. These wooden statues are by Unkei and his son Kaikei. Unkei is the most famous sculptor in Japan. Besides the gigantic Niō, he also carved smaller, sensitive masterpieces such as the Mujoku Bosatsu in Kofukuji Temple at Nara. All these pieces of architecture and sculpture are National Treasures.

Nara is also a treasure house of early Buddhist paintings. The seventh-century murals of Horyuji Temple still overwhelm you with their freshness and beauty (the surviving ones, that is; most were destroyed by a disastrous fire thirty years ago). There is a small museum at Horyuji Temple — small in size, but containing some of the most precious Buddhist art in Japan, including the "Dream Changing" Kannon, the Kudara Kannon, and the *Tamamushi Shrine*.

In Nara is another remarkable structure, the *Shosoin*, a building shaped like a log cabin on stilts. Inside are treasures belonging to an eighth-century emperor, including jewels, musical instruments, clothes, mirrors, masks, and other precious objects (some of them from as far away as Persia). After the death of the emperor they were locked up in this building and kept exactly as they were. During humid weather the logs expand, sealing the building; during dry weather they contract, when the air is less harmful to the objects. Once a year, during the dry days of late October and early November, these treasures are taken out and aired, and those lucky enough to be in Nara at the right time can view them.

Besides the temples and their treasures, Nara is noted for its beautiful countryside. Looking at the traditional farmhouses with thatched roofs, you would think you're back in the eighth century, if it were not for the TV antennas. Nara is an ancient city, with many traditional customs and festivals of interest to tourists. The most famous of these are the *On Matsuri* (December 16 and 17) of the Kasuga-Wakamiya Shrine, with its long procession of participants dressed in ancient costumes, and the *Yamayaki*, "Burning Mountain," of January 15, when the whole Wakakusa Hill is set on fire.

And of course you have heard of the tame deer, called the messengers of the gods. Every autumn their horns are cut off and made into chopsticks, brooches, knife handles, and other objects by local craftsmen. Everybody wants a picture of himself feeding the tame deer. If you go to Nara during the slack season, when there aren't too many tourists with handouts, you will find the deer hungry and aggressive. Before you know it, these divine messengers will be slobbering all over your cameras.

Takayama

Another museum city is Takayama, in central Japan at the foot of the Japan Alps. Nara is important because of its historical significance and its art treasures. Takayama, on the other hand, is interesting because you can get a vivid picture of the life of peasants and artisans. The city itself is quiet, old-fashioned, and has some marvelously preserved old wine stores and residences, most of them open to the public. Automobile traffic is light, but you may meet a rickshaw coming down the street, with a slightly self-conscious passenger seated in it, listening to the (literally) running commentary of the rickshaw boy. This rickshaw service was started a few years ago by an enterprising group of young men from Tokyo, who had become tired of the white-collar rat race. From their looks as they speed through the streets of Takayama, they seem to be having a wonderful time with their business venture.

By the side of a small river containing assorted colorful carp, farmers set up a morning market where they sell locally made utensils, clothes, souvenirs, and vegetables with improbably bright colors. With its scarlet-railed bridges, its vegetables and carp, Takayama is so full of color that if you try to buy black-and-white film the salesman looks at you as if you're mad. Here and there in the city you will see strangely shaped tall and narrow houses. They are storehouses for the tall, pointed carts used in the *Takayama Sanno Matsuri* (April 14 and 15), one of the famous festivals in Japan.

The city is very crafts conscious, with a large exhibition hall and salesroom for local handicrafts, but it's more fun to walk along the streets, peering into small shops and watching wood carvers at work. Wood and lacquer products are the local specialty.

Takayama's most famous attraction is the farm village outside the city. These farmhouses were originally located at a nearby village called Shirakawa, but when the site was flooded by dam construction, the whole village was moved to Takayama and painstakingly constructed as a museum. The tall, four-story thatched farmhouses are remarkable buildings that once accommodated as many as fifty people, in addition to domestic animals. Other farmhouses in the open-air museum are low and wide, with roofs made of plank and held down by heavy stones. The village is complete with water wheels, storehouses, charcoal firing hut, and Shinto shrine. In the shrine are images of the Seven Lucky Gods (see Chapter 10) made by local farmers out of rice straw. Everywhere you see the traditional farm equipment and tools for local handicrafts. In spirit the museum is a little like the Skansen folk museum in Stockholm, but the Takayama village looks more realistic because it is in the open countryside, with vegetable plots and rice paddies. In the proper season you can see farmers planting or harvesting.

To reach Takayama, go to Nagoya and take the Takayama Line of the JNR, a scenic route through mountain gorges with waterfalls and fragile suspension bridges. The whole area is wonderful for hiking, bike riding, and skiing.

Kyoto

The greatest museum city of all is Kyoto, the capital of Japan from 794 to 1868. Just as you get a picture of peasant life in Takayama, you get a picture of aristocratic life in Kyoto, the city of the emperor and his courtiers. Today the emperor lives in Tokyo, and the mainstream of Japanese culture is in that city. Tokyo is where most of the universities, museums, galleries, concert halls, and mass-media centers are. But Kyoto is still the center of traditional art and traditional handicrafts. If you have only about a week and want to see the "real" Japan, the most profitable way of spending your time is to go to Kyoto and stay there until it's time to go home.

But if you are so unfortunate as to have only a few hours in Kyoto, then a good place for a look at Kyoto arts and crafts is the Kyoto Handicraft Center. It is on Marutamachi Avenue, just north of the Heian Shrine. Many people are condescending about the Handicraft Center. It is true that the racks of gaudy nylon *happi* coats cheap atmosphere, and so do the large posters giving you latest exchange rate for your money. But the rates offer are really pretty good, and there is no denying the convenience of the place. It has a pleasant coffee shop, English-speaking salesclerks, and Western-style toilets. Best of all, there are craftsmen at work right before your eyes. You can see all stages of a woodblock print, from the carving of the woodblocks to the several printings it takes for all the colors. Or you can watch a jeweler pounding in gold wire with a small hammer to make cloisonné ware. Small wonder that the place is packed with tourists eagerly watching and eagerly buying.

If you have more time, you will enjoy strolling along a street and peeking into little shops specializing in Kyoto handicrafts. Some good streets for window-shopping are Shijo (Fourth Avenue) and Kawaramachi. You will see specialty shops featuring luxury products for which Kyoto has been famous for hundreds of years. The Kyoto lacquer ware, called *maki-e*, is distinguished by the gold or silver dust mixed with the lacquer. Even more glittering is the famous Kyoto damascene ware. The city produces sixty percent of the decorated fans in Japan, and on a winter day you can see the wooden fan ribs drying along the banks of the Kamo River. Kyoto dolls, portraying languorous court beauties or *maiko* (apprentice geisha) almost breathe decadence. Compared to the sturdy and plain folk craft, the artistic handicrafts of Kyoto seem effete. But they are beautiful, and some of the crafts shops are arranged like art galleries. On walking into a doll shop, you will be invited to sit on a rush-covered bench and served green tea. If you are so ill-advised as to try haggling, or even hint that the prices are too high, you will receive such a cold smile that years later you will still writhe at the memory.

For ceramics, try a walk along the narrow lane that

ENTERTAINMENTS

leads up to Kiyomizu Temple. Called Teapot Lane by tourists, this street has one ceramics shop after another overflowing with *Kiyomizu-yaki*, the name of the local pottery. (*Yaki* means "bake," "roast," or "broil," as we've seen in Chapter 3, FOOD). The shops here are less intimidating than the ones on Shijo, although haggling is still bad form. Occasionally a shopkeeper will give you a discount, but it's purely a gesture of good will on his part, and you must not expect it. The abundance of attractive inexpensive ceramics is irresistible. Some tourists, planning a quick dash to the famous Kiyomizu Temple, find themselves two hours later still only halfway up Teapot Lane.

If you love silk, you should visit the Nishijin District in the northwest section of the city, famous for its silk brocade weaving since the ninth century. There are nearly twenty thousand weavers in the Nishijin District, mostly working in their homes. The Nishijin Textile Museum at Imadegawa-Omiya has demonstrations and looms from the earliest models to the most modern. It also has Nishijin products for sale, including kimonos. The price of a good kimono can run into thousands of dollars. If you feel that a kimono is too expensive and hope to settle for just a sash, you will find that often the sash costs more than the kimono.

Another specialty of Kyoto is a method of dyeing called *yuzen*. The strips of silk are stencil dyed, steamed to set the colors, and then rinsed to get rid of the excess dye. Cold running water is best for the rinsing, and traditionally the strips of yuzen-dyed cloth were rinsed in the Kamo, Kyoto's main river. These days the brightly colored strips of silk are rinsed in the Katsura River, a tributary of the Kamo in the southwestern part of the city. At Katsura is a yuzen workshop where you can watch this unusual dyeing process. It is near the Nishi-Kyogoku Station of the Hankyu Electric Railway.

For fine arts you can go to the Kyoto National Museum on Shichijo (Seventh Avenue) and Higashiyama-dori. The museum has handicrafts as well as paintings and sculpture. But why go to the museum when the whole city is a museum? Even for paintings and sculpture, it is more rewarding to see them in the temple, palace, or villa where they were originally intended to be. If you take one of the painted screens of Kano Tayu and put it in a museum, it is nice enough. But when you see it in its proper place — an audience chamber in Nijo Castle — it is magnificent. The Golden Pavilion, if placed in the grounds of Expo '70, say, would look slightly cheap. But seen in its setting of landscaped gardens, hills and pond, it is the essence of Kyoto's overrefined elegance. The dry landscape garden of Daisen-in, said to be the highest achievement in garden design, makes sense only in its context — that of a great Zen Buddhist temple. You may have seen a picture of the Miroku Bosatsu of Koryuji Temple, and wondered why it is called the most beautiful piece of sculpture in Japan. But seeing it in the temple is an emotional experience, even for people who care nothing for Buddhism.

In the opinion of many, the greatest work of aristocratic art in Japan is the Katsura Imperial Villa, built in 1624 for an imperial prince. When you visit it for the first time you may have the strange feeling you've seen it before. That is because you've probably seen its influence in so many places already. There is a story of a man who went to see a performance of *Hamlet* for the first time. When asked afterward how he liked the play, he complained that it was too full of quotations. Quotations from the Katsura Villa can be seen in our present-day architecture and design. We can admire the painted screens, the grain of the wooden floors, the brocade borders of the tatami mats, the brass door fittings, the line of the roof, the moss in the gardens, or the arrangement of a stone bridge. But it is the whole, not the sum of its parts, that makes the impression.

The Katsura Villa is near the Katsura Station on the Arashiyama Line of the Hankyu Electric Railway (not far from the yuzen workshop mentioned earlier). It is open to the public, but you must apply to the Kyoto Office of the Imperial Household Agency for written permission to visit. You should do this two weeks in advance, and earlier during the busy season. For some tourists, this would mean writing to the Imperial Household Agency before leaving home. A few years ago, a foreign tourist stole one of the brass fittings from the villa, and the Imperial Household Agency was so outraged by this piece of vandalism that it temporarily banned all visitors except for a chosen few. Fortunately it has since softened its attitude, but advance application for permission is still necessary.

Another imperial villa is Shugakuin, built in 1658 for a retired emperor. Shugakuin's setting is considered by some to be even more beautiful than that of the Katsura Villa. It is also a treasury of exquisite paintings, scrolls, woodwork, lanterns, architecture, and gardens. But, like Katsura, it must be taken as a whole piece of art, not dissected into its components.

Permission to visit the Shugakuin Villa is obtained also from the Kyoto Office of the Imperial Household Agency. You can reach Shugakuin by the #5 Kyoto city bus, or you can walk from the Shugakuin-mae Station on the Eizan Line of the Keifuku Electric Railway. The walk takes about thirty minutes, but it goes through a quiet residential area and is very pleasant.

Lessons If you are in Japan for an extended stay, you may want to learn a particular traditional craft while you are there. It is not too difficult to arrange lessons if your ambition doesn't go beyond learning the rudiments of the craft. The best way to get a teacher is through the introduction of a Japanese friend. If you don't have friend, there are organizations that give lecture courses in English on Japanese arts and crafts. At these lectures you can inquire about lessons and teachers. In Kyoto, try the International Cultural Association of Kyoto at 517-32 Nagatani-cho, Iwakura, Sakyo-ku, telephone (75)-701-5356. Membership for the organization costs 1000 yen, and the course fee is 5000 yen. In Tokyo, the Tourist Information Center can recommend one closest to where you are staying.

Ceramics interest foreigners more than any other craft. As an introduction to Japanese ceramics, you can take a course at the Nihon Togei Club, 5-1, Jingu-mae, Shibuya-ku, Tokyo, telephone (03)-402-3634. In Kyoto, there is the Kyoto Togei Kyoshitsu, 9-6, Katsura Kamino Kitamachi, Ukyo-ku, Kyoto, telephone (75)-381-5835. Advance reservations are required for both these places, and the courses cost around 6000 yen, plus the cost of materials.

Advanced students of ceramics may want to go to one of the village pottery centers. The most famous is the village of Mashiko, northeast of Tokyo. To get there, take the Tohoku Line of the JNR from Ueno Station, get off at Utsunomiya (about two hours), and get on the Toya Bus for Mashiko (one hour). In Mashiko are Japanese-style inns that are not too expensive, but during the high season it is absolutely necessary to make reservations in advance.

It is one thing to arrive at the village. It is another thing to get accepted as a student by one of the masters. For that, an introduction is necessary. Master artists and craftsmen who speak English generally practice some form of Western or modern art. Traditional artists tend to be very conservative and speak only Japanese. They will accept a foreign student only if he speaks Japanese and is willing to work hard. Beginning students are given tedious work designed to weed out all but the most dedicated.

Still, a number of foreigners have succeeded in proving themselves and have become serious students of Japanese crafts. Japanese TV carried a program not long ago about an American potter working at Mashiko. Another young American became apprenticed to a swordmaker and is learning the difficult, exacting art of making a Japanese sword. These, of course, are craftsmen willing to devote years to their training.

9
CASTLES AND SAMURAI

(*For a chronology of Japan's historical periods, see page 211.*)

In the old days the social classes in Japan were ranked in the following order: warriors, farmers, artisans, and merchants. The feudal age ended in 1868, when the shogun (military leader) was deposed and power restored to the emperor. The new government abolished the warrior class and required the samurai to cut their hair short, put away their swords, and earn a living like other people. Not all the samurai wanted to obey this order, and the government had to put down several rebellions, the most serious of which we'll discuss a little later.

Even after the samurai had lost their status officially, they still retained a certain mystique. Until the end of World War II, being descended from an old samurai family was a definite asset for those pursuing a military or government career. It didn't do any harm socially, either. Even today, the samurai families continue to preserve the records of their family tree.

The warrior class didn't always carry prestige in Japan. Until the end of the sixteenth century farmers and warriors were sometimes indistinguishable. Some farmers took up arms when necessary, and went back to their land when the fighting stopped. But Hideyoshi (we shall say more about him later), upon mastering all of Japan, made the class structure more rigid by decreeing that henceforth farmers were to remain farmers, and warriors to remain warriors.

When the ancestors of the Japanese arrived from the Asian mainland, they had to wrest land from the native Ainu people, and naturally the successful warriors were the ones who rose to become tribal leaders. Even when one chieftain became pre-eminent, calling himself emperor and claiming descent from the Sun Goddess Amaterasu, he was still only one military leader among other military leaders.

In the sixth century, however, Chinese culture and writing were imported into Japan, and the rulers of the country decided to form a government after the Chinese pattern. Up to then there had been no permanent capital in Japan, and every time an emperor died the whole court moved to a new capital under a new emperor. But following the Chinese example, a permanent capital was founded — in Nara — with the streets laid out in a rectangular grid as in the Chinese capital of Chang-an. A hierarchy of civilians administered the government on behalf of the emperor. This system was elaborated further when the emperor and court moved to Kyoto.

The warriors were now no longer the rulers of the country. They became almost lackeys for the civilian administrators, and their function was to serve as guards for their masters. It was then that the term *samurai* began to be used. It came from the word *samurau*, or *saburau*, meaning "to serve" or "to attend." The term for warrior is actually *bushi*, where *bu* means "martial" and *shi* is "warrior" or "scholar." (We see the use of *bu* in such words as *budo*, "martial arts" and *bushido*, "way of the warrior.")

There was still a need for warriors to push back the aborigine Ainu people, to subdue rebellious chieftains, and to perform other disagreeable tasks with which the courtiers, preoccupied with elegant pastimes, didn't want to be bothered. As soon as they had done their duty, the uncouth warriors were supposed to take themselves back to the provinces where they belonged. Some of the leading military families were actually of noble descent: the Minamoto family traced its descent to the Emperor Seiwa, and the Taira family to the Emperor Kammu. But after generations of living in the country, the samurai were in a different world from the perfumed courtiers.

When an emperor wished to appoint a leader for some military expedition, he would confer on him the title *Sei-i-tai-Shōgun*, "Barbarian-subduing-great-General." The title of *shōgun*, "general," was temporary and good for only a specific expedition. But like the title *imperator*, conferred by a Roman Senate on a general, it eventually became permanent and hereditary.

In the beginning, a shogun had his title taken away after his job was finished, and frequently received little reward for his services. Minamoto Yoshiie, when he had subdued the northern barbarians, received no payment to help with the expenses of assembling his army. Infuriated, Yoshiie rewarded the army out of his own pocket after the campaign. As a result, the loyalty of the men turned to him and his family, rather than to the imperial court. Incidents of this kind built up loyalty for the provincial military leaders and weakened the authority of the central government, resulting in feudalism by the twelfth century.

Meanwhile, at home in Kyoto, the court was having other troubles. Various Buddhist sects had militant monks who fought with one another and made raids on the capital, trying to browbeat the court into submitting to their demands. The emperor finally decided that the samurai would be the perfect answer to the militant monks. Soon members of the Minamoto and Taira families were installed as guards for the nobility.

By then the emperors were puppets in the hands of various noble families, notably the Fujiwara family, who married its daughters to successive emperors. Whenever an emperor showed signs of having a will of his own, he would be forced to abdicate and make room for a younger, more pliable emperor. Since the imperial succession was not decided by primogeniture, disputes often arose about the succession. It wasn't long before some of the nobles decided to enlist the help of the samurai in their disputes. One faction used the Minamotos, and one faction used their arch rivals, the Tairas. Eventually civil war broke out between the two families, involving not only those members living in the capital, but also their satellite families living in the provinces. This war is called the *Gempei* War, from combining the two names *Genji* and *Heike*, which are the Chinese reading for the Minamoto and Taira respectively. But European writers like to call the war the Japanese War of the Roses, because one side used white and the other side red banners.

At the end of the war, when the Minamoto annihilated their enemies, their leader Yoritomo was appointed shogun by the emperor. Only this time the title was not to be taken away at the emperor's will. Instead, Yoritomo established a new military government at Kamakura in eastern Japan. In time the shogun also became a puppet in the hands of his advisors, and independent warlords grew powerful. Many of them had started as constables, whose job was to govern territory belonging to noblemen leading a soft life in Kyoto. These constables soon realized that they could ignore the absentee landlords and grab the territory for themselves. These territorial warlords, called

CASTLES AND SAMURAI

daimyo, literally "big names," gradually grew independent of the central government and ruled their territories like kings.

But unlike their European counterparts, the daimyo did not start building castles for themselves immediately. In the twelfth-century wars between the rival families (at a time when the Normans were building their immense stone fortresses), the battles were either in the streets of Kyoto or were pitched battles in the open. Sometimes noblemen tried to improve the defenses of their mansions by digging trenches around the house or plastering the windows and walls to reduce inflammability. But real castles were still years in the future.

One of the first defensive stone walls was built in the thirteenth century, not as part of a castle, but to repel a Mongol invasion. This was the only time Japan was ever invaded, if we don't count the American occupation after World War II. It was also the first time the samurai ever fought a foreign enemy. Although the Mongols were brought up short by the stone wall and by the bravery of the samurai, what really finished them was a typhoon, called *kamikaze*, "divine wind," which smashed the ships of the invaders. You can see remnants of this stone wall in the Genkai Quasi-National Park, near Fukuoka in northern Kyushu.

In the succeeding centuries the country suffered one civil war after another. For a time the emperor and his supporters tried to challenge the military government of Kamakura in eastern Japan. During the struggles between the imperial and the shogunal forces, warlords began to see the advantage of building forts on the tops of hills and mountains. These were called *yamajiro*, and they were a primitive form of the castle.

In the famous siege of Akasaka (1331), the defender of the hill fortress was Kusunoki Masashige, one of the most famous heroes of Japanese history. The fortress was a primitive affair surrounded by a wooden palisade enclosing only 650 square yards. It had simple wooden towers from which the defenders hurled rocks and poured boiling water on the attackers. The defenders also suspended huge logs and released them down the steep hill to crush the besiegers. But the food supply in the fortress gave out and, even worse, the stream supplying water was diverted by a trench cut by the besiegers. Knowing the end was near, Kusunoki evacuated his men by having them steal away in ones and twos. When they were nearly all gone, he had the corpses of his dead piled high and the whole fortress set on fire. The besiegers were misled into thinking the entire garrison had committed suicide.

Kusunoki's defense of Chihaya fortress in 1332 against the shogunal forces was even more brilliant. To prevent their water supply from being cut off, the defenders dug their own well inside the fortress, another step in the evolution of the true castle. After weeks of bitter fighting the besiegers had made no progress, and Kusunoki's defense of Chihaya became an outstanding victory for the imperial forces, because it tied up enemy men desperately needed elsewhere.

Eventually Kamakura, the capital of the military government, was taken and burned by imperial forces, but the triumph of the emperor did not last long. A new family of shoguns rose, the Ashikagas, and the shogunal government moved back to Kyoto. The Ashikaga shoguns were noted patrons of art, drama, and Zen Buddhism, but despite this the power of the central government steadily declined.

The civil wars raged on. At one point the city of Kyoto was reduced almost to rubble. As provincial warlords grew stronger, their castles grew stouter. Walls began to be built with a stone base, and moats became more elaborate. By the sixteenth and seventeenth centuries, castles reached their peak architecturally.

STRUCTURE OF A JAPANESE CASTLE

Many tourists feel that Japanese castles are like the German castles along the Rhine: photogenic and romantic on the outside, but disappointingly bare inside. The first time you see the many-tiered gables and the graceful curved roofs of a Japanese castle, your camera practically jumps into your hand fully cocked. But the closer you get to the castle, the less impressive it seems. Once inside, you see only bare wooden floors, with a few glass cases containing armor. After you've noted that the helmets have mustaches made of real hair, you wonder what else there is to see. There is a great deal to see, if you understand a Japanese castle's structure. You will know what to look for, and you can also get a good idea of life in feudal times.

TENSHU, OR DONJON

In many cases, what we see of a Japanese castle is only a small portion of the original structure. The handsome building with the curly roof is merely the watchtower, or as some European writers call it, the donjon. In a European castle, the donjon contains the great hall, as well as the private apartments of the lord and lady. In it the entire social life of the castle took place.

The feudal lord of a Japanese castle, on the other hand, seldom lived in the donjon. Called a *tenshu*, the donjon functioned as a watchtower and was very bare inside. But its exterior was made as impressive as possible, and since it was a towering structure, it could be seen for miles around as a symbol of the lord's prestige and power. The roof of the tenshu in Nagoya Castle was mounted by a pair of gold-plated dolphins that required more than a hundred and fifty pounds of pure gold. But the tenshu was not built just for show. If the castle was taken by the enemy, the defenders retired into the tenshu for their final struggle. The surviving samurai would try to hold off the enemy so that the lord and his family would have time to kill themselves and thus avoid capture.

Defense of the castle By the time the enemy got within shooting distance of the tenshu, the castle was well lost. Since the castles were largely built of wood and plaster, they had no defense against fire, and a fire arrow could set off a holocaust. That was why a castle had to cover much more area than just the region around the tenshu. A series of defensive structures was built to keep the enemy well away from the castle's heart.

As with European castles, one of the chief defenses of a Japanese castle was a moat, except that the Japanese were not satisfied with one moat, but often built a series of concentric moats. In addition, the defense depended on a number of walls. Like most of the fortification, the walls were built on a foundation of stone. Some of the stones were immense boulders weighing several tons, fitted together without mortar. Above the stone foundation, the walls were built of wood and plaster, and roofed with slate tiles. Holes in various geometric shapes — circles, triangles, diamonds, squares — were cut in the walls for shooting at the enemy.

To enter the castle, you have to pass through several gates, and these gates are arranged so that after passing through one gate, you turn 90° to face the next one. If the attackers should succeed in breaking through one gate, they wouldn't be able to use their momentum to charge against the next one. These gates are heavily studded with iron, and to protect them further from assault, defenders in gatehouses used to hurl rocks down from above. The gates, the plastered walls, and other fortifications of a Japanese castle could not compare in strength with the stone walls and towers of a European castle. Instead, the defense of a Japanese castle depended on the tortuous, maze-like approach whose purpose was to delay, confuse, and scatter the enemy. If an attacking army were to cross the outer moat and breach the outer wall, they found themselves facing a bewildering maze that led to blind corners and dead ends, with defenders ambushing them at every turn. Because frontal attack was so difficult for the besiegers, the most common methods of taking a castle were starvation and treachery. Of course, mobile heavy artillery could blast its way through a maze of fortification, but by the time heavy artillery reached Japan, castles had largely outgrown their military use anyway.

RESIDENTIAL QUARTERS

When gunpowder changed the nature of warfare in Europe, noblemen left their grim, drafty castles and built themselves comfortable chateaux and palaces. But the Japanese feudal lords did not have to leave their castles in order to be comfortable. They had luxurious quarters built right in the castle courtyards. In general, the location of a person's residence depended on his rank, and the higher his rank, the closer he lived to the tenshu, symbolically the castle's center. Let us look at the arrangement of the residential quarters for one of the elaborate castles with three or more concentric moats.

In a castle town the lowest-ranking samurai and the townspeople lived between the outermost and the middle moats. The townspeople were mostly artisans and their families, and their quarters were often arranged according to their trade — a street of armorers, another of gunsmiths, and so on. Then there were streets of houses for the low-ranking samurai. In older castle towns, the houses of the samurai were segregated from those of the commoners, but later the segregation was not so complete.

The higher-ranking samurai had residences between the middle and the inner moats. These were private houses with small landscaped gardens. (For a description of a private house, see Chapter 4, HOUSING.)

Enclosed by the inner moat were fortifications containing guardhouses and barracks for samurai on garrison duty. Finally, surrounded by the innermost fortifications were courtyards containing the residential mansions of the feudal lord, his family, relatives, and officers of the highest rank. The courtyard closest to the tenshu is called *hon-maru*, where *hon* is "origin" or "center," and *maru* is "circle" or "courtyard." The next courtyard is *ni-no-maru*, where *ni* is "second," and therefore ni-no-maru is "second courtyard." The more elaborate castles, such as the ones at Edo (the castle of the shogun), Osaka, Himeji, and Nagoya, had three or more courtyards.

NOTABLE CASTLES

Nijo Castle

If you want to see how a feudal lord and his household lived, you should visit Nijo Castle in Kyoto. The watchtower, or tenshu, of the castle was destroyed by lightning in the eighteenth century and never rebuilt, but Nijo has the best-preserved feudal residential mansion in the country. The mansion in the central courtyard, the hon-maru, is presently used by an imperial prince and closed to the public. But the residential mansion in the ni-no-maru is still kept in its original state and is open to visitors.

Western sightseers, used to the more cluttered stately homes of European noblemen, often find the rooms of the ni-no-maru mansion too bare and austere. All tourists, however, enjoy the famous "nightingale floors" that squeak to warn of a sneak assassin. The glory of the mansion is in its carved woodwork, paintings, screens, and gardens.

Among the interesting exhibits at Nijo Castle are wax

figures of the shogun and his court. There are tableaux of the shogun in his private apartments, and also of the shogun holding an audience. Nijo Castle was the residence of the shogun when he visited Kyoto. During the feudal period, the emperor was only the figurehead, while the shogun ruled the country from his capital at Edo (Tokyo). Nevertheless, the shogun felt it necessary to have a stronghold in Kyoto as well, to prevent potentially subversive forces from rallying around the emperor. Ironically, when the subversive forces did rally around the emperor and topple the shogunate, Nijo Castle was the site chosen by the last shogun to announce his surrender of power to the emperor.

When the feudal age ended in 1868, one of the first acts of the new government was to break the power of the feudal lords, and it ordered all castles dismantled. The residential buildings were the first to go, since they were the easiest to demolish. By the time the government woke to the fact that they were destroying valuable cultural monuments, it was almost too late to save the castles. Most of the fortifications had been torn down, and it was usually only the tenshu, or watchtower, that was left, plus a few odd bits of wall here and there. The surviving tenshu were later labeled National Treasures, but with so little left, it is difficult to get an idea of the size of the original castles.

HIMEJI CASTLE

Your best bet is to visit Himeji, because it is the most well-preserved castle in Japan. The first thing that hits your eye when you get out of the train station at Himeji is the tenshu looming at the end of a long avenue. Even the row of flowering cabbages in the middle of the avenue can't detract from the dignity of this stunning tower. It seems to float, and you can understand why another name for Himeji Castle is White Heron Castle.

The straight and broad avenue is not authentic, since in the old days there was no direct approach to the castle. In fact the train station is approximately where the outermost moat used to be. Throughout the city of Himeji there are ruins that turn out to be parts of the outer castle walls or turrets. Even some of the grassy walks are pieces of the outer and middle moats now filled in. Only by walking around the city do you get an idea of the true size of the original castle.

But all the time your eyes are drawn to the towering tenshu. Unlike the tenshu at Osaka (which is a reinforced concrete reconstruction), the Himeji tower is authentic. Most of the inner fortifications at Himeji have been carefully preserved as well, and you can get a good idea of the labyrinthine approach to the center. It is a pity that there is no trace of the residential quarters or of the landscaped gardens, although the courtyards — the hon-maru, ni-no-maru, and so forth — are still there. One of the wells has been preserved, because of its association with the castle's ghost. According to the story, a serving lady broke a plate from a priceless set, and for this she was brutally killed and her body thrown down the well. From that time on, a woman's voice would be heard at night counting plates, "One, two, three, four, five, six, seven, eight, nine . . ." And then the voice would break off into an anguished wail.

Himeji Castle looks beautiful and even fragile. Could it stand up to a siege, or was the extravagant White Heron really a white elephant? We don't know the answer, because the castle was never attacked. The irony is that the Golden Age of castle building began in the latter part of the sixteenth century, during a turbulent period of civil wars, but by the time the castles were completed, the country entered a long period of peace lasting more than two centuries. (We are reminded of the sixteenth-century ceremonial armor in European museums. Most of it was made long after soldiers stopped wearing full armor into battle.) Himeji Castle, and many others equally impressive, were never put to a real test. Were these airy, graceful structures defensible, or were they like the expensive toys in the Loire Valley?

OSAKA CASTLE

For an answer, let us look at the siege of Osaka Castle in 1615. The siege was the climax of a struggle that ended with the Tokugawa family in absolute control of Japan (a control lasting until 1868). In the sixteenth century, Japan finally moved toward unification after centuries of civil wars. The Big Three of the unification movement consisted of Nobunaga, Hideyoshi, and Ieyasu. The Japanese sum up these three men with the saying that Nobunaga planted the rice and reaped it, Hideyoshi made it into rice cakes, and Ieyasu ate them.

Of the three, Nobunaga received the best press from early European writers because he welcomed European merchants and missionaries with open arms. Although cruel and treacherous, he was a gifted leader, and soon made himself the most powerful man in the country. When he was assassinated, he was on the verge of making himself master of Japan.

Nobunaga's chief lieutenant, Hideyoshi, took up the work of unifying the country. His background was much humbler than Nobunaga's, but he was an even more brilliant soldier. He succeeded in bringing the whole country under his control — at least he forced the other warlords to acknowledge his supremacy. To demonstrate his power, he started building castles on a grand scale. Nobunaga had also built a magnificent castle at Azuchi, one of the few castles with a comfortably furnished tenshu. But it could not compare with Hideyoshi's mammoth castle at Osaka. As proof of their submission, the other warlords had to contribute money, materials, and labor toward its construction. When completed, Osaka Castle was supposed to be impregnable.

Hideyoshi died, leaving the country at peace and his son Hideyori (watch out for the similarity of the names) master of the strongest castle in Japan. The only trouble was, Hideyori was a little boy of five. To insure his son's safety, before his death Hideyoshi gathered the leading warlords of the country and made them swear to support his son. The most formidable of these was Tokugawa Ieyasu (Tokugawa is the family name).

Ieyasu was a patient man. There is another saying about the Big Three. When a nightingale refused to sing, Nobunaga threatened to kill the bird, Hideyoshi tried to use persuasion, but Ieyasu simply sat back and waited.

So, after Hideyoshi's death, Ieyasu waited. He quietly extended his influence over the entire eastern part of the country. Becoming alarmed at his growing power, the western warlords gathered their forces and challenged the eastern bloc under Ieyasu. At the crucial Battle of Sekigahara (1600), the western forces were decisively beaten, and Ieyasu's power was supreme. Those western warlords who still supported Hideyori withdrew until they were all concentrated in Osaka Castle. The castle was immense, and easily absorbed the refugees.

Ieyasu tried everything to lure Hideyori out of the castle. He had already arranged a marriage between the boy and his granddaughter, Senhime. He invited Hideyori to poetry parties, moon-viewing parties, and tea ceremonies. But Hideyori stayed put. Finally, when Ieyasu saw that there was no other way, he laid siege to the castle.

The siege went badly for the besiegers. They couldn't starve out the garrison, because the castle had access to a river that brought supplies. Periodically, soldiers from the castle poured out and inflicted casualties on the besiegers. Assault parties on the castle couldn't accomplish much against the broad moats and the strong walls. Even cannon, newly acquired from the Europeans, couldn't breach the defense, although some of the cannon shot did land in the women's quarters, injuring some serving ladies.

When Ieyasu saw that brute force didn't work, he decided to try cunning. He wasn't called the Old Badger for nothing. He sent a message to Hideyori's mother and suggested that there was no future for her son, living in perpetual isolation inside the castle. Why couldn't they come to an understanding? They could call a truce and talk over ways to divide the country between himself and Hideyori.

This approach tempted the defenders, who were becoming restless after being shut inside the castle for so long. Ieyasu then said that as proof of their sincerity, the defenders should fill in the outer moats and tear down some walls. With our advantage of hindsight, it is hard to understand how the defenders could have been so naive as to accept Ieyasu's terms. But Hideyori's mother was more outstanding for her beauty than for her brains, and she had become very nervous ever since some cannon shot had landed almost in her lap. She agreed to Ieyasu's proposal. The besiegers enthusiastically helped to tear down the walls and fill in the moats. If they got carried away and also destroyed some of the inner fortifications . . . well, they put it down to carelessness.

After the fortifications had been seriously weakened, Ieyasu soon found reason to accuse the defenders of violating the truce, and he mounted an all-out attack. The defenders fought with desperate courage, but they were overwhelmed and the castle was set on fire. Hideyori and his mother killed themselves in the burning tenshu. Ieyasu's granddaughter Senhime, who by now was married to Hideyori, was rescued from the burning castle and later married to the lord of Himeji Castle.

Ieyasu rebuilt Osaka Castle along different lines, but the new tenshu later burned down. In 1931 the tenshu of Osaka Castle was reconstructed in the form of Hideyoshi's original tower. You will often see Osaka Castle portrayed in Kabuki, TV, or the movies, since the siege is a favorite theme for historical plays.

AKO CASTLE

An even more popular theme for novels, plays, TV, and the movies is the history of the Forty-seven Ronin (a *ronin* is an unattached samurai). It is now more than two hundred and seventy years after the events took place, but the details are as fresh in people's minds as if they happened last month. December 14, the anniversary of the date when the forty-seven men accomplished their revenge, is still faithfully celebrated. Special tribute is paid to the forty-seven heroes, especially in Ako, their home. The only thing left of Ako Castle is a gate, a turret, and part of a moat and bridge. But because of its associations, this scene is one of the most photographed in Japan. There is also a museum at Ako containing relics of the ronin. A torn glove, a leather strap, a headband — these scraps are preserved with an almost morbid reverence.

Briefly, the story of the Forty-seven Ronin is as follows: Asano, Lord of Ako, was in attendance at the shogun's court in Edo (Tokyo). He was deeply insulted by a malicious courtier called Kira and, losing control of himself, he drew his sword and attacked him. He succeeded only in wounding Kira, but for committing the grave offense of drawing a sword in the shogun's castle, he was sentenced to commit seppuku (hara-kiri). After the death of their lord, his followers became ronin. A band of them resolved to avenge their lord by killing Kira. This was a difficult task, since Kira had powerful friends and his mansion was well guarded. Finally, after months of planning, forty-seven of the ronin mounted a successful attack on Kira's town house in Edo and killed their lord's enemy. The ronin deposited Kira's severed head at Lord Asano's tomb and then surrendered themselves to the authorities. They were sentenced to commit seppuku, a fate they fully expected.

Why did this story catch the imagination of the Japanese in such an extraordinary way? Perhaps because the events took place in 1701, when the country had been at peace for almost a hundred years under the firm rule of the Tokugawa family (descendants of the Old Badger, Ieyasu). The public had begun to think that the spirit of the samurai had declined. Therefore when these forty-seven men threw away their lives to avenge their lord, their display of loyalty and heroism aroused deep feeling.

The four castles we have suggested visiting are rich in historical associations and conveniently close together. You can see all of them in one or two days if you have a good pair of legs and an accurate railway timetable. But if you're interested in seeing more, there are other stunning castles, such as Matsumoto (situated at the gateway to the Japan Alps), Okayama (only a little farther west from Himeji), or Hirosaki (a pleasant northern old-fashioned city on the way to Hokkaido).

KANAZAWA

To immerse yourself in the atmosphere of a castle town, visit the city of Kanazawa (about two hours' train journey by JNR limited-express from either Kyoto or Nagoya). Most of the important castle towns have become so industrialized that they retain very little feudal-age flavor. The castle at Himeji is well preserved, but the city was badly bombed during World War II and after reconstruction, its crooked, maze-like streets became straight. In Kanazawa, on the other hand, many of the old streets and samurai mansions are intact. Closer to the central part of the castle, you can find pieces of the middle moat and several streets containing mansions of the middle-rank samurai. Farther out are the humbler homes of the lower-rank samurai. Walking along these streets is like being on the set of a Japanese period movie.

Kanazawa Castle belonged to the Maeda family, one of the wealthiest daimyo of the Tokugawa Era. The castle remains show evidence of Maeda money in the fine stonework and the lavish use of glazed tile. One well-preserved structure is the long, thirty-room building that served as barracks for the samurai on guard duty. The site of the castle is now being used as the campus of Kanazawa University, and it's startling to see students in jeans riding their bicycles out of the iron-studded castle gates.

KUMAMOTO

If your schedule allows a visit to the southern island of Kyushu, you can visit Kumamoto Castle. It dominates the central part of the city of Kumamoto, and is approached by a beautiful avenue of cherry trees. The castle was built by Katō Kiyomasa, a colorful sixteenth-century warlord who took part in Hideyoshi's invasion of Korea.

Kumamoto Castle was also besieged. Like Osaka Castle, it stood up magnificently to attack and proved itself more than a rich man's showpiece. The siege took place in 1877, and was led by Takamori Saigo, one of the tragic figures of Japanese history. Saigo played a leading part in deposing the Tokugawa shogun and restoring authority to the emperor. But the restoration also brought an end to the feudal age, turning thousands of samurai into civilians. Saigo was bitter at this destruction of his own class, and a rebel force of ex-samurai gathered under his command and attacked Kumamoto Castle. After fifty days of fighting, a relief force for the castle arrived and Saigo had to retire. The rebellion was eventually crushed, and Saigo committed suicide. He was a man of noble character, admired by both his friends and his enemies. He is called the last of the samurai.

10
SHRINES, CHURCHES, AND TEMPLES

There are four major religions in Japan: Shinto, Confucianism, Christianity, and Buddhism. About eighty-five million Japanese practice Shinto. Almost no one practices Confucianism as a religion, but its effect, though invisible, is profound. Christianity, on the other hand, is visible, but its practice is limited to a small, though influential, minority. Finally, Buddhism is the religion whose effect can be seen both tangibly in the temples, monasteries, and art works and intangibly in literature and the political and cultural history of the country. There are eighty-five million Japanese who practice Buddhism.

How can there be eighty-five million Shintoists, and eighty-five million Buddhists, when the total population of Japan is only slightly over one hundred and eleven million? The answer is that most Japanese practice both Shinto and Buddhism, but on different occasions. A wedding is usually a Shinto ceremony, while a funeral is usually Buddhist. (The reverse is possible, but not common.) On New Year's Eve, the Japanese listen to Buddhist temple bells toll out the one hundred and eight sins, but on New Year's Day they go to a Shinto shrine.

Following the general practice, we shall use the word "shrine" in connection with Shinto and Confucianism, "church" with Christianity, and "temple" with Buddhism.

SHINTO

Unlike Christianity, Confucianism, and Buddhism, Shinto is a purely native Japanese religion. Shinto literally means "The Way of the *Kami*." There are some eight million *kami*, usually translated as "gods," but a kami can be any power or spirit, and it can be associated with certain mountains, rocks, trees, legendary heroes, or any locality held to be sacred.

You can always recognize a Shinto shrine by its torii, a gate consisting of two upright posts topped with two cross beams. The older torii are made of wood. A stunning example is the one at the Itsukushima Shrine (on the island of Miyajima), which rises dramatically out of the sea and is pictured on so many travel posters. Later torii were sometimes constructed of stone, concrete, or even metal. The shrine with the greatest number of torii is the Fushimi Inari Shrine in Kyoto, dedicated to the Goddess of Food and Rice. It has more than ten thousand torii, placed one after the other, forming a vermilion tunnel nearly two and a half miles long. Most of these were donated in gratitude by successful merchants and businessmen, who like to patronize the Inari shrines.

Another sign of a Shinto shrine is a thick rope of plaited rice straw, fringed with rice stalks and strips of folded white paper. The rope sometimes hangs from the torii, but it can also be bound around a tree trunk or rock to indicate that the locality is sacred and protected. Small strips of white paper are also tied to tree branches. At a Shinto shrine you can get a strip of paper with your fortune on it. If you don't like your fortune, you tie the slip of paper to a tree and your fortune is supposed to improve.

Shinto shrines may have several buildings, and in the early shrines these are plain and austere. They are essentially huts constructed of unpainted wood, with simple thatched roofs. Two outstanding examples of this type of shrine are the Ise Shrine on the Kii Peninsula and the Izumo Shrine in western Japan, the two most sacred shrines in Japan, as well as the oldest. Later, under the influence of Buddhist architecture, shrine buildings became ornate. The Itsukushima Shrine at Miyajima, the Heian Shrine in Kyoto, and the Kasuga Shrine at Nara are splendid examples of the highly decorated style. Extravagant ornamentation reaches a peak at the Toshogu Shrine at Nikko.

Unlike a Christian church or a Buddhist temple, the shrine buildings do not contain statues or pictures of the kami. Instead, the kami is represented by an object such as a bead, a stone, a sword, but most often a mirror. This does not mean there is no sculpture. Often you will find a pair of guardian lion-like dogs at the entrance of the shrine. The Inari shrines always have statues of foxes, messengers of the Goddess of Food and Rice.

Very often, too, you will see hung in shrine buildings pictures painted on wood, called *ema*, "horse pictures." These are offerings from donors who may be asking for relief from sickness, a safe voyage, or a successful business venture, and the pictures take the place of offerings of real horses. Not all of them, however, must be of horses — they can depict other objects, depending on the donor's desires. Ema range from small, crude paintings to real works of art.

Primitive Shinto was basically a collection of legends, mostly to do with the origin and creation of Japan. The Goddess Amaterasu was worshiped as the ancestor of the imperial family. Later, when Confucianism and Buddhism were introduced, there was an attempt to give some structure to Shinto, so that it would look more respectable compared with the religions imported from the Asian

ENTERTAINMENTS

mainland. At one time Shinto and Buddhism were even combined, and the Shinto kami were identified with certain minor Buddhist deities. Many Buddhist temples included a Shinto shrine on their grounds, and vice versa. During periods of intense Japanese nationalism, Shinto was promoted over the other religions as the one purely native to the country. From the latter part of the nineteenth century to the end of World War II, Shinto was the official state religion, and the emperor was worshiped as a god. But after the war, state support for Shinto was withdrawn, and many shrines fell on hard times. Today some are used as playgrounds, some have tennis courts on them, and some have even been made into parking lots.

The more famous shrines, like the Meiji Shrine and the Yasukuni Shrine (dedicated to the war dead) never lack patronage. Others are crowded by worshipers only at certain times of the year. In January and February, the Tenmangu shrines are crowded with students preparing for entrance examinations. The Tenmangu shrines are dedicated to Tenjin, the posthumous name of Sugawara Michizane, a ninth-century statesman and scholar, who is the patron of learning.

New Year is one of the busiest periods at Shinto shrines. Another busy day is November 15, the day of the *Shichigosan*, "Seven-Five-Three." On this day parents whose daughters are three or seven and whose sons are three or five visit Shinto shrines with their children to pray for the future welfare of their offspring. The children are dressed in their best clothes, and it is a hard-hearted photographer who can resist a tiny three-year-old girl in her first kimono. Lately there is a regrettable trend to dress the children in more modern clothes. Boys have been seen in space-age costumes, replacing the traditional kimono and hakama (divided skirt). The Meiji Shrine in Tokyo is a good place to view the Shichigosan, but be sure to bring color film.

Shinto shrines reach their height of frenzy during their annual *matsuri*, or festival. Nowadays, a matsuri can be any festival, sacred or secular. But originally a matsuri was the occasion when the parishioners of a particular shrine threw a big party to honor that shrine's kami. A movable shrine, called a *mikoshi*, is carried around the district so that the kami can visit its "parish." This portable shrine is carried around by the youths of the district, who strip down to their loincloths for the occasion. Some festivals have, instead of one portable shrine, a parade of gorgeously decorated ones. If you want to see a matsuri with a lot of action, go to the *Kenka Matsuri* at Himeji (October 14 and 15). It has seven heavy shrines carried by the young men of the district, who push and shove at one another in friendly rivalry. For this reason the matsuri is called the "Roughhouse Festival."

During a festival, offerings of fruit, bales of rice, and barrels of sake are dedicated to the kami. (You can see the rice bales and sake barrels at many shrines.) Like any good party, a festival features a lot of music and dancing and bonfires. During rural festivals in the old days, some couples would retire into the woods after the bonfire died down and the festival would wind up as an orgy. The Japanese are not more promiscuous than other people, but during the excitement of a festival it was forgivable to get (literally) carried away.

These days the more famous festivals have become somewhat commercialized. The Big Three of the festivals are the *Sanno Matsuri* of Tokyo (June 15), the *Gion Matsuri* of Kyoto (July 16–24), and the *Tenjin Matsuri* of Osaka (July 24 and 25). These festivals are so crowded that you practically have to rent a helicopter to see anything. You should, of course, attend one of these huge spectacles, but don't leave Japan without going to at least one neighborhood matsuri (see Chapter 6, AMUSEMENTS). The tourist centers in Tokyo and Kyoto can give you information in English on local shrines and their matsuri. You'll have to make your own arrangements for fun and games in the woods afterward.

Between festivals, a Shinto shrine is a peaceful oasis in the frantic bustle of a modern Japanese city. Occasionally a lone worshiper comes and bows in front of the shrine and drops a coin into the offering box. If the worshiper wishes, he can wash his hands and rinse his mouth at a stone basin provided for the purpose. This is a symbolic act of purification. Some shrines have bells, which the visitor rings by pulling on some strips of cotton. Unlike churchgoers, who attend service together on Sunday morning, the worshipers at a Shinto shrine go whenever they feel the urge or need.

Many Japanese have a small family shrine in their living room. (They may have a small family Buddhist altar too.) But the family shrine and altar are mostly seen in more old-fashioned families of several generations living together. Younger Japanese rarely have them, and Shinto plays a relatively small part in their lives. New Year, the Seven-Five-Three, the festivals, a wedding, a sumo match (see Chapter 7, SPORTS) — these are about the only occasions when the younger Japanese have much to do with Shinto.

There is one other occasion that is always accompanied by Shinto rites: the start of a major construction project. A Shinto priest will solemnly perform the appropriate rites at the ground-breaking ceremony for a nuclear power plant or the launching of an oil tanker.

CONFUCIANISM

Of the four major religions in Japan, Confucianism is the least visible. Some people even argue it is not a living religion at all, since there is no longer much ritual or worship associated with it. Nevertheless, it has had a profound effect on Japanese behavior and society, and its influence is strong even in this modern age.

The Chinese sage Confucius (551–479 B.C.) believed in an orderly state in which everyone knew his place and was governed by a strict code of ethics. Confucianism was introduced into Japan during the sixth century A.D., together with Buddhism and Chinese culture. When Prince Shotoku (573–622 A.D.) drafted his Seventeen-Article Constitution, he was indebted to Confucianism as much as to Buddhism.

Later, Japanese feudalism showed the influence of the Confucian principle of the Five Relations: the relation between lord and retainer, between parent and child, between older children and younger children, between husband and wife, and between friend and friend. Contact with Confucianism helped form the principles of *Bushido*, "The Way of the Warrior." Being an elite group put certain obligations on the samurai, and they had to be models of virtue, self-discipline, and loyalty.

When the Tokugawa family took power at the beginning of the seventeenth century, they felt that the ideals of Confucius were what they needed to bring order to a country that had suffered centuries of civil wars. Under the Tokugawa regime, Confucianism was made the official cult of the ruling class. Shrines dedicated to Confucius were constructed in Edo (which later became Tokyo, "Eastern Capital," when the emperor moved there in 1868), where the shogun and his court attended ceremonies celebrating Confucius's birthday and the spring and autumn festivals. Following the example of the shogun, a number of the leading feudal lords had Confucian shrines constructed in their castles and founded academies for the study of Confucianism.

Eventually the influence of Confucianism spread to the common people as well. The relations between parent and child, between older and younger children, and between husband and wife were strictly observed among merchants and peasants, as well as among warriors. Today we can still see the respect Japanese children have for their parents. The low position of Japanese women is a result of Confucianism. In earlier days, before Confucianism became the official cult, Japanese women were not so subservient. (There were even a few reigning empresses in early Japanese history. During the tenth century, some of the court ladies were famous for their learning and for their uninhibited behavior, and during the medieval period there were several notable women warriors.)

Another effect of Confucianism is the Japanese respect for learning. Probably in no other country today is there such a direct relation between a student's academic achievements and his later success. Some companies have a policy of hiring only graduates from certain elite universities.

At the top of the list of elite schools is Tokyo University, which grew out of the Shōhei Academy, a Confucian university established in the feudal period for members of the Tokugawa family and their greater vassals. The site of the Shōhei Academy is still preserved as a Confucian shrine, and is called the Yushima Seido. It is on a small hill just across the Kanda River from Ochanomizu Station in Tokyo and is open on the first Monday of each month. The sanctuary of the shrine has bronze statues of Confucius and other Chinese sages. In spite of the fact that the location is one of the busiest in Tokyo, the high walls surrounding the shrine and the foliage of the trees in the courtyard give the place an extraordinary atmosphere of serenity and scholarly seclusion.

But there are very few Confucian shrines left in Japan. Nagasaki has a much-photographed Confucian shrine with brightly colored tile work. Called the Kōshibyo, it is patronized by the Chinese community in Nagasaki, and thus cannot rightly be considered a Japanese Confucian shrine.

CHRISTIANITY

Christianity was introduced in 1549 by St. Francis Xavier, a Jesuit priest working under a Portuguese mission. In a few short years, almost a quarter of a million Japanese were converted to Christianity, many of them of high rank. The early Portuguese were successful partly because they were welcomed by Nobunaga, the most powerful warlord of the day (see Chapter 9, CASTLES AND SAMURAI), who used the Christians to counter the power of certain Buddhist sects that were his bitter enemies.

After Nobunaga's assassination in 1582, the Portuguese missionaries, later followed by the Spanish, continued to thrive for a while under his successors. Then the Japanese rulers suddenly turned against the Europeans. One reason was the arrival of the Protestant English, enemies of the Catholic Spaniards and Portuguese. Soon the various groups of Europeans were busily slandering one another to the Japanese rulers, each claiming that the others were intending to conquer the country, and that the activities of the missionaries were a screen for eventual military occupation. Alarmed by these reports, the Japanese decided in 1639 to throw out all Europeans. (In view of what had happened to India and to the Inca and Aztec civilizations, perhaps the fears of the Japanese were justified.) Christianity was banned by the authorities and all Japanese Christian converts were ordered to renounce their belief.

These converts proved to be amazingly steadfast. Many of them suffered hideous tortures rather than give up their new faith. Others worshiped in secret by having statues of the Virgin Mary made to resemble the Buddhist Goddess Kannon. The government officials who were sent to root out Christianity devised a clever trick: they made little plaques, called *fumie*, that had a picture of Jesus or the Virgin on them. A suspect was ordered to step on the picture. If he refused to commit the desecration, it proved he was a Christian.

When Japan finally opened its doors to the outside world in the last century and Christian missions were permitted into the country again, thousands of people poured into Nagasaki and announced to the astonished missionaries that they were Japanese Christians whose ancestors had gone underground and practiced their faith in secret for two hundred years! Historians call this episode "The Finding of the Christians."

With the lifting of the ban against Christianity came a second wave of conversions. A Catholic cathedral was built in Nagasaki, the Urakami Cathedral — the largest church in the Far East until it was destroyed by the atomic bomb that fell on Nagasaki. Another Catholic church, the Oura Church, was built in 1865 and is still standing. In Nagasaki you can see many other traces of the city's historical associations with Christianity, among them a monument to the twenty-six martyrs (both Japanese and European) crucified in 1597 during the religious persecutions. Stores in Nagasaki sell replicas of the fumie plaques; you can also buy pictures of the "Mary" Kannon.

All through the latter part of the last century and the early part of this one, Protestant missions were sent to Japan from America and various European countries. But during the militaristic regime that seized power in the 1930s, Christianity again came under suspicion as a subversive and foreign religion and was suppressed. Although the suppression was lifted at the end of World War II, the number of Japanese Christians is today fairly small compared to that of other religious sects. The influence of

Christianity is stronger than the figures suggest, however, because of the Christian schools and colleges, many of whose graduates have gone on to become intellectual, social, and political leaders.

In Japan today there are about 744,000 Christians, equally divided between Protestants and Catholics (the Orthodox sects being counted as Catholic). There are more than six thousand churches, and many cities, including Tokyo, Yokohama, Nagoya, and Sapporo, have both Catholic and Protestant churches of various denominations. Affiliated with these churches are schools and centers of other activities. You may want to visit these Christian centers for social reasons, since many of the Japanese Christians speak good English, and the younger ones are eager to make friends with Westerners of their own age.

BUDDHISM

Buddhism, the last major religion of Japan, is also the most visible: its influence can be seen everywhere. It is all around you in architecture, landscaping, paintings, and sculpture. In literature, Buddhist influence is even greater. The classics make constant reference to *karma*, the Buddhist belief in cause and effect. Innocent victims accept their fate because it is their karma, the result of some misdeed in a past life. They also believe that the misdeeds in this life will rebound on some future reincarnation. Buddhism stresses the transitory nature of things. In the *Tale of Genji*, the characters talk about *mono no aware*, the desolate realization that all beauty will decay.

Buddhism was introduced to Japan in the sixth century along with Chinese culture and writing. This foreign religion became the national cult, largely through the efforts of Prince Shotoku (mentioned earlier in connection with

Confucianism), whose Seventeen-Article Constitution prepared the way for bringing the country under imperial rule. Prince Shotoku founded Horyuji Temple at Nara, whose buildings are the oldest surviving wooden structures in Japan. (See Chapter 8, ARTS AND CRAFTS.)

From the first, the Buddhist temples with their curly roofs showed the influence of Chinese architecture, which is strikingly different from the native Japanese architecture in such Shinto shrines as Ise and Izumo. One of the most conspicuous structures in a Buddhist temple is the pagoda, a multi-storied tower. Among the most famous and most photographed pagodas in Japan are the ones at Horyuji Temple in Nara and Toji Temple in Kyoto. They are made of wood and, being fitted together without nails, they can be taken apart for repairs and then reassembled. Smaller pagodas are made of stone. You often see pebbles lying on top of these stone pagodas, because it is believed that your wish will come true if you throw a pebble at a pagoda and succeed in making it stay on. (You can also make a wish by throwing pebbles at a Shinto torii.)

A temple has several buildings, one for holding images of Buddha, one for reading scriptures, one for the monks' quarters, and so on. If you walk past the scriptures hall while chanting is in progress, you may hear a *bok*, *bok* sound giving the tempo to the chanting, made by beating a hollow wooden fish with a stick. A delicate *ping* punctuates the *bok*, *bok* every now and then, and this is made by tapping a bronze bowl with a stick.

The temple bell, on the other hand, makes a lovely, booming sound that can be heard miles away. The huge bronze bell is suspended in a special bell pavilion, and instead of having a clapper, it is struck with a wooden log hung horizontally by a rope outside the bell. Since it takes time to draw back the log, push it forward to strike the bell, and repeat the process, the tolling of a Japanese temple bell is slow and majestic, unlike the frantic jangling of some Western church bells. In many temples the public is allowed to strike the bell, and you will find it gives you a marvelous feeling of satisfaction to do so. But some bells have a sign telling you to keep your hands off, since it may be one of the bells rung to mark the hours of the day, so that striking it at random causes confusion. (The Japanese for "It is forbidden" is found in the appendix.)

Worshiping at a Buddhist temple consists of lighting an incense stick in the bronze incense burner, striking a metal gong at the entrance to the main hall, and placing the palms together and bowing.

Sometimes a person with a special wish makes an offering of a thousand folded paper cranes. Mothers of sick children often bring offerings of food, flowers, or a cloth bib to Jizo, a minor Buddhist deity who is the patron of little children. You can often see in the street a small stone statue of Jizo with a red cloth bib tied around its neck. Jizo is an especially benevolent deity who is also the patron of travelers, and there are many stories of Jizo statues coming alive and going around to help travelers in need.

Another benevolent deity is Kannon, the Goddess of Mercy. The most famous Kannon temple in Japan is Senjoji Temple in the Asakusa district of Tokyo. Tourists know the temple as the one with the pair of huge red lanterns. In Kyoto there is a monumental concrete statue, called the Ryozen Kannon, erected in 1955 in memory of the war dead. Kyoto's famous Kiyomizu Temple is also dedicated to Kannon.

The truly devout make pilgrimages to distant temples, trips that can last for months. You can recognize pilgrims by their costume, which is made of white cotton, with white leggings and mittens. They also wear a big hat and carry a staff. Some temples stamp the clothing of the pilgrims when they arrive, a proof of the visit. A well-traveled pilgrim will have his white garment stamped all over. Spring is a good time to see pilgrims, and Shikoku Island is the place to go, because there is a circuit of eighty-eight temples, which annually attract more than a hundred thousand worshipers. Making a pilgrimage is an excuse to leave home in a cloud of sanctity instead of disapproval. Since olden times, people who have no other means of recreation go on pilgrimages for a change of scenery. Nowadays foreign tourists have discovered the fun of joining the throngs of Japanese pilgrims on Shikoku Island and they gleefully get their clothes and rucksacks stamped.

Many of the pilgrims going to Shikoku are followers of Kōbō Daishi (774–835), one of the most remarkable religious leaders in Japanese history. Among his other accomplishments, he is given credit for developing *hiragana*, one of the two phonetic syllabaries (see Chapter 2, LANGUAGE). He founded the Shingon sect of Buddhism, whose head temple is at Mt. Koya in the middle of the Kii Peninsula. The remoteness of the temple and its ancient cryptomeria trees give the whole area a feeling of mystery and awe.

Another mountain temple is Enryakuji, the head temple of the Tendai sect, strategically located on Mt. Hiei, northeast of Kyoto. It became so powerful that it began to interfere with the political affairs of the country. The warrior monks of Mt. Hiei did not hesitate to attack Kyoto, and in their periodic raids on the capital, they always carried a mikoshi, or portable Shinto shrine. This showed the former close relationship between Buddhism and Shinto.

Both these two Buddhist sects stress elaborate ritual, and have little to offer the common people. In the twelfth century, the Pure Land sects were founded, teaching that salvation is obtained through faith in the Amida Buddha (who watches over the Pure Land, or Buddhist heaven) without the necessity of costly ritual. These sects became immensely popular with the common people, and even today they have the greatest number of followers among the Buddhist sects. Temples of the Pure Land sects include Chion-in, Nishi-Honganji, and Higashi-Honganji in Kyoto. The huge bronze Buddha in Kamakura is situated in a temple of a Pure Land sect.

The thirteenth century was a troubled period for Japan, with two invasions by the Mongols and many natural disasters. Nichiren, originally a priest of the Tendai sect on Mt. Hiei, decided that these disasters were the result of spiritual decay, and that the only hope was to establish a truer, purer form of Buddhism. Because of his harsh criticism of all the other sects, he was persecuted and eventually exiled. But there were many who supported his reformist views. There is an almost evangelical zeal about the Nichiren sect that has kept it vigorous, and during recent years it has given rise to a number of new religions, one of which we shall discuss later.

The Zen sect was introduced from China during the beginning of the thirteenth century. According to Zen Buddhism, enlightenment (*satori*) is obtained through meditation. The emphasis of Zen on will power and self-discipline was a major influence in the development of Bushido, the Way of the Warrior (in addition to the influence of Confucianism, mentioned earlier).

A second Zen device for achieving enlightenment is the use of riddles (*koan*), such as "What is the sound of one hand clapping?" These riddles cannot be solved intellectually. Instead, one concentrates on them by gradually eliminating all extraneous thought, until enlightenment suddenly strikes. Sometimes this process takes years.

Zen Buddhism had the support of the shogun's government at Kamakura, and that city alone has five magnificent Zen temples. Under the Ashikaga shoguns (see Chapter 9, CASTLES AND SAMURAI), the military government moved back to Kyoto, and many richly endowed Zen temples were built there in the fourteenth and fifteenth centuries, including the Golden and Silver Pavilions and Ryoanji, famous for its garden of sand and rocks. Zen Buddhism, which discards non-essentials and emphasizes the abstract, has had a profound effect on Japanese landscaping.

Sitting cross-legged in meditation is called *zazen*. Many beginners find it all too easy to pass from meditation to a daze, and from a daze to a doze. Therefore a monk is assigned the duty of walking around with a stick and checking on the rows of meditators. If anyone shows signs of dropping off, the monk taps him on the shoulder with the stick. When tea was introduced from China, it was discovered that this drink helped keep people awake. Zen Buddhists drank tea for this purpose and developed *cha-no-yu*, the "art of tea" (sometimes called tea ceremony). Members of the warrior class were especially attracted to cha-no-yu, with its emphasis on concentration and self-discipline. Nowadays it has become largely a polite accomplishment for young ladies.

A beginner at zazen suffers not only from sleepiness, but also from an agonizing case of pins and needles. You wonder whether long periods of impeded circulation can actually harm your legs. Nor are your fears allayed when you hear the story about the Daruma, a roly-poly pear-shaped doll. According to legend, Daruma was an Indian saint who meditated for nine years, until his arms and legs became atrophied and shrank to nothing. Many Japanese buy Daruma dolls with blank eyes at New Year's time and make a wish. If their wish is granted, they paint the eyes in.

Also sold at the New Year are pictures of the Seven Lucky Gods, usually seen sailing in their *Takarabune*, or Treasure Ship. The Seven Lucky Gods are *Bishamonten* (God of Riches, usually depicted in armor), *Benten* (God-

SHRINES, CHURCHES, AND TEMPLES

dess of Music, Arts and Fortune, the only female of the group), *Daikoku* (bringer of good luck, a fat figure holding a sack of goodies and a hammer), *Ebisu* (son of Daikoku, Patron of Fishermen and the God of Food, depicted holding a large tai fish and a fishing rod), *Fukurokuju* (God of Longevity, an old bearded man with a staff, a crane, and a tortoise), *Hotei* (always shown with an enormous, naked belly), and *Jurojin* (another god associated with longevity, often confused with Fukurokuju. In fact, it is said that he was added merely to round out the number of gods to seven, which is a lucky number). These seven gods have their temples and shrines — they are a mixture of Shinto, Buddhist, and Chinese deities — but they are not worshiped with serious reverence. Rather, they are regarded as bringers of good fortune, and their pictures or figurines are lucky charms.

Although the festivals continue to be crowded and pictures of the Seven Lucky Gods continue to sell, many Japanese today feel a spiritual emptiness. This is partly the result of urbanization, which separates city dwellers from their family temples. Like the Shinto shrines, Buddhist temples have fallen on hard times. For many temples the chief source of revenue now comes from holding death anniversaries, for, in addition to celebrating birthdays, the Japanese observe death anniversaries of their relatives and illustrious ancestors. The temple containing the family graves holds a ceremony for important anniversaries, and the occasion may be a large family reunion bringing together members from all over the country.

At other times the younger Japanese tend to have little to do with traditional forms of worship. Various new religions have risen to fill the spiritual needs of city people and, unlike the traditional sects, these new sects are not tied to particular temples or localities. Some are so highly organized that they resemble business corporations. With their attention on practical matters, especially mental and physical health, and their missionary zeal, they have attracted millions of followers.

The one best known to Americans is probably the *Soka Gakkai*, because it has made thousands of converts in this country, especially in the Los Angeles area. In the last few years, it has been overshadowed here by Hare Krishna and later by the Church of Unification (under the Reverend Sun Myung Moon). But in Japan the Soka Gakkai continues to be a powerful force. It has even given rise to a political party, the *Komeito*, which received more than ten percent of the popular vote in recent elections. Its block of more than fifty seats in Parliament makes it a non-trivial factor in the formation of coalitions.

Zen Buddhism, however, has been of deeper and more lasting interest in the West since its introduction in the 1930s. There are Zen institutes in the West where one can practice meditation. Various groups have even formed communities where the members adopt the living style of a Zen monastery. A few Westerners have gone through the harsh discipline necessary to become Zen priests, but most prefer to try meditation sessions first.

Japanese temples often accept laymen as paying guests, but they prefer people who speak Japanese. It has been their experience that foreigners who speak no Japanese require too much special attention. Still, the Japanese realize that many foreigners have a sincere desire to experience Zen Buddhism. The Eiheiji Temple in Fukui Prefecture, one of the two head temples of the Soto Zen sect, has had so many Western applicants for zazen sessions that it now puts out an English pamphlet on Zen.

As tourists you are free to visit the temples any time, but if you want to stay in one, it is absolutely essential to submit a written application and receive confirmation before you show up with bag and baggage. It is recommended that your application be accompanied by a letter of introduction written by a Japanese friend (in Japanese).

One way of getting a taste of Zen Buddhism without staying as an overnight guest in a temple is to try a vegetarian dinner. There are several places near Nanzenji Temple in Kyoto that feature Zen cooking, and the Kyoto Tourist Information Center can give you their names and locations.

11
GENERALIZATIONS

We are always tempted to make sweeping statements on national character, and the less we know about a country, the more sweeping our generalizations. In the case of the Japanese, the temptation is especially great. Because of their economic successes, the Japanese have become more visible to the rest of the world, without being better understood. Very few Westerners have taken the trouble to study Japanese history, language, or culture, and this means that many of the assumptions they make about Japan have been acquired second or even thirdhand. In this chapter we'd like to talk about some of the common generalizations made about the Japanese.

THE JAPANESE ARE CONFORMISTS

We often hear that the Japanese have no individuality, and like to do things only in groups. Japanese sightseers spill out of tour buses and meekly follow the yellow flag of their guide, and after they've bought their souvenirs, they line up in neat rows for the obligatory group photograph. True, too true. Most Japanese do like to travel in groups, especially abroad, because they are afraid of getting lost in a strange land. They are not optimistic about finding a Japanese-speaking policeman or taxi driver in Athens.

In their own country, they are less timid. Since early times, it has been a popular custom for people, even the middle-aged and elderly, to make long journeys on foot. Sometimes they go in groups, but most go in ones and twos. People still do it, and if you're not scared of leaving your tour group and venturing into the mountains, you may run across one of these travelers. Even abroad, there are solitary Japanese travelers. Every now and then one of them sails across the Pacific, skis down Mt. Everest, or goes alone to the North Pole by dog sled.

In the West churchgoing is a group activity, and you see very few people going alone to the church on a weekday. But the Japanese go to a shrine or temple individually, whenever they feel the need. Try visiting a quiet, neighborhood shrine not flooded with tourists. You will soon see someone approach, throw money into the offering box, pull the red-and-white rope to ring the bell, and bow in silent prayer.

Another sign of the Japanese tendency to conform, people say, is the uniformity of their clothes. If you are in a Tokyo street at the noon hour, you will be engulfed by office workers pouring out for lunch. Suddenly you see nothing but a sea of white shirts. Doesn't anyone dare wear a plaid shirt, or even a blue one? And during the rush hour you see office workers by the millions in dark gray suits, nothing but dark gray. It's true that the white shirt and dark gray suit is the uniform of the office worker (like the bowler hat and tightly furled umbrella of the British civil servant). But that doesn't mean people want to wear this uniform all the time.

If you want to see a hodge-podge of clothing styles, wait

at a bus stop during an off-peak time. You will see a middle-aged man in a kimono, wooden clogs, and a straw hat, or a workman in leggings, bifurcated rubber boots, and woolen stomach warmer, or a farm woman wearing assorted cotton garments of different patterns, the ultimate layered look.

Another complaint is that Japanese businessmen have no individuality, and act only as a team or a group. This is undoubtedly true. Company and government decisions are made as a group, after consultation rather than confrontation. But this doesn't mean the Japanese frown on individuality. Hermits and mountain priests are highly respected, and after all, the archetypal hero in books, movies, TV, and comics is the wandering *ronin*, an unattached samurai — a loner.

THE JAPANESE WORK TOO HARD AND DON'T KNOW HOW TO ENJOY THEMSELVES

This is the explanation given for why the Japanese can price their products so cheaply: they use slave labor. It has to be admitted that the average Japanese worker puts in more hours than his counterpart in other countries. Instead of an hour for lunch, many workers take a fifteen-minute break to gulp down a bowl of noodles. They also come home much later at night. In one city a recent survey showed that twenty-five percent of office workers arrived home after ten at night. Japan is a small country, and competition is keen. If you want to get ahead, you simply have to work harder than others. But this doesn't mean people don't know how to go out and have fun. More and more firms have adopted the five-day week, and workers enjoy their weekends in window-shopping, sightseeing, and sports. Just try going to a ski resort on a weekend, and you'll find out how many people enjoy sports.

Students do have to study very hard. Employers attach great importance to educational background, and the prestige of certain universities is so great that high school students fight to pass the entrance exams for these schools. Certain high schools are known for their success in placing many of their graduates in the "good" universities. Therefore middle-school students fight to pass the entrance exams for these high schools. Certain middle schools are known for their success in placing their graduates in the "good" high schools, and so on. The end result is that even kindergarten students have to work. But not all Japanese youngsters are pale, nervous wrecks — except during the entrance-examination period. This period, from the end of January through February, is called "Examination Hell." During the rest of the year — well, see for yourself by stopping at a school and watching the youngsters on the playground. You will also run into school children on outings, all wearing caps and carrying water bottles and packages of rice balls. Chattering and laughing, they seem to be having a wonderful time.

THE JAPANESE CARE TOO MUCH ABOUT SAVING FACE

One of the most common tourist complaints is that when the Japanese don't know the answer to your question, they don't want to lose face by admitting their ignorance. Instead they give you a vague answer. Of course face is important in Japan. It's important in other countries too. How many of us like to admit we're ignorant? But a Japanese is reluctant to say "I don't know" partly because he considers such a blunt answer very impolite. It is less rude to say, "Yes, let's see," and then make a feeble stab at answering your question. Now, a fellow Japanese will immediately realize this man is no help, and will thank him and leave. It's only the inexperienced foreigner who stands around and watches the farce played to the end.

There is another common misunderstanding. Many travelers complain bitterly that the Japanese say "yes" when they mean "no" and vice versa. A traveler calls up a hotel and says, "You don't have a vacancy, do you?" The answer is "Yes," and the jubilant traveler hurries down to the hotel, only to find there is no vacancy. The explanation is that a Japanese says "yes" or "no" depending on whether or not he agrees with you. In this case, he means, "Yes, you are right: we have no vacancy." This misunderstanding is expressed perfectly by the title of the popular song, "Yes, We Have No Bananas."

THE JAPANESE ARE TOO POLITE

Tourists are always struck by the sight of people constantly bowing to each other in Japan. So much bowing seems excessively polite. The fact is that different cultures permit different degrees of physical contact. Frenchmen embrace and kiss each other, a custom regarded with suspicion by northern Europeans. With the Japanese, physical contact is rare even among close acquaintances, and bowing takes the place of shaking hands or an embrace. When you say "How are you?" you are not interested in medical details; you are only giving a standard greeting. A bow in Japan is not obsequiousness, but simply the standard way of greeting.

THE JAPANESE ARE ECONOMIC ANIMALS

This phrase was coined by those who claimed that since defeat in World War II forced the Japanese to disarm, their killer instinct is now channeled into making money. Even the tourist who is spending only a few days in Japan can soon see that this statement is false. How can you reconcile an economic animal with a mendicant monk who goes from door to door with his begging bowl, playing his mournful flute? If you enter a neighborhood store, you find that far from making a fast sales pitch, the owner is in a back room watching TV (in some countries this would be an invitation to shoplifting). You have to call out to get any service.

JAPANESE WOMEN ARE SLAVES

There is a general belief among foreigners that the function of Japanese women is to serve their menfolk, and they cite the example of geishas pouring wine or entertaining their male customers. One of the first things a tourist notices in a department store is the escalator girl, whose sole job is to bow to the customers riding the escalators. On the street, indignant tourists see the wife humbly following three paces behind her uncaring husband.

It is true that Women's Lib has not made much headway in Japan. One of the few national organizations for women's liberation had to disband from lack of support. The pay scale for female workers is far below that of the male, and few women reach managerial or executive positions.

But the position of women is far from insignificant. Women make up one-third of the total work force, and of the working women, two-thirds are married. Therefore the traditional image of the Japanese woman as a homebody is no longer valid. Even the housewife is not always bound to the house, and many of them are quite active in women's consumer movements. Moreover, the housewife controls the purse. Blondie has to wheedle money from

Dagwood for her shopping expeditions, but in Japan the husband hands over his entire pay envelope to his wife. She doles out a little pocket money for him after she has worked out the family budget.

In ancient days the position of women was even stronger. There were a number of reigning empresses in Japan, and one of them led an expedition to conquer Korea. Throughout Japanese history, the farm women have been tough, for they worked in the fields alongside the men. You'll find out how tough a farm woman can be if one of them has her eye on a bus seat you are making for. She may look scrawny, but in the collision you won't end up as the winner.

There are so many travel posters showing beautiful Japanese girls arranging flowers or conducting a tea ceremony that we tend to think of all Japanese women as poised and serene. That is certainly the impression they wish to convey. But if you attend a concert by a visiting rock group, you'll find the Japanese teeny boppers screaming as hysterically as their counterparts in other countries.

Are Japanese women more feminine than Western women? In a survey of high school students, thirty percent of the girl students said their favorite subject was mathematics, supposedly a male-dominated subject.

The status of women in Japan is not so high as that of certain Western countries. But it would be a gross simplification to think of all Japanese women as slaves.

THE JAPANESE ARE THE WORLD'S WORST LITTER BUGS

After a long journey, the interiors of even the best trains are often ankle deep in lunch boxes, bottles, and candy wrappers. Many scenic spots are disfigured with trash, and theaters are also bad. (I once went to a play and sat in front of a man who ate his way through a box of sandwiches, a bunch of bananas, and two oranges. The debris from his meal all went under his seat.) There is little defense against this accusation except to say that the Japanese love to eat whenever they go somewhere, and the trash containers are never equal to the load. But — next time you see a dog being walked, notice that the owner carries a bundle of newspapers. When the dog stops, he doesn't foul a neighbor's lawn, but is trained to use the newspaper, which his owner then folds up and takes away with him.

JAPAN IS TOO CROWDED

The most common complaint made by tourists is crowdedness. You feel suffocated in the subway and the bus, on the sidewalk and the department store escalators. How can you enjoy the serenity of a famous Buddhist temple when your view is obscured by mobs of people?

Tourists on a very short visit usually spend most of the time in Tokyo, which has the densest population in the world. Then they make a lightning foray to Kyoto, staying only long enough to see the Golden Pavilion, the Heian Shrine, and Gion. Since these places are precisely the targets of all the other tourists, both foreign and domestic, it is not surprising that you find mobs.

There are large portions of Japan that are virtually deserted. The countryside is peaceful and beautiful, and farmers still complain of crop damage by wild monkeys and boars. Even in Kyoto during the height of the tourist season, you can easily find back streets with hardly a soul. What if the most famous temples and shrines are crowded? There are many beautiful, lesser-known temples and shrines in Kyoto, where the only people you see are a monk hanging out his laundry, a little boy feeding pigeons, and an old woman lighting an incense stick. As for the famous temples, visit them on a drizzly day early in the morning. Many of them are more beautiful in the rain anyway.

JAPAN IS BECOMING WESTERNIZED AND TRADITIONAL CULTURE IS DISAPPEARING

Many tourists are disappointed to see Tokyo so modern and Westernized. Instead of little wooden houses, you see skyscrapers and modern thoroughfares. Instead of kimonos, you see blue jeans and tennis shoes. Young girls dye their hair red, and Western music blares in the night clubs, coffee shops, and bars. English words pepper the conversations and TV commercials.

The Japanese are often accused of being imitators and having no originality. Actually, most countries borrow culture from others. American music owes a debt to the German, Austrian, and African, and American art owes a debt to the Italian, French, and German. The very symbols of American culture — the automobile, hot dog, hamburger, pizza, and blue jeans — have their origins elsewhere. As Edwin Reischauer said in an interview, the English language is written with an alphabet borrowed from the Romans who borrowed it from the Greeks who borrowed it from the Phoenicians.

When the Japanese borrow culture, they usually do it with a lot of government fanfare. The adoption of Buddhism and Chinese writing in the sixth century was explicitly directed by the government. The first big wave of Westernization in the middle of the nineteenth century was part of the official policy of the Meiji government. In an effort to make their people as strong as the Westerners, the government even tried to make them eat beef, a sickening idea to traditional Buddhists. One reason why the

Japanese strike others as imitative is that when they swallow foreign culture, they take huge bites at a time, often leading to indigestion at home and ridicule abroad.

But traditional culture is also consciously preserved. We have already referred to the policy of honoring certain outstanding traditional craftsmen as Living National Treasures. We have also mentioned the National Theater in Tokyo, where performances of classical Japanese theater are held. Nor is it only the older people who prize the traditional culture. Many young people go off into small villages on weekends to take lessons in handicrafts. Girls who read fashion magazines on the latest Paris models nevertheless study tea ceremony and flower arrangement. Boys who like surfing and skiing still keep up their kendo and judo lessons.

Newly married couples may have adopted the Western custom of a honeymoon, but the wedding ceremony itself in most cases is still a Shinto rite. If you go to some famous shrine in October (a favorite month for weddings), you have a good chance of seeing a wedding party in progress. The groom is either in a Western morning suit or in kimono and hakama (divided skirt), but the bride is almost always in the traditional wedding costume, complete with a headdress to hide the horns of jealousy.

The kimono continues to be worn on most formal occasions. An interesting phenomenon is the kimono institute, where women learn not only how to put on a kimono, but also how to behave in one, how to bow, sit, and walk. There have been complaints that many younger Japanese girls seem wrong in a kimono, because they talk too loudly, walk with long strides, or sit with knees apart. To put on a kimono, a girl must put on the traditional persona as well.

It would be too hasty to say that the Japanese have embraced Western technology and culture wholesale and renounced their cultural heritage. But it would also be too hasty to say that Westernization is only skin deep and that a samurai lurks under every charcoal gray suit.

You should not believe everything you read about Japan. Too many facile generalizations have been written, and this book probably contains quite a few of its own. Don't take anyone else's word on what Japan and the Japanese are like. Go and see for yourself.

APPENDICES

APPENDIX A
MAJOR HISTORICAL PERIODS OF JAPAN

EARLY PERIOD (–710 A.D.)

When Japan was still connected to the mainland (around 150,000 years ago), it shared the Asian continental paleolithic culture.

Neolithic culture in Japan, called *Jomon* (after a type of pottery characterized by a wavy pattern), lasted for several thousand years.

Around 300 B.C., a new culture appeared called *Yayoi* (after a type of pottery found near the Yayoi district in Tokyo). The new culture used bronze for a short time, but quickly adopted iron.

Social units consisted of family groups called *uji*, and several uji formed small communities.

A number of communities coalesced to form the Yamato state (near present-day Nara) around the beginning of the fourth century A.D.

Frequent intercourse took place between Japan and the mainland, with Japanese interference in Korean civil wars.

APPENDICES

Buddhism was introduced in 552 A.D., together with Chinese writing.

Crown Prince Shotoku (572–621) framed the first code of laws in 604, initiated social reforms, and promoted Buddhism.

NARA PERIOD (710–784)

First permanent capital built in Nara.

Great flowering of Buddhist architecture, paintings, and sculpture, including the Great Bronze Buddha, or Daibutsu.

Literature included the *Manyoshu* (anthology of poems), the *Kojiki* (a record of ancient events), and *Nihongi* (chronicle of Japan).

HEIAN PERIOD (794–1185)

Capital moved from Nara to Nagaoka, but remained there only ten years.

Capital moved to Kyoto, called *Heian-kyo*, Capital of Peace.

Power passed from the emperor to the powerful Fujiwara family, who married their daughters to successive emperors.

Age of great scholars and writers, among them women writers like Murasaki-Shikibu *(Tale of Genji)* and Sei-Shonagon *(Pillow Book)*.

Toward the end of the period, many disturbances were caused by disputes over the imperial succession. Rival families of warriors, the Taira and the Minamoto, fought for supremacy.

KAMAKURA PERIOD (1185–1333)

Minamoto family emerged supreme, and their leader Yoritomo was created shogun.
Military government, called *Bakufu* (Tent Government) set up in Kamakura.
Rise of Zen, Pure Land, and Nichiren sects of Buddhism.
Invasion by Mongols in 1274 and again in 1281, ending in the destruction of the Mongol fleet by a typhoon.
Civil wars as Emperor Godaigo (1288–1339) attempted to regain power from the Bakufu.
Kamakura destroyed by imperial forces in 1333.

MUROMACHI PERIOD (1336–1575)

Ashikaga Takauji (1305–1358) seized power from the emperor and established himself as shogun in 1336, choosing the Muromachi district of Kyoto as headquarters.
Yoshimitsu (1358–1408), one of the Ashikaga shoguns, was a great patron of arts, Zen, and Noh, and built the Golden Pavilion.
Yoshimasa (1436–1490), another shogun, was also a great art patron and built the Silver Pavilion.
Era of masterpieces in landscaping, architecture, painting, and the decorative arts.
Toward the end of the period, unending civil wars as *daimyo* (powerful feudal lords) fought one another.
Arrival of the Portuguese in 1542, bringing Christianity and firearms.

APPENDICES

AZUCHI-MOMOYAMA PERIOD (1575–1598)

Rise of Oda Nobunaga (1534–1582), who began the unification of Japan and deposed the last Ashikaga shogun. Assassinated before completing the work. He built a castle at Azuchi.

Nobunaga succeeded by Toyotomi Hideyoshi (1536–1598), who mastered Japan and tried to conquer Korea. He built a castle at Momoyama (and also at Osaka).

Era of magnificent feudal architecture and decorative arts. Tea ceremony raised to a great art under Sen-no-Rikyu.

EDO (TOKUGAWA) PERIOD (1603–1867)

After the death of Hideyoshi, Tokugawa Ieyasu became the most powerful man in the country. He defeated supporters of Hideyoshi's son at the battle of Sekigahara (1600) and wiped them out at the siege of Osaka Castle (1615).

Ieyasu established a long era of stability and peace.

All foreigners were expelled by 1639 and the country was closed to the outside world. Christianity was banned.

Rise of the merchant class and its culture and entertainment, including Kabuki and the puppet theater.

Toward the end of the era, foreign pressure increased to end seclusion.

Commodore Perry arrived in 1853, demanding the opening of the country. In 1858, a treaty was signed with America, and Townsend Harris became the first American consul. Treaties were also made with other Western countries.

Shogun resigned power to the emperor in 1867, bringing an end to feudalism.

MEIJI ERA (1868–1912)

Emperor Meiji (1852–1912) moved the capital from Kyoto to Tokyo.
Westernization of the country, construction of railroads, and universal education system.
Constitution adopted in 1889 and the first Parliament convened in 1890.
War with China over Korea (1894–95) and with Russia over Manchuria (1904–05).

TAISHO ERA (1912–1924)

Emperor Meiji succeeded by Emperor Taisho.
Japan entered World War I on the side of the Allies, and received German possessions in China and in the Pacific at the end of the war.

SHOWA ERA (1925–)

Emperor Hirohito succeeded in 1925, and his reign became known as *Showa*, "Peace shines."
Japan took over Manchuria in 1932 and set up the puppet state of Manshukoku.
Attempted *coup d'état* by the military and assassinations of government leaders in 1936.
Armed conflict with China began in 1937, leading up to large-scale attempt at conquest.
Pearl Harbor in 1941 and the beginning of the Pacific War.
Atomic bombs on Hiroshima and Nagasaki, August, 1945, bringing World War II to an end.
New post-war constitution in 1947.

APPENDIX B
LIST OF CHARACTERS

These characters are some of the ones tourists are likely to meet. We hope that constant exposure will help you remember them.

Each character is given its meaning, together with first its Chinese reading and then its Japanese reading. There is no convention on when you use which reading. Japanese themselves sometimes don't know which one is used in proper names.

When there is no common reading in Chinese or Japanese, we leave a blank space.

For the numerals, the *ichi, ni, san,* . . . sequence is used as ordinals (telling the position), while the *hitotsu, futatsu, mittsu,* . . . sequence is used as cardinals (telling how many). The Chinese reading, however, is always used for numbers greater than ten.

APPENDIX B

KANJI	JAPANESE READING	CHINESE READING	MEANING	
一	hitotsu	ichi	one	
二	futatsu	ni	two	
三	mittsu	san	three	
四	yottsu	shi	four	
五	itsutsu	go	five	
六	muttsu	roku	six	
七	nanatsu	shichi	seven	
八	yattsu	hachi	eight	
九	kokonotsu	ku	nine	
十	tō	jū	ten	
百		hyaku bai	hundred	
千	chi	sen	thousand	
万		man	ten thousand	
上	ue, kami	jō	above, over	*Ue* occurs in *Ueno*, a district in Tokyo. *Kami* is in *Kamikamo*, a shrine in Kyoto.
下	shita, shimo	ge	under, below	*Shimo* is in *Shimokamo*, another shrine in Kyoto, founded simultaneously as the Kamikamo Shrine.
東	higashi	tō	east	*Tō* is in *Tōkyō*, "Eastern Capital." *Higashi* is in *Higashi Honganji*, a temple in Kyoto, the eastern one of a pair.

APPENDICES

KANJI	JAPANESE READING	CHINESE READING	MEANING	
西	nishi	sai	west	*Nishi* is in *Nishi Honganji*, the western one of a pair of temples in Kyoto.
南	minami	nan	south	*Nan* is in names like *Nanzenji*, "Southern Zen Temple."
北	kita	hoku	north	*Hoku* is in *Hokkaido*, name of the northernmost main island. The name is literally "North Sea Route."
出	de (-ru)	shutsu	go out	*De* is in *deguchi*, "exit."
入	i (-ru)	nyū	enter	*Iru*, or rather *iri*, is in *iriguchi*, entrance.
口	kuchi, guchi	kō	mouth	We have already seen *guchi* above in *deguchi*, "going out mouth" and *iriguchi*, "going in mouth."
左	hidari	sa	left	*Sa* occurs in Sakyō, that part of Kyōto which is left of the Imperial Palace.
右	migi	u	right	*U* is in *Ukyō*, that part of Kyōto right of the Imperial Palace.

APPENDIX A

KANJI	JAPANESE READING	CHINESE READING	MEANING	
山	yama	san, zan	mountain	Both *yama* and *san* are commonly used for Mt. Fuji, as in Fujiyama and Fujisan.
川	kawa, gawa	sen	stream	*Kawa* is very common in surnames, as in Ogawa.
日	hi	nichi	sun, day	*Ni* is in *Nihon*, "Origin of the Sun," name for Japan. *Nichi* is also in *Nichiyōbi*, Sunday.
月	tsuki	getsu	moon	*Getsu* is in *Getsuyōbi*, Monday. It becomes *gatsu* when used for the months, as in *Ichigatsu*, January, *Nigatsu*, February, *Sangatsu*, March, etc. (Recall that *ichi*, *ni*, *san*, etc. are one, two, three, ...)
火	hi	ka	fire	*Ka* is in *Kayōbi*, Tuesday.
水	mizu	sui	water	*Mizu* occurs in *Kiyomizu*, "Temple of Pure Water." In the form of *sui*, it's in *Suiyōbi*, Wednesday.

APPENDICES

KANJI	JAPANESE READING	CHINESE READING	MEANING	
木	ki	moku	wood	*Moku* is in *Mokuyōbi*, Thursday.
金	kane	kin	gold	*Kane* is in *okane*, "Money." We see *kin* in Kinkakuji, Temple of the Golden Pavilion. *Kin* is also in *Kinyōbi*, Friday.
土	tsuchi	do	earth	*Do* is in *Doyōbi*, Saturday.
銀	shirogane	gin	silver	*Gin* occurs in Ginkakuji, Temple of the Silver Pavilion. *Ginkō* means "bank," and *gin* is also in the name Ginza, "Silver Assembly."
大	ō (-kī)	dai	big	*Dai* is seen in Daimaru, the department store.
小	ko, chi, o	shō	small	*O* is in names like Oda, Ogawa.
子	ko		child	*Ko* is in *kodomo*, "child." It is very common in names for girls, like Akiko, Michiko, etc.
人	hito	jin	person	We've already seen *jin* in *gaijin*, foreigner.
男	otoko	dan	male	This is one of two kanji you *must* learn.

APPENDIX B

KANJI	JAPANESE READING	CHINESE READING	MEANING	
女	onna	jo, nyō	female	This is the other one.
屋	ya	oku	house, store, establishment	*Ya* occurs in the names of many stores, such as Takashimaya, "High Island House." It also occurs in Nagoya.
門	kado	mon	gate	*Mon* is used in *sammon*, "mountain gate," the huge, tall gate in front of some temples. It's also in the name Rashōmon.
寺	tera, dera	ji	temple	*Ji* is in the names of temples, such as Ryōanji.
京	miyako	kyō	capital	We see *kyō* in Tōkyō, Kyōto
市	ichi	shi	city, market	You will see this kanji at bus stops which are operated by the city. *Shi* is in *shidensha*, streetcar.
田	ta, da	den	(cultivated) field	*Ta* is very common in surnames, such as Tanaka.
洋		yō	ocean	Since the Western countries are across the ocean from Japan, *yō* has come to

221

APPENDICES

KANJI	JAPANESE READING	CHINESE READING	MEANING	
				mean Western, especially used for toilets, hotels, cooking, etc., which are Western-style.
和		wa	calm	Wa is in Showa, the name of the present reign. But wa is also used to denote anything Japanese-style, such as toilets, hotels, cooking, etc.
円	maru	en, yen	circle	It's used to denote a unit of money, the yen.

The following pairs of characters are found on many posters, signs and walls. It's a good idea to know what they mean.

休日	kyū jitsu,	"closed for business," or "on vacation."
禁止	kin shi,	"not permitted" or "forbidden."
急行	kyū kō,	"express," used for trains, buses
特急	tokkyū,	"special-express" or "limited-express," used also for trains, buses, etc.

Table of the Japanese syllabaries — hiragana and katakana — and their transliteration (katakana on the right of hiragana)

a	あ ア	i	い イ	u	う ウ	e	え エ	o	お オ
ka	か カ	ki	き キ	ku	く ク	ke	け ケ	ko	こ コ
sa	さ サ	shi*	し シ	su	す ス	se	せ セ	so	そ ソ
ta	た タ	chi*	ち チ	tsu*	つ ツ	te	て テ	to	と ト
na	な ナ	ni	に ニ	nu	ぬ ヌ	ne	ね ネ	no	の ノ
ha	は ハ	hi	ひ ヒ	fu*	ふ フ	he	へ ヘ	ho	ほ ホ
ma	ま マ	mi	み ミ	mu	む ム	me	め メ	mo	も モ
ya	や ヤ	i	い イ	yu	ゆ ユ	e	え エ	yo	よ ヨ
ra	ら ラ	ri	り リ	ru	る ル	re	れ レ	ro	ろ ロ
wa	わ ワ	i	い イ	u	う ウ	e	え エ	o	を ヲ
n*	ん ン								

*In other Romanization systems spelled differently.
Namely, shi=si, chi=ti, tsu=tu, fu=hu, and n=m.

ga	が ガ	gi	ぎ ギ	gu	ぐ グ	ge	げ ゲ	go	ご ゴ
za	ざ ザ	ji*	じ ジ	zu	ず ズ	ze	ぜ ゼ	zo	ぞ ゾ
da	だ ダ	ji*	ぢ ヂ	zu*	づ ヅ	de	で デ	do	ど ド
ba	ば バ	bi	び ビ	bu	ぶ ブ	be	べ ベ	bo	ぼ ボ
pa	ぱ パ	pi	ぴ ピ	pu	ぷ プ	pe	ぺ ペ	po	ぽ ポ

*ji=zi, zu=dzu.

kya	きゃ キャ	kyu	きゅ キュ	kyo	きょ キョ
sha*	しゃ シャ	shu*	しゅ シュ	sho*	しょ ショ
cha*	ちゃ チャ	chu*	ちゅ チュ	cho*	ちょ チョ
nya	にゃ ニャ	nyu	にゅ ニュ	nyo	にょ ニョ
hya	ひゃ ヒャ	hyu	ひゅ ヒュ	hyo	ひょ ヒョ
mya	みゃ ミャ	myu	みゅ ミュ	myo	みょ ミョ
rya	りゃ リャ	ryu	りゅ リュ	ryo	りょ リョ

*sha=sya, shu=syu, sho=syo, cha=tya, chu=tyu, cho=tyo

gya	ぎゃ ギャ	gyu	ぎゅ ギュ	gyo	ぎょ ギョ
ja*	じゃ ジャ	ju*	じゅ ジュ	jo*	じょ ジョ
bya	びゃ ビャ	byu	びゅ ビュ	byo	びょ ビョ
pya	ぴゃ ピャ	pyu	ぴゅ ピュ	pyo	ぴょ ピョ

*ja=zya, ju=zyu, jo=zyo

APPENDIX C

MISCELLANEOUS ADDRESSES

As soon as you've made your decision to visit Japan, you should write to the nearest office of the Japan National Tourist Organization (JNTO) and get as many brochures as you decently can. They will automatically include booklets like *Traveler's Companion*, *Your Guide to Japan* and *Exploring Japan*. Then according to your specific desires, you can ask for regional guides (Japan Alps, Kyoto-Nara area, Kyushu, Hokkaido, etc.). If you have special interests, such as pottery, weaving, Zen Buddhism, judo, Kabuki, etc., you can ask for literature on these subjects. Finally, the JNTO can also supply you with lists of hotels, inns, youth hostels and restaurants. All these brochures are free. The addresses of JNTO in the U.S. are:

    45 Rockefeller Plaza, New York, NY 10020
    333 North Michigan Ave., Chicago, IL 60601
    1420 Commerce St., Dallas, TX 75201
    1737 Post Street, San Francisco, CA 94115
    624 South Grand Ave., Los Angeles, CA 90017
    2270 Kalakaua Ave., Honolulu, HI 96815.

APPENDIX C

After you reach Japan, it's a good idea to head for the Tourist Information Center (TIC) operated by the JNTO. The staff at these places speak English and can help you plan itineraries, suggest places to stay which fit your budget and give you ideas on interesting places to visit and things to do. There are three major TIC operated by the JNTO, and their addresses are:

> Tokyo Airport Office: Airport (Haneda) Terminal Bldg., Ota-ku, Tokyo, Tel. (747)0261-2
> Tokyo Office: 6-6 Yurakucho 1-chome, Tokyo, Tel. (502)1416
> Kyoto Office: Kyoto Tower Bldg., Higashi-Shiokoji-cho, Shimogyo-ku, Kyoto, Tel. (371)5649.

Osaka city operates a Tourist Information Center, and its address is Osaka Station, Kita-ku, Tel. (345)2189.

There are Tourist Information Centers operated by local governments in other cities, but since most tourists start with Tokyo, Kyoto or Osaka, it doesn't seem worthwhile to list all the local ones.

If you are interested in visiting one of the two imperial villas, the Katsura Imperial Villa or the Shugakuin Imperial Villa, you must get written permission from the Imperial Household Agency, whose address is Imperial Household Agency, Kyoto Office, Kyoto Gyoen-nai, Kamigyo-ku, Kyoto, Tel. 211-1211.

There are many travel agencies in Japan with English-speaking staff, and you can inquire about these at your hotel or at the TIC. But you can find an office of the Japan Travel Bureau (JTB) at any major train station or airport. At the bigger offices there is usually someone who speaks enough English to cope with your needs, if they are not too strange.

Lodging is better arranged by a travel agency such as the JTB, but if you are interested in staying at an inexpensive *minshuku*, or "people's lodging," you can get in touch directly with the Tokyo Minshuku Center, Tokyo Katsu Kaikan Bldg. near the Yurakucho JNR Station, Tel. (216)6556.

For cheaper lodging yet, there are youth hostels. As we've said, the JNTO can send you a free brochure with a list of hostels, but for more information you can write to the Japan Youth Hostels, Inc., 1-2 Ichigaya Sadoharacho, Shinjuku-ku, Tokyo, Tel. (269)5831/3.

American tourists with unusual problems can get in touch with the American Embassy at 1-10-5 Akasaka, Minato-ku, Tokyo, Tel. (583)7141.

If you decide to stay beyond the time limit specified on your visa, you can extend your stay by getting in touch with the Tokyo Immigration Office, 3-20 Konan 3-chome, Minato-ku, Tokyo, Tel. (4471)5111/6.

If you need an ambulance, dial 119 and ask for a *kyūkyūsha*. When you're in trouble, you can dial 110 for police to come and help. Japanese policemen, like the English Bobbies, present a benign image. They are not armed, and they are courteous and helpful. The officers tend to be very well educated. Even if they don't speak English, they can quickly find someone who does.

You won't need to dial 110 for police if you are close to a police box. There are many of these tiny police boxes and they are found at many busy street corners and stations. Called *kōban*, they can be identified by a small red light in the front. People commonly go to a kōban if they are lost or need to borrow small change.

APPENDIX D

SUGGESTED READING

The list of books here merely reflects my personal tastes and bias. I don't even attempt to make a complete list. But many of these books include their own lists of books for suggested reading, so that the interested reader can pursue those subjects further. In this list all the authors' names, both Japanese and Western, are presented with given names first, followed by surnames.

For the serious tourist, there is no better introduction to Japan than Edwin O. Reischauer's scholarly but highly readable book, *The Japanese* (Belknap Press of Harvard University Press, 1977). The author describes Japanese geography, history, culture, religion and society, but the most thorough treatment is on political processes.

Of the general guide books, the foremost is undoubtedly *Japan: The New Official Guide*, compiled by the Japan National Tourist Organization. If you intend to spend more than two months in Japan, this book will become a second Bible to you. My only complaint is that the book does not include any kanji, or characters. Anybody who wants the kind of detailed information included in the book will want to know the kanji for many of the names.

There are other comprehensive guides to Japan. Some of them tend to put emphasis on telling you where to get Irish coffee and where to buy cultured pearls, and they have a "This summer we're doing Japan, and next summer we're doing Greece" sort of tone. But there are also some excellent guides. I like the *Sunset Guide to Japan* because it's nicely illustrated and packs a lot of information for the money. The Fielding Guide is beautifully arranged. It has well-written sections by foreign residents in Japan, and these give you more insight than mere lists of hotels, restaurants, department stores and sightseeing "musts."

There are many good books on various aspects of Japanese life. Among the most interesting and entertaining are *Things Japanese* by Mock Joya (Japan Publications, 1971), *Japanalia* by Lewis Bush (Tokyo News Service, Ltd., 1965) and *Japanese Things* by Basil Hall Chamberlain, an old book first published in 1905, but still fascinating (reissued by Tuttle, 1964). Jack Seward's books *The Japanese* and *More about the Japanese* (Lotus Press, 1977) are fun to read as well as very informative.

If you want a more scholarly treatment of Japanese society, you can read Chie Nakane's *Japanese Society* (University of California Press, 1973). There is also *The Chrysanthemum and the Sword* by the anthropologist Ruth Benedict. It was written right after World War II, when there was a need to understand a defeated but baffling enemy. The book has become a classic, and much of it is still relevant today.

For Japanese history, read Reischauer's *Japan; The Story of a Nation* (Knopf, 1974) or Sir George Sansom's *Japan: a Short Cultural History* (Appleton-Century, 1944). If you are really hooked on Japanese history, there is Sansom's monumental three-volume *History of Japan* (Stanford University Press, 1958, 1961, 1963). Bradley Smith's

APPENDIX D

Japan: a History in Art (Simon and Schuster, 1964) is a beautiful coffee table book which is also informative.

Books on Japanese art tend to be gorgeously illustrated, but too heavy to hold comfortably. One exception is the thirty-volume series put out by Heibonsha on every aspect of Japanese art. Fortunately each volume is a manageable size. But I can't resist mentioning the two-volume *The Arts of Japan* by Noma Seiroku (Kodansha, 1967) because the books are so beautiful, even though they are unwieldy. If you are interested in woodblock prints, *The Floating World* by James Michener (Macmillan, 1954) gives a good introduction to the artists and their milieu.

Most of the English books on Japanese religion are on Zen Buddhism. It's not unusual for a college bookstore to have fifty or more different books on Zen (there is even a book called *Zen in the Art of Archery*). Usually about a dozen of these books are by Alan Watts, and another dozen by D. T. Suzuki, who was largely responsible for arousing Western interest in Zen. For a more general book on Japanese religion, you can read *Religions in Japan* by William K. Bunce (Tuttle, 1955).

If you want to know about the Japanese samurai, you can start with *Tales of Old Japan*, by A. B. Mitford, or Lord Redesdale, to give him his title (first published in 1871, but reissued by Tuttle, 1966). The author was one of the few Westerners to witness someone committing seppuku, or hara-kiri, which he describes in some detail. Another book about the samurai is H. Paul Verley's *The Samurai* (Weidenfeld & Nicholson, 1970). *The Samurai* by S. R. Turnbull (Macmillan, 1977) is lavishly illustrated and very readable, full of battles and tales of heroism.

You can find a good general introduction to Japanese drama in *Theaters of Japan* by Peter Arnott (Macmillan, 1969), but if you are interested in Kabuki particularly, there is *The Kabuki Theater of Japan* by A. C. Scott (Macmillan, 1955). Movie fans should not miss Donald Richie's *The Japanese Movie* (Kodansha, 1965).

Every tourist should get *Eating Cheap in Japan* by Kimiko Nagasawa and Camy Condon (Shufunotomo, 1972). It has a detailed and illustrated list of all the foods you commonly come across in Japan. Camy Condon and her husband Jack also wrote a very entertaining book called *The Simple Pleasures of Japan* (Shufunotomo, 1975), which tells about some off-beat ways to have fun Japanese fashion. And don't forget to read *Japanese Inn* by Oliver Statler (Random House, 1961), a fascinating account of an inn plus historical anecdotes served in a very palatable form.

Making a list of books about Japan is hard enough, but attempting to list works of literature is even more foolhardy, because people's tastes differ so much. Still, you can't claim acquaintance with modern Japanese literature if you haven't read some works by authors like Yasunari Kawabata, Yukio Mishima, Junichiro Tanizaki and Soseki Natsume.

Among older works I recommend Lafcadio Hearn for people who like things spooky. One of his short-short stories, *Mujina*, is just about the scariest story I've ever read. You might also like the stories of Ryunosuke Akutagawa, that strange genius who committed suicide at the age of thirty-five. The movie *Rashomon* is based on his story *In a Grove* (he wrote a story called *Rashomon*, but the plot is different). The prolific writer Edogawa Rampo also likes the macabre. Edogawa is his surname, but we give his name in this order because if you read it fast enough, it comes out like Edgar Allan Poe, and that's no coincidence.

For a vivid picture of the seventeenth-century, I recommend the works of Saikaku Ihara. He is famous for his erotic writing, such as *The Life of an Amorous Man*, *The Life of an Amorous Woman*, and *Comrade Loves of the Samurai*, but in his stories about townsmen, he has a sardonic humor which is quite irresistible.

APPENDIX D

For humor of a broader kind, there is *Hizakurige*, or *Shanks' Mare* by Ikku Jippensha. It's about the misadventures of two fellows who travel up and down the Tokaido highway. Much of the humor is scatological, but there is one episode which is unforgettable: the two men somehow wind up with a long, awkward ladder, and they can't get rid of it no matter what they do. Try the experiment of saying "Hizakurige" and then "ladder" to a Japanese. The chances are that he will burst out laughing.

Nobody with a serious interest in Japanese literature should miss *Tale of Genji*, by Lady Murasaki Shikibu. Written in the tenth century, the book is considered by many people the greatest novel ever written. The translation by Arthur Waley is a masterpiece in its own right, but is not scrupulously faithful to the original. There is a new translation by Edward Seidensticker which is more faithful (Knopf, 1977).

Another tenth century court lady is Sei Shonagon, whose *Pillow Book* is a witty commentary on court life. Among the delightful things in her book are lists of things she particularly likes or dislikes. Sample dislike: someone who is late washing his hands in the morning.

I realize that this is a very mixed bag, but I hope that these books will serve in stimulating you to read more.

INDEX

Actors, Kabuki, 106–7
Acupuncture, 98
Addresses
   for information about Japan, 224–26
   in Tokyo, taxi travel and, 8
Agar-agar, 54
Aikido, 139
Aikikai, 139
Ainu, 162, 163
Air pollution, 11
Airlines, domestic, 16–17
Akasaka, siege of, 165–66
Ako Castle, 176–77
Akutagawa, Ryunosuke, 230
Alcoholic drinks, 55–57, 103
Alcoves, 67
All-girl revues, 110–11
All Japan Kyudo Federation, 141
All Nippon Airways (ANA), 17
Alps, Japan, 4, 132, 133
Amado, 68

Amaterasu, 162, 181
Ambulance service, 226
American Embassy, 226
Amida Buddha, 192
Amma, 98
Amusement parks, 116
Amusements, 103–25
   chindonya, 119
   festivals, 121
   flower viewing, 122–24
   geisha parties, 41, 111
   Go, 115–16
   indoor games, 114–16
   Kabuki, 105–8
   komuso, 119–20
   Kyogen plays, 109–10
   mahjong, 114–15
   matsuri, 121
   movies, 104–5
   night life, 103–4
   Noh plays, 109
   pachinko, 114

INDEX

Amusements (*continued*)
  puppet shows, 108-9
  reading, 111-13
  revues, all-girl, 110-11
  stores, 117-19
  street entertainment, 119-21
  television, 113
  theaters, 104-11
  vendors, 120
  yomise, 120
  zoos, 117
Aomori, 21
Apartments, 75-76
Apāto, 75
Arcades, shopping, 118
Archery, 140-42
Architecture
  Buddhist temple, 190
  castle, 167-70
  in Nara, 151, 152
  shrine, 180-81
Arigatō, 25, 28
Art, 145-60
  books on, 229
  Buddhist, 151
  ceramic, 155-56, 159
  fine, 150-51
  folk, 147-50
  of Kyoto, 154-57
  museums, 150-58
  National Treasures in, 146-47
  "People's," 148, 149
  shrine, 181
  Western influences in, 145
Artists, as National Treasures, 146-47
Asano, 176
Ashikagas, 166, 213
Atami spas, 99

Automobiles
  pedestrians and, 9, 11
  rental of, 11-12
Awa Odori, 121
Azuchi, castle at, 173
Azuchi-Momoyama Period, 214

Baggage. *See* Luggage.
Bakufu, 213
Barē mama, 127
Barriers, highway, 5, 130
Bars, 55-57, 103-4
Baseball, 126-27
Basins, wash, 96
Baths, 89-100
  famous spas for, 99-100
  health-center, 98
  hot-spring (onsen), 96-100
  jungle, 98-99
  medicinal, 97-98
  preliminary washing for, 89-90
  public, 92-96
  sento, 92-96
  temperature of water for, 90-91
  tubs for, types of, 92
Beaches, 128-29
Bedding in homes, 66
Beef, 41-42, 47
Beer halls, 55-56
Bells, temple, 190-91
Benedict, Ruth, 228
Benjo, 86
Benten, 194-95
Bento, 53-54
Beppu

INDEX

ferry to, 22
hot springs of, 99
Bicycling, 12, 131–32
  pedestrians and, 9
  rentals for, 132
Biggu Makku, 47–48
Bijinesu hoteru, 83
Bikology, 131
Bīru, 56
Bishamonten, 194
Blind pedestrians, 10
Blossoming seasons, 122–24
Bon Odori, 121
Books, 111–13
  on art, 229
  comic, 112–13
  on drama, 229
  on food, 230
  phrase, 27–29
  on religion, 229
  on samurai, 229
  suggested list of, 227–31
Bookstores, 111–12
Bow, Japanese (for archery), 141
Bowing, 202
Bowling, 129
Breakfast, 55, 77
"Bring-along" hotels, 83
Buckwheat noodles, 52
Buddhism, 179, 189–97
  art and, 151
  books on, 229
Buddhists, militant, 163–64, 192
Budokan Hall, 138
Bullet trains, 17–20
Bunraku, 108–9
Buns, 57
Buses, 12–13
  luggage racks on, 6

Bushi, 162–63
Bushido, 163, 185, 193
Business hotels, 82–83

Cabarets, 103–4
Carpeting, 76
Cars. *See* Automobiles.
Castles, 165–78
  Ako, 176–77
  Azuchi, 173
  courtyards of, 170
  defense of, 168–69
  gates of, 168
  Himeji, 171–73
  Hirosaki, 177
  history of, 165–66
  Kanazawa, 177–78
  Kumamoto, 178
  Matsumoto, 177
  maze-like approach to, 169
  moats of, 168
  Nagoya, 167
  Nijo, 157, 170–71
  notable, 170–78
  Okayama, 177
  Osaka, 173–76
  residential quarters of, 169–70
  structure of, 167–70
  watchtower (donjon or tenshu), 167–68, 171
Catholicism, 187–89
Ceramics, 155–56, 159
Chanko-nabe, 137
Cha-no-yu, 194
Characters in language, 32–34
  list of, 216–22
Charms, 104

235

INDEX

Checking stations, 5, 130
Cherry blossoms, 123–24
Chess, 115
Chicken, 46, 56
Chihaya, 166
Chikamatsu, 108
Chikatetsu, 13–15
Chindonya, 119
Chinese characters, 32–34, 216–22
Christianity, 179, 187–89
Churches, 188–89
Chushingura, 107
Civil wars, 164–66
Classes, social, 161, 169
  language and, 27
Climate, 3
Clogs, wooden, 9
Clothing
  conformity of Japanese, 199–200
  in homes, 69–71
  Shinto, 182
Coffee houses, 55
Comic books, 112–13
Commuter trains, 15–16
Condon, Camy, 230
Conformity of Japanese, 198–200
Confucianism, 179, 184–87
Confucius, 185
Consonants, Japanese, 30
Construction rites, 184
Cooking. *See also* Food.
  in homes, 73–74
Costs
  airline, domestic, 16, 17
  bus, 13
  bicycle rental, 132

craft lessons, 159
ferry, 21, 22–23
food, 44, 45, 49, 50, 51, 53–54, 55
hostel, 81
hotel, 82, 83
inn, 78
Kabuki theater, 108
kokumin, 80, 81
minshuku, 79
movie theater, 105
night club, 104
Noh and Kyogen, 110
public bath, 93
revues, all-girl, 111
subway, 14–15
swimming, 128
taxi, 7
train travel, 15, 19, 20
Countryside, 130–31, 152
Courtyards, 170
Crafts, 146, 148–50
  in Kyoto, 154–55, 159
  lessons in, 158–60
  in Takayama, 153
Crowded conditions, 205–6
Cryptomeria trees, 192
Culture. *See also* Art; Books; Crafts; Drama; Food; Museums; Traditional culture.
  borrowing of, 206–8
Curry, 46
Cycling. *See* Bicycling.

Daigoji, 123
Daikoku, 195

INDEX

Daimyo, 165
Daisen-in, 157
Daishi, Kōbō, 192
Damascene ware, 155
Daruma, 194
Deer, 152
Department stores, 117–18
Depāto, 117–18
Desserts, 54
Deva Kings, 151
Dining. *See also* Food.
  etiquette for, 59–63
  in inns, 66, 77
  towers, 44–45
Dōgo Spa, 97, 99
Dogs, 10–11
Doll Festival, 123
Dolls, Kyoto, 155
Donburi, 47
Drama, 105–10
  books on, 229
  Kabuki, 105–8
  Kyogen, 109–10
  Noh, 109
  puppet shows, 108–9
Dress. *See* Clothing.
Drinks, 55–57, 103–4
Driving, 11–12
Dyeing, 156

Early Period, 211–12
Eating. *See* Food.
Ebisu, 195
Economics, aggressiveness in, 202–3
Edo. *See* Tokyo.
Edo (Tokugawa) Period, 130, 214

Education, respect for, 186, 201
Eiheiji Temple, 196
Ema, 181
Embarrassment, 78, 94
Embassy, American, 226
Emperors, history of, 162–64
English, Japanized, 36–37
Enlightenment, 193
Enryakuji, 192
Entertainments. *See* Amusements; Art; Drama; Festivals; Sports.
Entrances, house, 64–65
Etiquette
  dining, 59–63
  sword, 142–43
Examination Hell, 201
Expenses. *See* Costs.

Face-saving, 201–2
Fares
  airline, domestic, 16, 17
  bus, 13
  ferry, 21, 22–23
  subway, 14–15
  train, 15, 19, 20
Farmers, social status of, 162
Farms, 131, 152
  of Takayama, 153–54
Federation of All Japan Karate Organizations, 140
Ferries, 21–23
Festivals, 121
  blossoming seasons and, 122, 123
  Buddhist, 195
  kemari demonstrations at, 144

237

Festivals (*continued*)
  Kyogen, 110
  Kyoto, 121, 183
  Nara, 152
  Osaka, 183
  Roughhouse, 183
  Shinto, 183
  Takayama, 153
  Tokyo, 183
  yomise, 120
Feudal age, 161, 171, 185
Fish, 43, 50–51, 58
Flower viewing, 122–24
Flying, 16–17
Folk art, 147–50
  buying, 148–50
Food, 41–63
  authentic Japanese, 48–54
  beer hall, 55–56
  bento, 53–54
  breakfast, 55, 77
  chicken, 46, 56
  coffee house, 55
  costs of, 44, 45, 49, 50, 51, 53–54, 55
  in department stores, 118
  dining towers, 44–45
  at festivals, 121
  fish, 43, 50–51, 58
  in homes, 73–74
  in inns, 66, 77
  kissaten, 54–55
  literature on, 230
  manners and, 59–63
  meat, 41–42, 47
  model dishes of, 45
  nomiya, 56–57
  noodles, 51–53, 59
  pancakes, 58
  pickles, 44
  place setting for, 60
  poisoning, 50–51
  rice dishes, 46–47, 49–50, 53
  salads, 43
  school lunches, 63
  shokudō, 45–46
  snack, 54, 58–59
  soups, 43
  street vendors of, 58–59, 120
  sukiyaki, 48
  for sumo wrestlers, 136–37
  sushi, 49–50
  take-out, 47–48
  tempura, 48–49
  traditional, 42–44
  vegetables, 43–44
  vending machines, 57
  Western-style, 47–48
  yakimono, 57–58
  yogurt, 57
  Zen, 197
Football, 144
Fortresses, 165–66
Forty-seven Ronin, 176–77
"Four o'clock," 54
Francis Xavier, 187
Fruit, 54
Fugu, 50–51
Fuji. *See* Mt. Fuji.
Fujiwara family, 164, 212
Fukui, Buddhist temple at, 196
Fukurokuju, 195
Fumie, 188
Furniture, 66
Furo, 89
Furoshiki, 6
Furūtsu, 54
Fushimi Inari Shrine, 180

Fusuma, 68
Futon, 66

Gagaku, ix
Gambling
    mahjong, 114–15
    pachinko, 114
Games, indoor, 114–16
Gardens
    department store, 118
    home, 74
    in Kyoto, 157
Gates, castle, 168
Geishas, 41, 111
Gempei momo, 123
Gempei War, 164
Generalizations about Japanese, 198–208
Genkai Quasi-National Park, 165
Geography of Japan, 4–6
Geta, 9
Getting around. *See* Transportation.
Gion Matsuri, 121, 183
Globe fish, 50–51
Go, 115–16
Gochisōsama deshita, 62
Godaigo, 213
Golden Pavilion, 157
Golf, 128
Government, development of, 162
Government-supported lodging, 80, 81
Gozaimasu, 28
Green Car, 19
Grills, 71, 73
Guide books, suggested, 227–28

Hachiman Shrine, 141
Haitsu, 75
Hakata, 18
Hakodate, 21
Hakone, 130
    spas (onsen), 97, 99
Hamada Shoji, 147, 148
Hambagu suteki, 47
Hanami, 122–24
Hanamichi, 106
Handicraft Center in Kyoto, 154–55
Hankyu, 126
Hara-kiri, 142, 229
Harris, Townsend, 214
Health centers, 98
Hearn, Lafcadio, 230
Heat Bath, 100
Heating
    of bath water, 91, 92
    of houses, 70–72
Heian Period, 212
Heian Shrine, 181
Heibonsha, 229
Help, phrases to ask for, 38–39
Herusu sentā, 98
Hibachi, 71
Hideyori, 174, 175
Hideyoshi, 142, 162, 173–74, 214
Highways, 5, 130
Hikari, 18
Hiking, 130–31
Himeji
    castle at, 171–73
    festival at, 183
Hina Matsuri, 123
Hinomaru bento, 53
Hiragana, 35, 192
    table of, 223

239

INDEX

Hirohito, 215
Hirosaki, castle at, 177
Hiroshige, 130
Historical periods, 211–15
  Azuchi-Momoyama, 214
  Early, 211–12
  Edo (Tokugawa), 130, 214
  Heian, 212
  Kamakura, 213
  Meiji, 138, 206, 215
  Muromachi, 213
  Nara, 212
  Showa, 215
  Taisho, 215
History of Japan, 162–78, 211–15
Hizakurige, 231
Hokkaido, 4
  ferry to, 21
  onsen of, 99
Holidays, 24
Homes. See Housing.
"Honorable three o'clock," 54
Hon-maru, 170
Honshu, 4–5
  mountains of, 132
  trains of, 18, 20
  undersea tunnel from, 21
Hormones, 56
Horseradish, Japanese, 50
Horumon, 56
Horyuji Temple, 151, 190
Hostels, 81, 226
Hotei, 195
Hotels, 82–83
  "bring-along," 83
  business, 82–83
  luxury, 82
Hoteru, 82–83

Hot springs, 96–100
Hotto kēki, 58
House numbers in Tokyo, 8
Housing, 64–84
  alcoves in, 67
  apartments, 75–76
  baths and, 90, 92
  in castles, 169–70
  clothing and, 69–71
  entrance, 64–66
  flexible room use and, 66–67
  furniture and, 66
  gardens and, 74
  heating of, 70–72
  hibachi and, 71
  hostels, 81
  hotels, 82–83
  impermanence of, 67–69
  inns (ryokan), 76–78
  kitchen in, 73–74
  kokumin kyuka-mura, 80–81
  kokumin shukusha, 80
  kotatsu and, 71–72
  minshuku, 78–80
  mosquitoes and, 72–73
  motels, 84
  openness in, 72–73
  pensions, 84
  pillows and, 67
  present-day, 74–76
  shoes and slippers and, 65, 76
  shoji and, 68–69
  sliding screens and, 68
  tatami mats and, 65–66
  toilets in, 88
  tokonoma and, 67
  traditional, 64–74
  Western-style, 82–84
Humidity, 3, 9, 93

240

INDEX

Hydrofoil, 22
Hyoshigi, 105

Ieyasu, 174–75, 214
Ihara, Saikaku, 230
Imadegawa-Omiya, 156
Immigration Office, 226
Imperial Household Agency, 158, 225
Imperial villas, 145, 157–58, 225
Important Cultural Properties, 146
Ina, 148
Inari shrines, 180, 181
Individuality in Japan, 198–200
Information sources, 224–26
  books suggested as, 227–31
Inland Sea, 5
  ferries across, 22
Inns, 76–78
  clothing in, 70
  dining in, 66, 77
International Cultural Association, 159
Ise Shrine, 181
Islands of Japan, 4–6
Itadakimasu, 61
Itsukushima Shrine, 180, 181
Izumo Shrine, 181

Japan
  history of, 162–78, 211–15
  unification of, 173
Japan Airlines (JAL), 17
Japan Alps, 4, 132, 133

Japan Karate Association, 140
Japan National Railway (JNR), 15
Japan National Tourist Organization (JNTO), addresses of, 224
Japan Travel Bureau (JTB), 225
Japan Youth Hostels (JYH), 81
Japanese (language). See Language.
Japanese (people), 198–208
  conformity of, 198–200
  crowdedness and, 205–6
  as economic animals, 203
  education and, 186, 201
  embarrassment and, 78, 94
  face-saving and, 201–2
  generalizations about, 198–208
  littering by, 204–5
  overwork of, 200–201
  politeness of, 202
  traditions of. See Traditional culture.
  travel by, 198–99
  Westernization of, 206–8. See also Western influences.
  women's status, 186, 203–4
Japanized English, 36–37
Jidaimono, 106
Jigoro, Kano, 138
Jippensha, Ikku, 231
Jizo, 191
Jogging, 129
Jomon, 211
Jozankei Spa, 99
Judo, 138
Jujitsu, 138
Jungle baths, 98–99
Jurojin, 195

241

INDEX

Kabuki, 105-8
  literature on, 229
Kabukiza Theater, 107
Kaerazui, 133
Kaikei, 151
Kaki furai, 47
Kamakura, 164, 166, 213
  Buddhist temples of, 193
Kamakura Period, 213
Kami, 180, 181
Kamikaze, 165
Kamikochi, 133
Kammu, 163
Kamo, 156
Kana, 34-35
Kanazawa, castle at, 177-78
Kanji, 32-34, 217-22
Kannon, 191
Kano Jigoro, 138
Kano Tayu, 157
Kansai, 5
Kantō, 5
Kanze Kaidan, 110
Kanze Nohgakudo, 110
Kappa, 128
Karate, 139-40
Kare raisu, 46
Karma, 189
Kasuga-Wakamiya Shrine, 152, 181
Katakana, 35-36, 45
  table of, 223
Katori senko, 72
Katsura, 156
  Imperial Villa at, 88, 145, 157-58, 225
Keio, 127
Keisatsu-sho, 143
Kemari, 144

Kendo, 142-44
Kenjitsu, 143
Kenka Matsuri, 183
Kiai, 138
Kiga, 97
Kimonos, 69, 70-71, 117
  of Nishijin, 156
  traditional behavior and, 207
Kinokuniya, 112
Kira, 176
Kissaten, 54-55
Kitanoumi, 137
Kitchens in homes, 73-74
Kiyomasa, Katō, 178
Kiyomizu Temple, 191
Kiyomizu-yaki, 156
Koan, 193
Kōban, 143, 226
Kobe, ferry from, 22
Kodama, 18
Kodokan Judo Hall, 138
Kokumin kyuka-mura, 80-81
Kokumin shukusha, 80
Kokusai Theater, 111
Komeito, 196
Komuso, 119-20
Komusubi, 137
Konro, 71, 73
Konyaku, 59
Kōrakuen Yuenshi, 116
Kōrin, 146
Koryuji Temple, 157
Kōshibyo, 186-87
Kōshien Stadium, 127
Kotatsu, 71-72
Kuhaulua, Jesse, 137
Kumamoto Castle, 178
Kurame Kokugi Kan arena, 137
Kurashiki, 149-50

242

Kusatsu
  hot spring at, 99–100
  skiing at, 134
Kusunoki Masashige, 165–66
Kyobunkwan, 112
Kyogen, 109–10
Kyoto, 5, 12, 154–58, 212
  bookstores in, 112
  Buddhist temples in, 190, 191, 193–94, 197
  crafts of, 154–55, 159
  crowdedness in, 205–6
  dolls of, 155
  festival in, 121, 183
  gardens of, 74
  Imperial Household Agency of, 158
  Kabuki plays in, 108
  militant monks of, 163–64, 192
  Movie Village in, 105
  as museum city, 154–58
  Noh-Kyogen in, 110
  shrines in, 180, 181
  Tourist Information Center in, 225
  warlords and, 164–65
Kyudo, 140–42
Kyūkyūsha, 226
Kyushu, 5, 18
  castle of, 178
  undersea tunnel to, 21

Lacquer ware, 148, 155
Lamien, 52
Language, 25–40
  basic phrases of, 37–40
  characters in, 32–34, 216–22
  class distinctions and, 27
  consonants in, 30
  difficulties of speaking correct, 26–29
  Hiragana, 35, 192, 223
  Japanized English, 36–37
  Kana, 34–35
  Kanji, 32–34, 217–22
  Katakana, 35–36, 45, 223
  phonetic symbols in, 35–36, 223
  phrase books for, 27–29
  pitch in, 31
  pronouns in, 27
  pronunciation, 29–31, 32, 36–37
  reading and writing, 31–37
  Romaji, 32
  stress in, 30–31
  verbs in, 28
  vowels in, 29–30
  women's speech and, 26–27
Leach, Bernard, 145
Learning, respect for, 186, 201
Lessons in crafts, 158–60
Liquor, 56
Literature, 230–31. *See also* Books.
  Buddhist influence in, 189
  suggested list of, 227–31
Littering, 204–5
Living National Treasures, 146–47
  puppeteers as, 108
Lodging, 76–84, 226
  baths and, 96
  hostels, 81
  hotels, 82–83
  inns (ryokan), 76–78

INDEX

Lodging (continued)
   Japanese-style, 76–81
   kokumin kyuka-mura, 80–81
   kokumin shukusha, 80
   minshuku, 78–80, 226
   motels, 84
   pensions, 84
   people's, 78–80, 226
   Western-style, 82–84
Luggage, 6
   airlines and, domestic, 17
   taxis and, 7
   train travel and, 20–21
Lunch boxes, 53–54
Lunches, school, 63

Maeda family, 178
Maegashira, 137
Magazines, 111
Mahjong, 114–15
Maid service, 76–78
Main Hall of National Theater, 107
Maki-e, 155
Makizushi, 49
Manchuria, 215
Manners
   sword, 142–43
   table, 59–63
Manshon, 75
Manshukoku, 215
Mansions, 170
Maple blossoms, 124
Marathons, 129
Maruzen, 112
Masashige, Kusunoki, 165–66
Mashiko, 148, 159

Masseurs, 98
Mats, tatami. *See* Tatami mats.
Matsumoto, 133
   castle at, 177
Matsuri, 121, 183. *See also* Festivals.
Mattresses, 66
Mazes, 168–69
McDonald's, 47
Meals. *See also* Food.
   traditional Japanese, 42–44
Meat, 41–42, 47
Medicinal springs, 97–98
Meditation, 193, 194
Meiji Era, 138, 206, 215
Meiji Shrine, 182
Mibu Temple, 110
Michener, James, 229
Michizane, Sugawara, 122, 182
Midori-no-madoguchi, 19
Mie, 106
Mikoshi, 183, 192
Minamoto family, 163, 164, 213
Minamoto Tametomo, 140–41
Mingei, 148, 149
Minshuku, 78–80, 226
Miroku Bosatsu, 157
Missionaries, 187–89
Mitford, A. B., 229
Mitsu-mame, 54
Miyajima, shrine at, 180, 181
Moats, 168
Momiji Matsuri, 144
Mongols, 165, 213
Mōningu sābisu, 55
Mono no aware, 189
Morihei, Ueshiba, 139
Morioka, 148
Mosquitoes, 72–73

Motels, 84
Mountaineering, 132-34
Mountains of Japan, 4
Mt. Fuji, 4, 132
  climbing of, 133-34
Mt. Hiei, temple of, 192, 193
Mt. Kaerazui, 133
Mt. Koya, temple of, 192
Mt. Norikura, 133
Mt. Tanigawa, 133
Mt. Yari, 133
Mt. Yoshino, cherry blossoms of, 123
Movies, 104-5
Movie Village in Kyoto, 105
Mujoku Bosatsu, 151
Muromachi Period, 213
Musashi, Miyamoto, 143
Museums, 150-58
  cities as, 151-58
  fine-art, 150-51
  folk-art, 149-50
  in Kyoto, 156, 157
  in Nara, 151-52
  in Takayama, 153-54
  in Tokyo, 150
Musicals, 105-8
Musicians, street, 119-20

Nagaoka, 212
Nagasaki
  Christianity and, 188
  Confucian shrine at, 186-87
Nagasawa, Kimiko, 230
Nagoya Castle, 167
Nanzenji Temple, 197
Nara, 151-52, 162
  Buddhist temple at, 190
  shrine at, 181
Nara Dreamland, 116
Nara Period, 212
National Museum, 150
National Theater, 107
National Treasures, 146-47
  Living, 108, 146-47
Neolithic culture, 211
Netsunoyu, 100
NHK, 113
Nichiren, 193
Night life, 103-4
Nihon Togei Club, 159
Nijo Castle, 157, 170-71
Ni-no-maru, 170
Niō, 151
Nishijin District, 156
Noboribetsu, 99
Nobunaga, 173, 174, 187, 214
Noh, 109
Nomiya, 56-57, 103
Noodles, 51-53, 59
Noren, 52
Norikura, 133
Nudity, embarrassment about, 78, 94

Oden, 59
Ōhara gallery, 150
Ohayō, 28-29
Okayama, 22
  castle at, 177
Okinawa, 6
  karate and, 139-40
Okonomi yaki, 58
O-Kuni, 106

INDEX

On Matsuri, 152
Onnagata, 107
Onsen, 96–100
Osaka, 5
   castle at, 173–76
   ferry from, 22
   festival at, 183
   information center in, 225
   museum in, 150
   puppet theater in, 109
   siege of, 174–75
Osanji, 54
O-shibori, 17
Otsu, 148
Oura Church, 188
Oyako donburi, 47
Oyattsu, 54
Ozeki, 137

Pachinko, 114
Pagoda, 190
Paleolithic culture, 211
Pancakes, 58
Panels in homes, 68–69
Panshion, 84
Parks
   amusement, 116
   hiking in, 131
   lodging at, 80–81
   museums in, 150
Peach blossoms, 123
Pedestrians, 8–11
Pensions, 84
People's Art, 148, 149, 150
People's lodging, 78–80, 226
Periodicals, 111
Perry, Commodore, 214

Phonetic symbols, 35–36, 223
Phrase books, 27–29
Phrases, basic Japanese, 37–39
Pickles, 44
Pilgrimages, Buddhist, 191–92
Pillow Book, 231
Pillows, 67
Ping-pong, 129
Pitch in pronunciation, 31
Place setting for dining, 60
Plains, 4
Plays. *See* Drama.
Plum blossoms, 122–23
Plums, sour, 53
Police, 226
   kendo bouts of, 143–44
Politeness of Japanese, 202
Pollution, air, 11
Pools
   health-center, 98
   jungle, 98–99
   soaking, 95
Porters, railway station, 21
Portuguese missionaries, 187
Pottery, 147, 148, 156
   in Mashiko, 159
Priests, itinerant, 119–20
Pronunciation, 29–31, 32
   of Chinese characters, 32
   of consonants, 30
   of Japanized English, 36–37
   stress and pitch in, 30–31
   of vowels, 29–30
Protestantism, 187–89
Puppet theater, 108–9
Pure Land sects, 192–93

Quilts, 66, 71–72

Railway. *See* Trains.
Rain, 3, 9–10
Ramen, 52–53
Rampo, Edogawa, 230
Reading, 111–13
   in Japanese, 31–37. *See also* Language.
Redcaps, railway station, 21
Reischauer, Edwin, 206, 227, 228
Religion, 179–97
   books on, 229
   Buddhism, 179, 189–97
   Christianity, 179, 187–89
   Confucianism, 179, 184–87
   Shinto, 179, 180–84
Reservations
   for hostels, 81
   for inns, 78
   for kokumin, 81
   for minshuku (people's lodging), 79
Resorts
   hot-spring, 96–100
   ski, 134–35
Restaurants. *See also* Food.
   model dishes in, 45
   phrases for use in, 39
   shokudō, 45–46
   tower, 44–45
   traditional meal in, 42–44
Revues, 110–11
Rice dishes, 46–47, 49–50, 53
Rickshaws, 153
Riddles, Buddhist, 193
Romaji, 32
Rondon yaki, 58
Ronin, 176–77
Roughhouse Festival, 183
Running, 129

Rush hours, 15–16
Ryoanji Temple, 194
Ryokan, 76–78
Ryoriya, 42
Ryozen Kannon, 191

Saigo, Takamori, 178
Sake, 56, 57
Salads, 43
Samisen, 105
Samurai, 141, 142, 161–65
   archery training of, 141, 142
   books on, 229
   class, 161–63
   definition of, 162–63
   Forty-seven, 176–77
   history of, 161–65
   housing for, 169–70
   last of, 178
   Noh plays and, 109
   swordsmanship of, 142–43
Sanitary napkins, 89
Sanjusangendo Temple archery contest, 141–42
Sanno Matsuri, 183
Sansom, George, 228
Sapporo
   bicycling in, 132
   skiing in, 134
   underground shopping center in, 119
Sararimen, 57
Sashimi, 43
Satori, 193
School lunches, 63
Screens
   painted, 157
   sliding, in homes, 68

INDEX

Sculpture
  in Kyoto, 157
  in Nara, 151
Sea of Japan, 4
Seasons, 3
  blossoming, 122–24
  busy travel, 23–24
  housing decor and, 67, 68
Seaweed as food, 49
Seiroku, Noma, 229
Sekigahara, 214
  Battle of, 174
Sekiwake, 137
Senhime, 174, 175
Senjoji Temple, 191
Senshu University, 129
Sento, 92–96
Seppuku, 142, 229
Seto Naikai, 5
Seven-Five-Three, Day of, 182
Seven Lucky Gods, 194–95
Sewamono, 106
Shakuhachi, 119
Shape of Japan, 4–6
Sharaku, 106
Shichigosan, 182
Shikibu, Murasaki, 231
Shikoku, 5
  ferries to, 21–22
  pilgrimages on, 192
Shingon sect, 192
Shinjuku Station, 16, 79
Shinkansen, 17–20
Shinto, 179, 180–84
  festivals, 121
  sumo matches and, 136
Shirahama hot springs, 99
Shochiku Kageki-dan, 110–11

Shoes, 9
  removal of, in homes, 65, 76
Shōgi, 115
Shogun, 161, 163, 164–66
  castle of, 171
Shōhei Academy, 186
Shoji, 68–69
Shoji, Hamada, 147, 148
Shokudō, 45–47
Shonagon, Sei, 231
Shopping. *See also* Stores.
  arcades, 118
  centers, underground, 118–19, 149
  phrases used in, 40
Shosoin, 107, 152
Shotoku, 185, 189–90, 212
Showa Era, 215
Shrines, 180–84
  Confucian, 185, 186–87
  family, 184
  festivals of, 121
  individual attendance at, 199
  Kyoto, 180, 181
  Nagasaki, 186–87
  portable, 183
  Shinto, 180–84
  Takayama, 154
  Tenmangu, 122–23, 182
  Tokyo, 182, 185, 186
Shugakuin, 158, 225
Sidewalks, 9, 10, 12
Silk, 148, 156
Skewers, street-vendor food on, 59
Skiing, 134–35
Skymate, 16–17
Sleepers, 20
Slippers

INDEX

in houses, 65, 76
toilet use and, 87
Small Hall of National Theater, 108–9
Smith, Bradley, 228–29
Snacks, 54, 58–59
Soba, 52
Soccer, 144
Social classes, 161, 169
   language and, 27
Social phrases, 38
Soetsu, Yanagi, 149
Soka Gakkai, 196
Somen, 52
Soto Zen, 196
Soups, 43
Sour plums, 53
Souvenir shops, 149
Spas, 96–100
   famous, 99–100
Speech. *See also* Language.
   pronunciation in, 29–31, 32, 36–37
   women's, 26–27
Sports, 126–44
   aikido, 139
   archery (kyudo), 140–42
   arena, 137
   baseball, 126–27
   bowling, 129
   cycling, 131–32
   football, 144
   golf, 128
   hiking, 130–31
   judo, 138
   karate, 139–40
   kendo, 142–44
   mountaineering, 132–34
   running, 129
   skiing, 134–35
   soccer, 144
   sumo, 135–37
   surfing, 128–29
   swimming, 128
   table tennis, 129
   tennis, 127–28
   traditional, 135–44
   volleyball, 127
   walking, 130
   Western, 126–35
Springs, hot, 96–100
   medicinal, 97–98
Statler, Oliver, 76, 230
Stone walls, 165, 168
Stores, 117–19
   in arcades, 118
   book, 111–12
   department, 117–18
   folk art in, 149
   in Kyoto, 155–56
   underground, 118–19, 149
Straw mats. *See* Tatami mats.
Streetcars, 12
Street entertainment, 119–21
Streets, 9, 10
Street vendors, 58–59, 120
Stress in pronunciation, 30–31
Subway, 13–15
Suitcases. *See* Luggage.
Sukiyaki, 48
Sumo, 135–37
Surfing, 128–29
Sushi, 49–50
Sweet potatoes, roasted, 59
Sweets, 54
Swimming, 128
Sword Hunt, 142
Swordsmanship, 142–44

249

INDEX

Syllabaries, table of, 223
Symbols, phonetic, 35–36, 223

Table manners, 59–63
Table setting, dining and, 60
Table tennis, 129
Taira family, 163, 164
Taisho Era, 215
Tai yaki, 58
Takamatsu, 22
Takamiyama, 137
Takarabune, 194
Takarazuka
   all-girl revues in, 110
   amusement park in, 116
Takauji, 213
Takayama, 148, 152–54
Takayama Sanno Matsuri, 153
Takeda family, 139
Tako, 58
Tale of Genji, 231
Tametomo, Minamoto, 140–41
Tampons, 89
Tanigawa, 133
Tanzen, 71
Tatami mats, 65–66
   on ferryboat, 23
Taut, Bruno, 145
Taxis, 7–8
Tea bowls, 148
Tea ceremony, 194
Teapot Lane, 156
Tea shops, 54–55
Teine Olympic Ski Grounds, 134
Television, 113
Temples, Buddhist, 190–96
Tempura, 48–49

Tendai sect, 192, 193
Tenjin, 182
   Tenjin Matsuri, 183
Tenmangu shrines, 122–23, 182
Tennis, 127–28
Tenshu, 167–68, 171
Theaters, 104–11
   Kabuki, 105–8
   Kyogen, 109–10
   movie, 104–5
   Noh, 109
   puppet, 108–9
   revues, all-girl, 110–11
Thermal springs, 97
"Three o'clock," 54
Tickets. *See also* Fares.
   public bathhouse, 93
   restaurant (shokudō), 46
   theater, 108, 110, 111
Time, phrases for, 39
Tipping, 78, 82
Toa Domestic Airlines (TDA), 17
Todaiji Temple, 151
Tofu, 120
Tohoku, 4
   skiing in, 134
Toilet paper, 88–89
Toilets, Japanese, 85–89
   advantages of, 87–88
   posture for using, 87
   slippers and, 87
Toire, 89
Toji Temple, 190
Tōkaidō highway, 5, 130
Tōkai Nature Trail, 131
Tokonoma, 67
Tokugawa family, 173, 174, 177, 178
   Confucianism and, 185

Tokugawa Period, 214
Tokushima, festival in, 121
Tokyo, 4, 5
   amusement parks in, 116, 117
   bicycle borrowing in, 132
   bookstores in, 112
   Buddhist temple in, 191
   crowdedness of, 205
   ferries from, 22
   festival at, 183
   house numbers in, 8
   information centers in, 225
   judo in, 138
   Kabuki theaters in, 107
   karate in, 140
   museums of, 150
   night life in, 103–4
   Noh and Kyogen in, 110
   puppet theater in, 108–9
   revues in, all-girl, 110–11
   shrines of, 182, 185, 186
   sumo matches in, 137
   tennis courts in, 127–28
   transportation in, 6–16
Tokyo University, 186
Ton katsu, 47
Toothbrushes, Japanese, 82
Torii, 180
Toshiya, 141–42
Tourist Information Center (TIC), 225
Tours, bus, 13
Towels, public baths and, 93
Toyonaka Folk Museum, 150
Traditional culture, 206–8
   food and, 42–44
   housing and, 64–74
   kimonos and, 207
   sports and, 135–44

Traffic
   bicycles and, 12
   pedestrians and, 9, 11
   signs, 11
   taxis and, 7–8
Trails
   hiking, 131
   mountaineering, 134
Trains, 15–21
   baggage and, 20–21
   bullet, 17–21
   interurban, 15–16
   long-distance, 17–21
   luggage racks on, 6
   sleeper, 20
   underground (subway), 13–15
Transliteration of syllabaries, 223
Transportation, 6–24
   bicycling, 12
   buses, 12–13
   driving, 11–12
   ferries, 21–23
   flying, 16–17
   taxi, 7–8
   streetcars, 12
   subway, 13–15
   trains, 6, 15–21
   walking, 8–11
Travel
   agencies, 225
   busy seasons for, 23–24
   by Japanese, 198–99
   phrases for use in, 39–40
Trays, food, 60
Tsugaru Straits, 4
Tsuyu, 3
Tunnels, undersea, 21
Turnbull, S. R., 229

INDEX

Uda, 148
Udon, 52
Ueno Park, 150
Ueno Zoo, 117
Ueshiba Morihei, 139
Uji, 211
Umbrellas, 9–10
Umeboshi, 53
Unagi donburi, 47
Underground shopping centers, 118–19, 149
Underground trains (subways), 13–15
Unkei, 151
Uno, 22
Unzen hot springs, 99
Urakami Cathedral, 188

Vacation villages, 80–81
Vacations, busy season for, 23–24
Valuables
　inns and, 77
　public bathhouses and, 94
Vegetables, 43–44
Vending machines, 57
Vendors, street, 58–59, 120
Villas, imperial, 84, 145, 157–58, 225
Volcanoes, 134
Volleyball, 127
von Baelz, Erwin, 100
Vowels, 29–30

Wajima, 137
Wakakusa Hill, 152

Walking, 8–11, 130
Walls
　defensive, 165, 168
　in home, 68–69
Warlords, 164–66, 173–74
War of the Roses, 164
Warrior class, 161–63
Waseda, 127
Wash basins, 96
Washi, 148
Watchtowers, 167–68, 171
Water sports, 128–29
Watering cans, 9
W.C. *See* Toilets, Japanese.
Weather, 3, 9
Weddings, 21, 207
Well of Himeji Castle, 172
Western influences in Japan, 206–8
　in art, 145
　in food, 47–48
　in lodging, 82–84
　in sports, 126–35
　in toilets, 85, 86, 88
Wheat noodles, 52
Whisky, 56
White Heron Castle, 171–73
Women
　speech of, 26–27
　status of, 186, 203–4
Woodblock prints, 148, 155
Wooden structures, oldest, 151
Work, Japanese devotion to, 200–201
Wrestling, Japanese-style, 135–37
Writing in Japanese, 31–37. *See also* Language.

252

INDEX

Yabusame, 141
Yaki imo, 59
Yakimono, 57–58
Yakitori, 56
Yamagata, 148
Yamajiro, 165
Yamato state, 211
Yamayaki, 152
Yanagi Soetsu, 149
Yanaka, 150
Yari, 133
Yasukuni Shrine, 182
Yatai, 58–59
Yayoi, 211
"Yes," as answer, 202
Yogurt, 57
Yojimbo, 11
Yokozuna, 137
Yomise, 120
Yomiuri, 126
Yomiuriland, 116
Yoritomo, 164, 213
Yoshiie, Minamoto, 163
Yoshimasa, 213
Yoshimitsu, 213
Yoshino, cherry blossoms of, 123
Youth hostels, 81, 226
Yukata, 69–70
Yushima Seido, 186
Yuzen, 156

Zao Spa, 134
Zazen, 194
Zen Buddhism, 193–97
    books on, 229
Zoos, 117